Praise for *7*

Stories of faithfulness in the service o those who read. *The Quiet Leading* is that kind of story. Read with joy in His goodness.

Gerry Breshears, professor of theology
Western Seminary, Portland, OR

In *The Quiet Leading*, Scott Winters shows us what a life in constant conversation with God looks like. John Samson, Winters' good friend and mentor, challenges him (and us) to live a life that is fully engaged with the Savior and that depends solely on the goodness of God. This story never insists on the spectacular, though sometimes the spectacular happened. Rather, it opens us up to the real possibility of hearing God's voice in our daily lives—if we are willing to listen. *The Quiet Leading* is a testament to God's trustworthiness and to the fact that truth is never really learned until it is lived.

Thomas G. Moon, pastor
Shepherd of the Valley Bible Church, Hood River, OR

Scott Winters' personal journey of spiritual growth is warm, inspiring, and sometimes brutally honest. The lives of his dear mentors and loved ones weave through his story and, ultimately, it all becomes God's Story.

God loves to reveal Himself! He also delights in flexing His muscles and displaying His greatness. Scott Winters paints a literary portrait of what total dependence on God looks like. Be inspired by reading what "less of me, more of Jesus" looks like fleshed out. Be encouraged to know that God desires you to join His work, as he enlists all kinds of people in His adventure. How wonderful, when He chooses to reveal His power through the lives of people—transformed people, tender people. *The Quiet Leading* inspires and encourages.

Dave Abbatacola, pastor
Gold Canyon Community Church, Gold Canyon, AZ

The Quiet Leading

THE QUIET LEADING

SCOTT W. WINTERS

The Quiet Leading
© 2013 Scott W. Winters

All rights reserved. No part of this book may be reproduced or transmitted in any form or by any means, electronic or mechanical, including photocopying and recording, or by any information storage and retrieval system, without permission in writing from the publisher.

Unless otherwise noted, all Scripture quotations are from *The Holy Bible,* King James Version. Public domain.

Scripture quotations marked "NASB" taken from the *New American Standard Bible,* © Copyright 1960, 1962, 1963, 1968, 1971, 1972, 1973, 1975, 1977, 1995 by The Lockman Foundation. Used by permission.

Scripture quotations marked "NKJV" are taken from the *New King James Version.* Copyright © 1982 by Thomas Nelson, Inc. Used by permission. All rights reserved.

Published by
Deep River Books
Sisters, Oregon
www.deepriverbooks.com

ISBN – 13: 9781937756949
ISBN – 10: 1937756947

Library of Congress: 2013947096

Printed in the USA

Cover design by Joe Bailen, Contajus Design

"I know when the proposition comes from God because of its quiet persistence."
Oswald Chambers, *My Utmost for His Highest*

"In quietness and trust is your strength."
Isaiah 30:15, NASB

Contents

	Preface	11
Chapter 1	A Man Sent from God	13
Chapter 2	Wait and See	17
Chapter 3	A Small Giant from Scotland	21
Chapter 4	Beit Shalom	29
Chapter 5	Through God by Prayer Alone	37
Chapter 6	The Challenge of Beit Shalom	61
Chapter 7	My Personal Beit Shalom Challenge	69
Chapter 8	A Swiftly Changing Life	85
Chapter 9	Faith Building in Pensacola	91
Chapter 10	Pendleton and Beyond	99
Chapter 11	A School and Church in Hood River	105
Chapter 12	A Death and a Birth	113
Chapter 13	A Storm in the Valley	119
Chapter 14	A Little Angel and a Long Silence	125
Chapter 15	Angels Around the World	131
Chapter 16	The Road to Romania	135
Chapter 17	Romania	147
Chapter 18	A Daughter and a Dog	155
Chapter 19	The Call of Russia	161
Chapter 20	Cuba!	185
Chapter 21	Back to Britain	201
Chapter 22	The Final Chapter (But Not the End)	205
	Postscript: Where the Winters Family Is Now	223

Preface

Although this account is written in first person, it is more a biography than an autobiography. It is the story of two men whose influence on my life and the lives of many others was tremendous, two men whose stories bring glory to God. It is not only an account of two men who lived their lives before God with extreme influence and effectiveness, but of God Himself and how He is still working today in loving, mighty, and unique ways.

May you, dear Reader, deepen your walk with the Savior as you read through these pages. And may You, dear Lord, be glorified by this book. It is dedicated to You.

Chapter 1

A MAN SENT FROM GOD

Larry Gordon was indeed a rare soul. Words cannot adequately define him. The kindest description of Larry I ever heard was spoken by the man we both recognized as our spiritual father and mentor, John Samson. After John and I had listened together to an audiotape which Larry had mailed to John years earlier, John mused aloud, "He was just like Jesus!"

We were not the only ones who thought so highly of Larry. We must, however, go back much further to come to the fullest understanding of just how accurate that expression by John Samson really was.

Larry Gordon came to Pendleton sometime around March of 1980. Pendleton was a fairly quiet farming community in northeast Oregon with about fifteen thousand people. Larry's arrival was almost completely unnoticed by the town in general, but to a few of us his relatively short stay would have a profound and lasting effect.

An attractive young man about thirty-three years old, Larry was on a unique pilgrimage. He had left his hometown of Tyler, Texas, about two years previously and had been traveling as an itinerant preacher, living his sermons more than preaching them. He told us he had been following, as closely as he could, the leading of the Holy Spirit. When the Spirit led him to go, he went; when the Spirit led him to stay, he stayed. And the Spirit of God had now brought him to Pendleton.

Larry found a job as the assistant manager of an assisted-living facility for the elderly, which provided him with a residence as well as an income. In his first few months, Larry enjoyed visiting various churches and conversing with business employees and owners as he walked the streets with his walking stick and Bible. The man of God with the walking stick quickly became well-known and well-liked in our little eastern Oregon town.

One of the locals who met Larry was my wife. She worked after classes each weekday and full-time during the school's summer breaks at a little drive-through dairy store. At certain times of the day, the dairy store got quite busy because it had two drive-up windows and a counter. Larry happened to be there during one of these exceptionally busy times, and without being asked, he jumped behind the counter and began to help.

"What color are the tops of the two percent?" he shouted across the store, followed by, "How much is it?" This, I would learn, was typical Larry Gordon. He was always helpful, kind, and a good listener; most of all, he loved to talk about Jesus Christ.

I met Larry shortly after the encounter at the little dairy store, and a close friendship quickly developed. Early on, he invited me to come to his little apartment at the assisted-living facility any time I wanted to talk or just hang out, and he meant it. I took Larry up on his offer one night as I was driving home from a church function. It was fairly late, and I barely knew him, so I was a bit apprehensive about dropping in. The Spirit of the Lord seemed to lead me there, so I drove on. My fears were allayed as Larry warmly welcomed me into his comfortable little apartment at Camlu. We talked for over two hours. Mostly, I sat and listened as he shared about the Lord. I was not offended or overwhelmed; rather, I felt drawn to Jesus through Larry's words.

I began spending a lot of time with Larry around the facility where he worked during his off-duty hours. We got into deep discussions about the Lord, even though most of the depth was on Larry's part. On three different occasions, I was so struck by the depth of his love for the Lord that I could almost *see* the Holy Spirit pouring down from heaven through Larry toward me.

Once, Larry mentioned a man named John Samson, whom he considered his spiritual father. I was awestruck that a man this godly would refer to someone that way! I determined that very moment to meet this man, and the sooner the better.

I would indeed meet John Samson in the not-too-distant future, but little did I know how costly it would be for that to happen.

When I met Larry I was already a Christian, but I had never known anyone quite like him, and I had no idea how he would expand my world. My life started in a fairly small town. I grew up in Pendleton with my two sisters, my brother, Phil, and a dog named Smokey on a little two-plus-acre farm on the edge of town. Smokey was part husky but mostly Australian shepherd. He was a boy's dog, tough and loyal. I had loved the husky part of him since the time my fourth-grade teacher read to our class about a dog named Silver Chief, who was half-husky and half-wolf.

My father passed away from a second heart attack when I was twelve years old. My mother did a remarkable job taking care of us and the farm while teaching full-time. She provided us with a predominantly pleasant life until we all went off to college to begin adulthood for ourselves.

We all did well enough academically at college, but my sister Judy and I headed down the wrong road there. She got into drugs and alcohol and would call me at random times, even in the middle of the night, to discuss her personal problems. I was headed down the same road as Judy, but during my first year of college, I made the most important decision of my life: I committed myself to follow Jesus Christ as my Lord and Savior. Still, due to my own poor choices, I had some rough patches during the next five years before Phil helped me make my way back to Pendleton in August of 1978. He helped the family a lot after my father's death.

The best thing I did during that period was to marry my lovely wife, Debbie, in June of 1977. Shortly after we moved back to Pendleton, I recommitted my life to the Lord and began to steadily grow in Him. Within two years, I had become the upper-grades teacher and administrator of the Christian school which was a ministry of our little Baptist church. I had also become the chairman of the board of deacons. Debbie and I desired to have children, but the Lord seemed to be withholding them from us, so Debbie also worked at the school as an aide.

The weeks and months passed swiftly, and Larry and I spent much time together. He shared with me how he would spend a weekend or a week alone with the Lord in the wilderness. He spent most of his time on these retreats fasting, praying, and reading God's Word. He told me that he'd had some very unusual experiences with the Lord during these times. On one occasion, he shared about an encounter he'd had in Yosemite Park in California. While he was resting in his tent one night, a bear came into his campsite and jostled his tent. Amazingly, the bear left without harming Larry. I remember trying to decide if Larry was brave or foolish to continue on these retreats in the wilderness after such an event. I finally realized that Larry just did not fear death.

Larry continued to visit various churches around Pendleton, including frequent visits to our little church. Once, Larry and I were standing together at the back of the sanctuary just before the Sunday morning service, quietly observing the hubbub of people talking. I turned to him and said, "Larry, what do you do with all of them?" Without hesitation, Larry calmly said, "Just love them." I was amazed at how profound, yet simple and Christlike, that answer was.

Another time, as Larry was walking through town with his now-famous walking stick, he stopped by my house as I was trimming the front hedge. We chatted for a few moments, and then Larry, watching me clipping away, commented on how the Lord often prunes things from our lives. I had already accepted this truth, but Larry went on to say the Lord not only prunes the things from our lives that might imperil our walk with Him, but that He also prunes some of the good things from our lives in order that we might experience the best. I was very familiar with the text on pruning from the Gospel of John (see John 15:12), but I had never thought of it this way before. I was amazed at the constant insight that Larry had into such things. Later, I would also be amazed at how personal this application would become. In a short time, Larry had become the most influential person in my life. I could not have imagined the turn our relationship was about to take.

Chapter 2

WAIT AND SEE

By September of 1980, Larry and I had known each other for a little over five months, but it seemed much longer than that, as close as we had grown in our friendship. Early in the month, Larry shared with me that he sensed the Lord calling him to move on. He didn't know exactly where he might end up, but he said he was going to meet a couple of close friends somewhere back east in late September. He would see what the Lord had for him after that.

I never doubted Larry in his pursuit of God's will; he always took great care in it. He loved the Lord immensely. What amazed me was that Larry had known the Lord for just a little over three years. I had been a Christian for about seven-and-a-half years, and I was not even close to the maturity level Larry had reached in his walk with the Lord.

A few years before I met Larry, he had been a pilot in the Vietnam War and had used the G.I. Bill to go to college to get a degree in psychology. Afterward, he went back to his first love and became a copilot for a small commercial airline that was headquartered in Dallas, Texas, about seventy-five miles from his hometown. Larry grew up with an alcoholic father and began something of a drinking habit himself while in Vietnam, but he never let this interfere with his flying. During one of his flights with his good friend and fellow pilot, Harold West, all this changed. Harold helped Larry come to faith in Jesus Christ. Larry never took another drink, and about a year and a half later, he left his job as a copilot to become an itinerant preacher for the Lord. Larry didn't preach very often, but he lived in such dedication to the Lord that his life was a continual sermon.

The Lord had led Larry to Pendleton, and now He was leading him away. This was very disconcerting to me. Larry had revealed much deeper aspects of personal faith to me, and we had grown so close in our friendship. I would sorely miss our deep talks about the Lord. I didn't want to let go, but I told Larry that I felt we would see each other in the future. He told me he appreciated that, yet I felt very little comfort in those words. I wanted to trust the Lord in this, but the sense of loss I felt was great. It would, however, be much greater in just a few short weeks.

Larry decided to go up through Banff and Jasper National Parks in Canada and come back down through Glacier National Park in Montana on his way to Vermont. He loved spending time in the beauty of God's creation, and there are few places as beautiful as these. Debbie and I, along with friends from our church, were going up to visit our dear friends Ben and Mary Gribble in northern Washington, so we offered Larry a ride that far.

Ben and Mary were the first couple to welcome Debbie and me at Pendleton Baptist Church and had almost instantly become our best friends. After a few months of close friendship and fellowship, Ben had offered me a teaching position in the school ministry of the church, beginning a career of teaching and administrating in Christian schools that has spanned more than three decades at the writing of this book. Ben had resigned his position at Pendleton at the end of my first year to take a teaching position at a larger Christian school in Kettle Falls, Washington, just fifteen miles from the Canadian border.

Larry accepted our offer to drive him and said he would hitchhike the rest of the way through Canada and back east, as was his normal mode of travel. So we began the trip early on what turned out to be a warm, beautiful mid-September day. We had a lot of fun on the way up just talking, joking, and enjoying each other's company. I was especially thankful for the extra time with Larry.

About two-thirds of the way on the long drive to the Gribbles', a tire blew out on the trailer we were pulling. We didn't get to their home in northern Washington until after two in the morning, and we stayed up visiting until almost four. It was a happy reunion even at those extreme hours. Everyone slept in until about midmorning the next day except me. I set an alarm and got up at six. I thought it was a sign of spiritual maturity to get up early. Larry assured me later that day that it was all right for me to get the rest I needed, especially during this little vacation. I felt a little silly, but I appreciated Larry's concern and wisdom. Our final few days together passed all too quickly, and the time neared for Larry to part from us on his journey to Vermont.

Larry spoke almost exclusively about the Lord, and at one point in our conversations together I looked off into the distance as he spoke. He must have detected my deflection because he responded gently and almost immediately, "You know, Scott, people sometimes get tired of me because all I want to do is talk about Jesus." Even though Larry did not intend it as such, it was a mild, well-deserved rebuke. I marveled at how he experienced such joy in the Lord.

The next day, Larry was ready to set out on his journey. He put a generous monetary gift into my hand and told me it was a "seed." We gave each other a long, hard embrace; then Larry headed down the road, his walking stick in hand, with only a backpack, a bedroll, and a small tent strapped to his back. I took a short walk in the woods to be alone with my grief. A short while later, I felt hungry and went into town to get something to eat. Larry was still there trying to hitch a ride. We waved to each other as I drove by. On the way back, Larry was still there, so I stopped to pick him up. He was a bit confused by this, so I explained to him that I thought he would be able to get across the Canadian border a little more easily if I drove him across. Anything for a little more time with Larry.

We crossed the border with little trouble, and once again we hugged and parted ways. A few days later, my wife and I headed back to Pendleton. There I tried to bury myself in the school ministry. A few days later, I got a postcard from Larry explaining that someone had picked him up shortly after I let him off and had given him a ride to the main highway, where he got a ride to Banff National Park. It was the last time I would hear from him on this side of heaven. About two weeks later, early on a Sunday morning, I received the most stunning phone call of my life. Larry had been killed by a grizzly bear while camping in Glacier National Park.

I literally began to go into shock. My mind raced: *Wha...? No! It couldn't be!* It was. I put the phone back on the receiver after fumbling out some sort of response. I didn't know what to do except to call Debbie, who was out of town, and share the horrifying news. I was not able to speak to her at first; I just cried. She tried to get out of me what was the matter, and I finally choked it out. I was only able to give her a few details before I hung up and completely broke down sobbing, crying as hard as I had when my father died.

After several minutes, I was able to get some composure. I called Debbie back to assure her that I would be all right, though I felt anything but. I could only think enough to ask the Lord, "Why?" I simply could not understand why God would allow anyone to die in such a horrible manner, especially someone like Larry. I had never known anyone as Christlike as Larry Gordon, and *this* was his reward? Suddenly Christianity made no sense to me at all, and I asked God the ultimate question: "Are You real?" He did not react to my question with shock, horror, or wrath, just the patience of His deep love. His answer was composed of three words: "Wait and see." I did not hear the words audibly, but it was as if I had. I did not understand what the Lord meant, but with the little faith I could muster, I decided to trust His quiet leading.

I somehow managed to ready myself for church. I sat in stunned silence while the service proceeded around me. The pastor announced the tragic news about Larry during the service, and after the sermon the congregation sang, "Blest Be the Tie That Binds." When they began to sing the third verse, beginning with the words, "When we asunder part; it gives us inward pain," I noticed a friend who had also been very close to Larry leaving the room crying. I left to find her and give her some comfort.

I found Myrna sitting on the stairs leading to the lower floor of the church, crying softly. I sat quietly next to her and put my arm around her shoulders. After a few moments she asked me the same question that had been tumbling tortuously in my own mind: "Why?"

I wasn't able to give her an answer, but the quiet leading came to me once more. So I told her that I didn't know why, but the Lord had given me the words, "Wait and see."

There was a brief pause; then Myrna sat up straight and said slowly and thoughtfully, "Yes, yes, the Lord is going to bring something good from this."

I was amazed at her words, but it began to sink into me. Yes, the Lord was going to bring something good from this, as horrible as it was. This was His pruning, and he had something to bring through it. Just how he was going to do it, I could not imagine; but I would learn, through the years, that this event was to be the watershed of my entire Christian life.

Chapter 3
A SMALL GIANT FROM SCOTLAND

Larry died on September 26, 1980, even though we did not hear of his death until October 4. We held a memorial service for him at the assisted-living facility where he had worked about a week after hearing of his death. We tried to move on with our lives, even though our hearts ached terribly. For those of us who had been close to Larry, the loss was hard to absorb.

A few weeks after Larry's memorial service, Debbie and I turned onto the church's driveway on what promised to be a warm, sunny mid-October Sunday morning. The driveway lay long and straight for about a hundred yards before it opened up into a larger parking area just beyond the church building. As we started up the gentle incline, I noticed a nicely dressed gentleman talking with our good friend and my fellow deacon, Tommy Burton. As I continued to drive, I fixed my eyes on the gentleman and felt strangely drawn to him—so much so that I did not take my eyes off of him until I turned to park at the top of the parking area. Then I said to Debbie, "There's something about that man. I don't know what it is, but I'm going to find out." I left her at the car and hurried over. I walked up and stood silently while Tommy finished talking to the gentleman. Then Tommy, in his usual polite manner, said, "Scott, I'd like you to meet John Samson."

John Samson! This was the very man Larry had said was his spiritual father and mentor. After the trauma of Larry's death, I had all but forgotten my determination to find him. And here he was, standing right in front of me in our church parking lot!

"Brother John," as he was called by most, was a sturdy man, though only about five feet four inches tall. (He always joked that in his native Scotland, a man was measured from the chin up.) He was in good shape for a man in his late sixties. Having been raised in the lowlands of Scotland, he spoke with a kind and gentle Scottish brogue, and his voice was marked with genuine humility. He had also been stunned by Larry's death and was retracing the path Larry had trodden during the last two years of his life. That path had now brought him to Pendleton.

Debbie soon joined us and was introduced to Brother John as well. After a few moments of conversation, we took him into the church to meet our pastor. Our church was fairly small and informal, and after speaking with Brother John for a while, our pastor graciously asked if he would like to speak during our Sunday morning service in a little over an hour. Brother John then did something I had never seen before. He said he first needed to check with his Father for permission. He hurried from the room. I remember wondering if he was looking for a phone to call his earthly father, and then it began to dawn on me exactly what he meant. After a few moments, he reappeared and said that it was all right for him to speak during the service. His willingness to yield to his heavenly Father made a deep impression upon me.

I sat mesmerized as Brother John spoke that morning. I had never heard anyone speak with such an intimate knowledge of the Savior and His Word before. I did not yet realize it, but the "wait and see" was beginning to unfold before me that day. Though we may not ever fully understand why God allows some things to happen, He is able to bring beauty from ashes. Sometimes He uses these things to deepen our walk with Him or deepen our trust in Him, though I don't believe He would ever allow tragedies *solely* for those reasons. Some things will remain a mystery to us as long as we are on this side of heaven, but if we will continue to trust God *in spite of them*, He will continually draw us closer to Himself and deeper into His purposes.

Brother John's visit, during that October of 1980, lasted for two weeks; and while he was with us, he shared a stirring experience regarding Larry's death. He and another close friend of Larry's, Rob Nichols—another pilot employed by the same airline as Larry—were the friends Larry had planned to meet in Vermont after he toured the parks. They were to meet at a small priory led by a group of spiritual monks who held a daily communion service attended by people from all over the world. John had arrived early at the priory to visit with some of the brothers, and as the time for beginning the service neared, he found three seats together for them. As John waited alone, he sensed Larry's presence, so he turned to look for him. He didn't see Larry, so he turned back around to wait. After a few moments, John felt a hand on his shoulder. When he turned to look, he saw Larry and thought, "Oh, good, he's here." He wondered why Larry was wearing a red windbreaker jacket rather than his usual blue one. Larry, though, did not sit down. Rob had some car trouble and didn't make it to the service, and Larry never came and sat with Brother John.

After the service, Brother John looked for Larry but could not find him anywhere. This was all very unusual, so he called Larry's mother in Texas to see if she had heard from Larry or if anything was wrong. She hadn't. A few hours later, she called back weeping and said that Larry had been killed a few days before. Brother

John found out later that the windbreaker Larry was wearing when he was killed was red.

Brother John also shared with us about the memorial service in Larry's home church in Tyler, Texas. He had not only attended the service, but had spoken at it. He was astounded when he saw the hundreds of cards, letters, and flowers that had poured in from all over the country. These all came from people whose lives had been affected by Larry much like ours, whose lives Larry had touched in some profound way over the past three years.

Brother John pointed out to us that Larry had first put his faith in Christ when he was thirty years old, and he had died when he was thirty-three. We all marveled at the incredible level of maturity Larry had reached in a little over three years. It was a maturity that had found a great balance, combining God's love and God's holiness with the abundance of grace and humility that made Larry so approachable by anyone. In subsequent visits, Brother John shared more details about Larry's death and life, as he had known Larry about two years longer then we had. In his second visit to us, Brother John shared the effect Larry had on the park ranger he met just outside Glacier National Park in Cutbank, Montana. Larry had inquired with the ranger about staying in the park, and the ranger was so impressed with Larry that he invited him to stay at his home for a day or two.

Five years after Larry's death, a nationally known magazine carried a large article on encounters between humans and bears. A large part of the article was dedicated to Larry's story, and strangely enough, the article in this fairly secular magazine quoted the park ranger on his impression of the kind of person Larry was. He said the love of Jesus Christ just radiated out of Larry and that he had the sort of thing good Christians strive for.

Brother John had met Larry through flying on a plane which Larry co-piloted in the spring of 1978. They had just deplaned, and Larry saw John first and noticed that he was wearing a lapel pin in the shape of a dove on his suit jacket. Larry commented, "Either you're a lover of birds or a lover of Jesus." John replied that he was both, and a friendly conversation ensued. After they parted, Brother John was disturbed with himself that, even though they had exchanged names, he had not gotten Larry's address or phone number. The unique way Larry had struck up the conversation intrigued John, and he really wanted to see Larry again. So, after attending to the affairs he had while in the States, John inquired at the desk of the airline he and Larry had flown in on to see if someone could help him find Larry. Now, the Dallas International Airport was one of the largest airports in the US, with hundreds of planes flying in and out every day. But as Brother John was trying to describe Larry to the man at the desk, the man abruptly pointed beyond John and said, "There's your pilot." Such was the beginning of a friendship which became very deep in the Lord and took both men to many places throughout the world.

Because Larry was a pilot, he had access to inexpensive air travel. He spent time with Brother John in Israel at a youth center he directed, spending three months there at one stretch attending a Hebrew language school so he could learn the original language of the Old Testament. Sometimes Brother John's schedule was so busy that he didn't get back to the center until late into the night. Larry always turned back the covers on John's bed and had a pot of simmering tea waiting for him on those nights.

Larry also spent time at Brother John's home in Hove, England, with John and his amazing wife, Rosalie. Larry always stayed in the upper room, which was known as "the Prophet's Chamber." John also spent much time in Larry's hometown of Tyler. When they could not be together, they mailed mini cassette tapes to each other that could hold about thirty minutes of conversation on each side.

On one occasion while staying at Brother John's home, Larry brought out a handful of letters from his former fiance and showed them to John. John knew what they were. Larry had broken off the engagement because he wanted to completely dedicate himself to the Lord in accordance with 1 Corinthians 7:32–33. Larry knew it was not wrong to marry; he simply wanted to commit himself wholly to the One he loved more. It was a painful choice, and Larry had kept the letters and read them occasionally to get some comfort from the loss. Now, Larry built a small fire and burned the letters. John told me years later how he appreciated what Larry had done. It was a huge sacrifice, but Larry wanted to give himself completely to the Lord, and in burning the letters he cut the last tie with any other choice. John felt privileged to be present at such a moment.

When Brother John left us, many in Pendleton felt the beginning of a great bond of friendship. We begged him to come back to see us, and he did so three times over the next year and a half. We were starting to comprehend a great life that had been a major influence in Larry's relatively short yet amazingly deep spiritual life.

The friendship between Larry and John Samson was one of the most Christ-centered I have ever seen. But Brother John had a storied history of his own with the Lord.

John Samson was born in the lowlands of Ayrshire, Scotland, near the small town of Cumnock, in 1912. He was the youngest of five brothers. When he was five, his father left his mother to raise the boys alone. Brother John tried to help the family and earn a little pocket money for himself by gathering sticks and selling them for a penny a bundle and by caddying for golfers whenever he could. He knew from this very early age that the hand of the Lord was upon him, so he tried to do his best with whatever responsibility he was given.

One day when he was caddying, he was not able to find a golf ball that had been hit into the rough. This really bothered him, as it was an important part of being a good caddy. That night, while he was lying in bed trying to sleep after the hard day's work, the Lord gave him a vision of where the golf ball was. Early the next morning, Brother John hurried off to the golf course and found the lost ball just as it had been revealed to him. He joyfully returned it to the golfer, but more importantly, he understood from this and other such experiences that the Lord was with him ("a Father to the fatherless," as Psalm 68:4–5 promises) in a special way.

When Brother John was about twelve years old, an unfortunate accident caused a severe injury to his right hand. He found a blasting cap on his way to school one morning and carried it into his elementary school classroom. He began to pick at it with his pen while holding it with his right hand. The cap exploded. Only Brother John's right hand was injured, but it was injured severely. He lost his right thumb down to the first joint, about half of his pointing and middle fingers, and the tip of his ring finger. In spite of this loss, Brother John still wrote with his right hand and did so quite well. In time he also learned to play the piano at a fairly accomplished level. Brother John never allowed this small disability to slow him down in the least.

After Brother John finished his schooling, he went off to be trained for the ministry at a Bible college in Glasgow. He knew the Lord wanted him in the ministry, but after his third year of training, he felt the Lord calling him to leave college and enter immediately into the pastorate. He obeyed and became the pastor of a church in the northern Scottish city of Inverness. Brother John was never bothered by not finishing the degree program he had started at Glasgow; he understood well that his adequacy came from God and not from men or institutions.

Wherever the Lord led John, he threw himself fully into the responsibilities given to him. His pursuit of excellence was driven by his immense love for the Lord. During these early years of Brother John's adulthood, the Lord brought him to Hove, England, where he founded the Aldrington Free Church. Hove is situated on the southern coast of England and runs into the more famous southern English city of Brighton. Both are beautifully set about fifty miles due south of downtown London, overlooking the English Channel. It was here that John met the love of his life, humanly speaking. Rosalie Cole was the talented and witty daughter of an English builder. John and Rosalie were married in September of 1939 and began forging their life together in Christ at the end of the Great Depression and the beginning of World War II.

For years, Brother John led a large troop of boys in an organization known as the Boys' Brigade. During the same period, Rosalie led a group of girls through the Girls' Guild. John would organize and go on camping trips with the boys while teaching them outdoor skills. Rosalie would direct the girls in performing community plays and would teach them domestic skills. Together they would organize parades, and they marched through the town while the girls and boys were playing instruments and singing Christian hymns and fun songs. Character development was always at the fore, but it was modeled much more than it was preached or taught.

At the end of each year, several troops from the region would meet for an awards ceremony. A half-dozen or more trophies would be presented for excellence in various areas of skill and citizenship. The troop judged to have performed the best in a given area would win the trophy for that area. In most of the ceremonies throughout the years, Rosalie's Girls' Guild troop won most, if not all, of the trophies. At one particular ceremony, held in a local church, the director of the winning troop had to shimmy out of the row, walk down the aisle to the front of the sanctuary, climb the steps up to the platform, accept the trophy, and go back to her seat. On this year, Rosalie's troop won seven out of seven trophies. By the time Rosalie had been called to accept the final trophy, she was so wearied of the arduous journey to the platform that she simply climbed over the rows of seats to get to the front. This was quite typical of Rosalie's great sense of humor.

After years of winning so many trophies with her girls, Rosalie decided to start a new troop in a very poor area in the district. Brother John thought the task would be too much for her. Each of the girls would need a uniform, and most could not afford one. Rosalie sewed a uniform for every girl in the troop. When it came to putting on a community play, she sewed all of the costumes needed while the girls helped her make all of the props. Some wondered if Rosalie could keep up her string of successes at the awards ceremony that year. Once more, Rosalie's troop was awarded seven out of seven trophies.

As the Lord called Brother John deeper into His purposes, Rosalie became distressed because it was causing him to be away from her and their home more than she wanted. So she sought the Lord, and He gave her John 3:30: "He must increase, but I must decrease." Rosalie understood what the Lord was implying, so she decided she would become a prayer warrior for her husband. We will only know for sure when we get to heaven, but it is my estimation, as it was Brother John's, that a great number of the many wonderful things we saw the Lord do through Brother John were the results of Rosalie's prayers.

Brother John and Rosalie were never able to have children of their own, but this allowed them to devote themselves more fully to the Lord and His work. As the Lord's enterprises are always focused on people, they invested themselves in those God brought into their lives. In a spiritual sense, they had many children. I personally heard no fewer than seven men claim that Brother John Samson was their spiritual father.

After some time in Hove, the Lord took Brother John and Rosalie back to a local church in East Kilbride, Ayrshire, Scotland. Upon arrival, Brother John found that there were no living accommodations at the church, and there was only one house for sale in the entire area. The house, called "The Orchards," was a fairly imposing estate with a main residence, a ruined castle, stables, and a gatehouse. Brother John thought it would be nice to live there but had no money to buy it, and the price was seven thousand pounds sterling (about the equivalent of $250,000 to $450,000 in 2013). So, doing what he knew would give him a solution, he prayed to his heavenly Father about the fact that he was homeless and was expecting his wife to join him shortly. The Lord told him to buy The Orchards. Since he had no money, it really wasn't the answer he was looking for! However, his relationship with the Lord was founded on faith, so he entered into an agreement with the owner of the house. He explained that his funding would be coming later and that he could take immediate possession of the house as his wife was about to join him. Brother John and Rosalie moved in, having no money to pay for the house. As the time neared to pay, Brother John continued to pray. He was becoming quite concerned, but the Lord reassured him, "Have faith; trust in Me." And the Lord delivered. Someone offered to buy the gatehouse from Brother John, and the amount he offered was *exactly* seven thousand pounds.

I have included this episode in this book, not to validate any kind of "health and wealth" or "name it and claim it" gospel, but to show that when the Lord takes us into His purposes, there are divine reasons why He leads us down certain pathways. Sometimes these paths come in the way of great (or modest) blessings; at other times, they take us down the road of suffering. Either way, He is lovingly developing our character, if we will yield, in order to use us more and more for *His* purposes. Brother John shared with me later that he was sure the Lord gave him the responsibility of caring for this fairly large estate to prepare him for an even greater responsibility and ministry in the future. Brother John's many hours spent taking care of the gardens and the house and at times entertaining large groups of people, besides all of his pastoral responsibilities, did in fact prepare him well for a future ministry that would bring much glory to God and many blessings for many people from all over the world—and that would become an inspiration for my own journey of faith.

Chapter 4

BEIT SHALOM

In the nearly twenty-one years that I knew Brother John, we had hundreds of conversations about his season of directing a youth center in Israel called Beit Shalom. During his time in Oregon, he also gave six or seven slide presentations about it while I operated the slide projector for him. The account of this youth center and its place in Brother John's life inspired and challenged me as I continued to grow in the Lord.

As the years passed, the Lord saw Brother John and Rosalie through the end of the Great Depression and World War II, meeting their physical needs as well as keeping them safe and warm. During the war, they took care of a little girl for three years until she could be reunited with her parents. Brother John could not serve in the military because of the injury to his right hand, so he served as the warden of a district (called a ward) in Hove. His main responsibility was to make sure that everyone safely reached a bomb shelter during the many air raids over England. While Hove was never a main target, many times the German planes would dump the bombs they had left over along the south coast of England after bombing London. Brother John led many groups to pray for the safety of the Hove area throughout the war. They prayed intensely when the nightly bombings of London occurred in the fall and winter of 1941 during the Battle of Britain. Many bombs were dropped throughout these times, but only one landed in their area during the entire war, and it landed in a cemetery. The only damage was to those who could no longer be hurt.

After the war, in the 1950s and early 1960s, Brother John and Rosalie spent thirteen years in South Africa doing some mission work there. South Africa's apartheid policy disillusioned Brother John, so he went back to England and worked in London for three years.

In 1967, the couple went on a two-week tour of Israel. While there, Brother John came to the realization that the Lord had a special work for them in that nation. About a year later, the Lord led him to a "temporary position" that turned into an eleven-year stay in Israel. It was during this time that the Lord accomplished His most amazing work through them, even though Rosalie eventually went back to their home in England to care for her aging sister.

The Quiet Leading

Sometime in 1968, Brother John took a position in Israel through the Church of Scotland and was put in charge of a Scottish hospice and a church in Jerusalem near the Mount of Olives. While carrying out his responsibilities there, he began to learn the layout, customs, and culture of Israel. He also began to make many close friends and acquaintances. After about a year at the hospice and church, Brother John resigned his position. He was soon asked to take another as a guide at the Garden Tomb just outside the walls of the Old City of Jerusalem. He loved this job, as it afforded him the opportunity to share with people from all over the world about the death, burial, and resurrection of Jesus. It also gave him more free time on days off (the hospice had required his attention seven days a week), which he used to tour and visit places and areas outside of Jerusalem.

It was during a particularly busy time in his second year working at the Garden Tomb that John felt the need to get away for a quiet weekend somewhere. He had heard that the Latrun Monastery, situated in the Ayalon Valley about eighteen miles out of Jerusalem, would take guests, but he had made no arrangements to stay there. So he committed it to the Lord to undertake in such a way that he could be sure it was God's will for him to go. He drove out to the monastery, and when he entered the gate, he was met by one of the approximately thirty Trappist monks who lived there. When Brother John saw the monk, he recognized him from a meeting at the Garden Tomb two or three weeks previous (he was the *only* monk Brother John knew at the monastery at that time). The monk greeted him with the words, "Oh, how nice to see you! I hope you have come to stay for a time." Brother John felt this invitation was the confirmation he was seeking from the Lord. The story is an example of a major principle I learned through Brother John's life: sometimes yielding to the Lord in even the smallest thing can lead to great opportunities. We can be sure that if we are not mindful of God concerning the little things, in the course of our days on earth, we will most assuredly miss the greater opportunities.

So the monk showed John to his room, and after spending some time there, he decided to go on a walk to spend some time in the Word in a little piece of woods behind the monastery. He sat down in the shade of a tree and began to read from the book of Haggai. In the second chapter, beginning in verse 7, he read:

> And I will shake all nations, and the desire of all nations shall come:
> and I will fill this house with glory, saith the LORD of hosts. The silver is
> mine, and the gold is mine, saith the LORD of hosts. The glory of this latter

house shall be greater than of the former, saith the LORD of hosts: and in this place will I give peace, saith the LORD of hosts. (Haggai 2:7–9)

Brother John had learned long ago the value of listening to God through His Word. Now the Lord was impressing the words of this passage upon him, but he didn't understand what they were getting at. He asked the Lord to be patient with him and help him understand.

A short while later, John got up to go back to the monastery. As he was walking through the front garden, he was met by the abbot, who engaged him in a brief conversation. After the usual introductions, the abbot said to Brother John, "You know, we're praying that that place over there will become a Christian center one day." As he said this, he pointed over to a group of trees about a mile away. All they could see was the roof of a building, but the remarkable thing was that as the abbot spoke, the words of Haggai came immediately to Brother John's mind: "The glory of this latter house shall be greater than of the former, saith the LORD of hosts."

So Brother John asked the abbot about the building's history, and the abbot said that it had been erected on the supposed site of the house of Cleopas (see Luke 24:13–35—Cleopas was one of the disciples Jesus joined on the road to Emmaus after the resurrection). Brother John asked him who owned the building, and the abbot responded that it was owned by a Roman Catholic organization. When Brother John heard that, he thought to himself, *This is not the place for me.* His father had been an anti-popery preacher, and anything to do with Catholicism had been considered taboo in their home. For Brother John himself, visiting a monastery was not a big issue, but entering into a partnership or legal agreement was something else altogether. And now he was being confronted with the possibility of contacting a Roman Catholic priest about this building. Brother John tried to push the whole thing from his mind, telling himself he had imagined everything about the building.

Quickly ending his retreat at the monastery, Brother John drove back to Jerusalem and continued guiding tours at the Garden Tomb. But during that week, the Lord persisted through the quiet leading of His still, small voice, "You *must* go and see that place." So without giving any details, Brother John talked his only coworker, John Vanderhoven, into going with him, and they drove out to Emmaus.

As they approached the site, they saw a large, beautiful white stone building with arches in the middle and a wing at each end. A large circular window was built into the right wing of the building with stone crosses carved right into the window, signifying that this wing was probably a chapel or a church. When they came to the gate pillars of a stone wall, they saw some ancient ruins between themselves and the building. They would later find out that these were the ruins of a church from the twelfth century which were built over the ruins of a church dating back to the seventh century. That church was built upon the site of yet another church, which was built in the fourth century. There were also some mosaics, some with Greek texts in them from one of the Gospels, that dated back to a second-century Roman villa that had been built over what was believed to be the site of the house of Cleopas.

Brother John and John Vanderhoven walked past the ruins and up the driveway to the front of the building. The years and the lack of care had taken a fairly serious toll on the building. They couldn't get inside the front door (they later found it had been barred from the inside), so they entered through a side door in the left wing. As they pushed the door open, they found the floor covered with rocks, bricks, glass, plaster, and all sorts of debris several inches deep. Walls had been knocked down so that there wasn't a whole room inside the entire building. They found out later that the Israeli army had been using the building for a campsite for many years and left their rubbish whenever they finished staying there. It had been accumulating for several years.

The two men were amazed at the extent of the damage that had been done, but they were also amazed at the beauty of the front of the building. It had been built by the Roman Catholic Church over a three-year period beginning in 1933 and used to house the senior students studying for the priesthood from a seminary near Bethlehem. They would spend their final year of seminary in this building before going into the priesthood or onto a mission field. The building had thirty-six rooms, including thirteen bedrooms, a dining room and kitchen area, a chapel, and a huge room which later became a music room. Not one room had been left entire.

They made their way down a corridor toward the front door and found a stairway leading up to the second floor. A long, arched balcony stretched out in front of the building. Ascending the stairway, they stepped out onto the balcony and found another stairway leading up to a flat roof.

On the rooftop, they decided to get down on their knees and claim the building for the Lord. They asked for guidance as to how He wanted to use the building and claimed it for His glory. Then they climbed back down, got into the car, and drove back to Jerusalem. On the way back, they laughed and called each other all sorts of names for having such wild, imaginative thoughts. What could they do with a place like that? It would cost hundreds of thousands of pounds sterling, the British monetary unit which was approximately twice the value of the American dollar at the time. If they did rebuild it, what could they do with it? How could they furnish it? Where would they get people to support it? All these thoughts kept going through their minds. Brother John finally said, "John, let's forget it." But the Lord didn't say so. The words of Haggai came back once more:

> The silver is Mine and the gold is Mine, saith the LORD of hosts. The glory of this latter house shall be greater than of the former, saith the LORD of hosts: and in this place will I give peace, saith the LORD of hosts.

All the next week, the Lord kept insisting, "You must go and find out more about that place." So Brother John decided to go back to the monastery and ask the abbot if anyone was interested in it. He also decided that if the abbot were to say that no one was interested and the building was available if he wanted it, that would be enough of a miracle to indicate the Lord was indeed leading the way. So he went back to the monastery and inquired of the abbot as to whether anyone was interested in the building, and the abbot said just those words. Brother John asked the abbot who owned the place, and the abbot replied that it was owned by the Latin Fathers of Beit Jala near Bethlehem.

Brother John still struggled a bit with having to go before a Roman Catholic priest to inquire about the building, but the Lord said, "You go and see that man." So Brother John inquired of the abbot as to whether he could arrange for a meeting.

Shortly thereafter, Brother John went to see Father Mine Al b'Train, a Frenchman, at the seminary. He found him to be one of the most gracious men he had ever met. All thoughts of him being a Roman Catholic disappeared. To Brother John, this man was simply a servant of God. He spoke so graciously and so kindly, and when Brother John mentioned the building, he asked, "What do you want it for?" Brother John replied that he didn't have much of an idea, and it sounded crazy, but he thought it would make a splendid youth center. Father Mine Al said, "Yes, it's a very good idea." Then Brother John asked what the possibility of such a venture coming to fruition might be. Father Mine Al said there was no reason Brother John could not have the building, but first he must get permission from the bishop in Jerusalem; second he must get permission from Rome; and third he must get permission from the military authorities, because the building was in an occupied area under a curfew. This meant that no one was allowed to enter the area an hour before dark or leave until an hour after sunrise. He warned Brother John that it could be risky because there were soldiers watching all the time.

What Father Mine Al said next nearly floored Brother John. He said, "You know, it's strange; I'm going to Rome next week, and I'll bring it before the authorities there." He continued to say that he was meeting with the bishop in Jerusalem the very next day, and he would speak to him regarding the building as well. John thought to himself, *What am I getting into here?* Then he conveyed to Father Mine Al that he would carry on until he heard back from him. At this, Father Mine Al asked Brother John if he would look after the place and see what he could do about cleaning it up until he returned from Rome. He said there had been a lot of vandalism going on, and he mentioned that the Israeli soldiers occasionally stayed there and always left the place in much worse shape than they found it. Brother John agreed to watch the building, and he and a friend stayed at the place for the next two or three nights.

A few weeks later, Father Mine Al sent for Brother John. "I don't understand it," he told him, "but when I presented your proposition to the authorities in Rome, they said, 'Yes, let him have the place.' The bishop in Jerusalem is quite willing for you to have it as well." So now there was only one obstacle left: the military authorities. Father Mine Al told Brother John that he would have to approach Moshe Dayan, who was in charge of the entire military in Israel.

The thought of meeting Moshe Dayan thrilled Brother John. He had done so much for the Israeli military, and he was considered a hero in Israel. Father Mine Al, however, thought it would be best to first write a letter.

A letter was sent off, and three weeks later Brother John received a reply from Moshe Dayan. He said he didn't have any objections to Brother John using the building so long as it was not used to hold any sort of public meetings to discuss political issues. This suited Brother John just fine. He wanted to use the building to glorify the Lord.

Now Brother John was faced with the enormous task of restoring the building. How would he raise the funds for such a project? Every time he got down on his knees to ask for guidance about it, the Lord brought to mind three hundred pounds sterling he had saved up to get a flight out of Israel in case a war broke out (a very real possibility at that time). So Brother John said, "All right, Lord," and he put the money into the building. Now he was ready to start.

Before Brother John started any work on the building, he went out to it alone one day, knelt down in the rubble in the main hallway downstairs, and said, "Lord, You have challenged me to do something about this place. I'm going to take Hudson

Taylor's motto as a motto for this place: to move man through God by prayer alone. I promise You now that I will never ask anyone to help. There will never be any appeals for funds of any kind. No one will be told outside this building what the needs are. To You alone, who have brought me to this place and challenged me here, I hand back the challenge, and I promise You that I will in no way receive any human effort to raise funds." For the eight-and-a-half years Brother John was at the building, that promise was kept.

It didn't take long for God's plans to begin coming to light. Young people and adults came from all over the world to help in the rebuilding of Beit Shalom or just to stay for a youth retreat. Sometimes world-famous Christians would come to lead week-long seminars. Top-rated musicians, like members of the Israeli Philharmonic Orchestra, would come to give concerts of praise. All willingly joined in with the daily cleaning, preparing of meals, or whatever task needed to be done.

Over sixteen hundred young people stayed at that building from over twenty different nationalities. Many of them are now on the mission field. Others are doctors, nurses, and lawyers scattered all over the world. Over half a million dollars came in by prayer *alone*. People would come to Brother John and say, "Tell me what your needs are, because we want to help." Every time Brother John would reply, "If you want to help, you go and ask the Lord. It's His building, not mine. He'll tell you what the needs are." Never, at any time, did Brother John mention to anyone what they needed.

On one occasion, a man came to Brother John while he was at home in Hove, England, and told him that he wanted to give him a gift of two thousands pounds sterling every year until the completion of the building, provided that Brother John would appoint a committee to help him with that place because it was too big for him to run alone. He said this while they were sitting in Brother John's front sitting room. Brother John excused himself to go to the back room, but halfway there the Lord told him to have nothing to do with it. So he turned on his heel and went back and told the man, "Thank you, but the Lord says no." The man said, "How? Why?"

Brother John replied, "I don't know, but he said no, so I must do exactly what he says." The remarkable thing was that, in spite of it, the man sent Brother John two thousand pounds a year without question, and without stating what it was to be used for. In addition, he sent his three sons, one after another, when they had reached the age of seventeen and had left the public school, to stay with Brother John at the building for six months, each to learn this life of faith before being sent out into his life's work. The building eventually became known as *Beit Shalom*, which means "The House of Peace."

Chapter 5
Through God by Prayer Alone

While Brother John was still working at the Garden Tomb, he would go out to Beit Shalom and work each evening. He began by cleaning the rubble and working on replacing the hundreds of broken panes of glass in the building. The broken windows were allowing birds and bats and mice and rats to get in. When he and those helping him finished, they had replaced more than five hundred panes of glass.

One evening when Brother John came back to Beit Shalom after working all day, he went into the chapel and found that two of the three stained-glass windows had been pried out of the chapel wall. One of them was lying smashed and twisted on the floor, and the other was completely gone. Brother John was distraught at the thought of losing any of these windows because they had been specially made and could not be replaced. Even if they could, the glass in them was very expensive. They were beautiful windows with steel frames that stood about six feet tall and eighteen inches wide, with golden glass set in an ornate design. They had a convex shape, and when the sun was setting, the chapel was stunningly illuminated in gold. But how could they find the missing window? Where could it possibly be?

For almost a year, Brother John prayed that the Lord would guide him to that window. He knew it had to be somewhere nearby because it was too big and clumsy to be carried very far. One day, the secretary from a kibbutz about two miles away sent for Brother John and asked him to come and talk to him about cooperation between the young people at the kibbutz and the young people who came to Beit Shalom. He wanted the young people from the kibbutz to come to Beit Shalom and help there with whatever was needed, and then the young people from Beit Shalom could go to the kibbutz and help them in the same way.

Brother John arrived early for the appointment, so he walked around the grounds. Suddenly, he stumbled upon the chapel window lying in the grass! He joined the secretary for their meeting, and when the secretary was finished talking, Brother John said, "Well, before we can enter into any negotiations, there has to be complete trust and understanding between us." The secretary replied, "Oh, yes, of course." To that Brother John asked, "Can I have my window back?" The secretary answered, "What do you mean?" Brother John answered, "Come outside and I'll show you." So he took him to where the window was lying in the grass. The secretary very innocently asked, "Well, how did that get there?" Brother John replied, "I don't know, but I would like it over at my place." The next day when Brother John got to the building, the window was lying on the front steps waiting to be taken into the chapel.

After another week or two of working at the Garden Tomb during the day and cleaning and repairing the building in the evenings, two young fellows from America came out. They had heard something about the place becoming a youth center and wondered if they could help. Brother John said, "Yes, of course. What do you do? Are you qualified in anything?" They replied that they were not qualified in any particular skill but that they could do things generally. They had previously worked alongside a carpenter as he did different tasks. Brother John asked, "Do you know how to glaze? Put in windows?" They said they didn't. So they prayed that the Lord would guide them regarding replacing the panes of glass.

Brother John left the boys to the work while he stayed in Jerusalem and worked at the Garden Tomb. After about four days, Brother John went out to the building to see how the work was progressing, and the young fellows told him of an episode that had happened. The younger of the two was chipping away at the glass in one of the windows, and a piece of glass flew into his eye. He was instantly in great agony, and he called to the other fellow to come and pray with him. They got down on their knees and prayed. When they finished praying, the younger fellow took his hand away from his eye, and the piece of glass was lying in the palm of his hand.

When Brother John heard this, he realized how gracious the Lord had been even though he had not thought to ask for the protection of Jesus while they worked on the place. Immediately the three of them went through the building, into every room, and asked the Lord to protect the location and anyone who would be coming to work there so there would be no accidents.

There were no other accidents during the eight-and-a-half years they were in the building. Brother John quipped later that if anyone had seen some of the equipment and rickety scaffolding they used to paint the high walls and ceilings (sixteen feet high), they would have realized just what a miracle that was! They used some of most ramshackle structures that were ever put together, and neither of the boys had ever climbed on such things before. Sometimes they had to climb up and walk along a plank about a foot wide. At first Brother John had to go up and help them along and hold them up until they got their balance. Then they would begin scraping and painting the upper walls and ceilings. Every wall and ceiling in the entire building had to be scraped.

On another occasion, Brother John had gone into Jerusalem for the day to do some shopping. When he returned, he found armored cars and all kinds of military vehicles parked at the house and four hundred soldiers already established inside the building. When he went to see one of the officers, he was asked, "What are you doing here?" To which Brother John replied, "I want to know what *you* are doing here!" Brother John explained that he had been asked to take over the place and was making it into a youth center. When the officer heard that, he apologized profusely. They slept there that night in different rooms on the floor and left the next day. Once again, though, there was much more trash left there than when the soldiers had come.

A little later, while working at the Garden Tomb, Brother John met a group of Christians who were part of a choir. They had heard about Beit Shalom, and they asked if it would be all right if they came out and stayed for a couple of days to help with the work there. Brother John told them they could come and stay on the condition that they sang while they were there. Now, there was still no electricity at all at Beit Shalom, and the chapel had not yet been worked on. Yet after working during the day, the choir gathered in the chapel amidst candlelight, and standing with rubble all around and water dripping through a leaky roof, they sang, and they sang, and they sang. It was glorious to hear. In fact, one night the abbot of the monastery was in the area and heard them singing. He asked Brother John if the choir could come and sing at the monastery. So they also went and sang to the monks.

Later on, with the help of some others, Brother John took on the dreadful job of sealing the entire roof with tar to stop the leaks when it rained. He had never done anything like this before, and the old tar was pealing in places, but they managed to seal up all the cracks and leaks until the whole roof was watertight. Once this was done, they were able to clean and repair the chapel. After they cleared away the rubble, they cleaned and polished the floor, which was made of beautiful grain-gold and cream-colored tiles set in designed panels. A communion table stood on a slightly raised platform at the front of the chapel. After it was cleaned up, the beautiful marble, which had been quarried near Jerusalem, was stunning. The monks also gave Brother John a prayer desk, which he put in the chapel in front of the communion table. Now people could come up to the front to kneel and pray.

A young man who came from Virginia Beach, Virginia, heard about the place while at the Garden Tomb and asked if he could come out to help. Before he left, he gave Brother John a gift of five hundred dollars for chairs for the chapel. Next came the chapel curtains. On one of his trips back to England, someone said, "What about curtains? You must need curtains for that place." Brother John replied that his wife didn't want him to say anything, but yes, they did need curtains. In fact, he told the man he had the measurements for the curtains with him, and he gave them to him. So the man went to one of the biggest shops in Hove and bought the most expensive velvet material he could find. The curtains were readied to be taken to Israel, but Brother John had a lot of other things to take as well. The airline he was flying on allowed only twenty kilograms (about forty-four pounds) of luggage per passenger. He had over sixty kilograms of luggage, and he didn't have any money left to pay the charge for the extra weight. So Brother John just committed it to the Lord.

When he got to the airport and approached the desk of the airline, two or three people were ahead of him in line, and a few followed behind him. As they moved forward, Brother John inching his heavy bags along, he saw how those ahead of him were putting their bags on the weighing machine to be weighed and then taken off to be loaded onto the plane. The lady in front of him put her luggage onto the machine, had it weighed, and then watched as it was taken off. Brother John was about to follow suit when the girl at the desk paused for a moment to talk to someone. When she looked again, he put his baggage onto the machine, but it didn't work. She approached someone at the next desk, but that desk was quite busy, and people were piling up behind Brother John. So she said, "On you go," and he got through with all his luggage. When he looked back, the next person in line put his luggage onto the weighing machine, and it worked. When Brother John told us the story at one of our slide presentations, he said, "The Lord had even taken care of the luggage. That's how the Lord works. Is anything too hard for the Lord? He's in control of everything. Every detail He has taken care of."

Brother John also felt that the chapel needed some Bibles. So he decided that on his next return to England, he would go to the British and Foreign Bible Society to see if they had copies of the New International Version. He knew where the organization had been located in London a while back, but he wondered if it was still there. He left for England and was met at the airport by a friend who was going up to Scotland and wanted Brother John to accompany him. Brother John agreed, so they put the car on a train and rode to the Midlands. From there, they continued by car. Then they spent the night at a farm nearby and continued on to Scotland the next day.

When they began the trip, Brother John was asked to take charge of an elderly gentleman and to share his sleeping chamber with him. He graciously agreed to this also. On the way back down, they stayed again at the same farm, then caught the train from Maxport down to London. However, the older gentleman had decided he wasn't going to return to London, which meant there would be a sleeping compartment available in Brother John's sleeping chamber. Brother John went to find his sleeping chamber when they got onto the train, but when he found the one that matched the number on his ticket, there was a gentleman standing just outside. As Brother John approached, the man asked if this was his compartment. The man was trying to get a booking because his son was speaking at a large meeting in London, and he wanted to surprise him by coming to hear him speak. He explained that the train was full, there were no accommodations even in first class, and he was hoping someone had canceled their booking. Brother John offered to share his chamber.

After they got settled the gentleman introduced himself, and in the course of conversation asked Brother John what he did. Brother John told him that he was in charge of a youth center in Israel and asked if the gentleman knew whether the British and Foreign Bible Society was still on Queen Victoria Street. The gentleman replied that it was, and he asked Brother John why he wanted to know. Brother John replied that he wanted to buy Bibles to take them back to Israel. To this the gentleman asked how many Bibles he wanted, and Brother John said forty. The gentleman took a card out of his wallet and wrote on it, "Please give John Samson forty Bibles and charge it to my account." That gentleman was one of the directors of the British and Foreign Bible Society! "How perfectly the Lord works when we are walking in His way!" Brother John told us years later, and he quoted from Genesis 24:27: "Being in the way, the Lord led me."

With the addition of the chairs and the Bibles, the chapel was complete. There was a chapel service held every evening at six o'clock. Everyone was required to be clean, washed, and dressed well for the service, but Brother John rarely had to enforce this because the people so willingly entered into the special spirit that God so impressed upon those who stayed at Beit Shalom. The first service in the chapel was a candlelight service because there was no electricity yet. Only Brother John, a friend of his, and a young man from Holland attended. As time progressed, there were sometimes thirty in attendance at chapel; occasionally there would be as many as sixty or seventy, but usually fifteen to twenty attended. Brother John said it was wonderful to see the people coming to chapel all prepared, and they had many times of wonderful fellowship. A different person from the group or groups staying at Beit Shalom would lead the chapel service each night. Then, at the end of each service, all would come forward to kneel at the prayer desk to receive the elements of communion.

While Beit Shalom was in the early stages of being rebuilt, Brother John stayed in a small room at the top of the stairs. He had two pots and a hot plate for cooking, a bowl for a washbasin, a lamp, and a portable oil stove to provide heat during the cold Israeli winters. He borrowed a set of bunk beds from a youth center in Jerusalem to sleep on.

One day a young lady from the youth center was at Beit Shalom and saw the beds. She said to Brother John, "You say that you are trusting the Lord to meet your needs. It's not very much like faith, taking a couple of beds from the youth center on the Mount of Olives." Brother John replied, "No, you're quite right." As he said that, the word of the Lord came to him from the book of Genesis, chapter 14. After Abraham had rescued Lot and the goods and people from Sodom and Gomorrah, the king of Sodom told Abraham he could keep the goods. Abraham replied that he would not even take a thread or a sandal strap.

Brother John understood what the Lord was getting at, and the next day he borrowed a truck and took the beds back to the youth center. For the next three months, he slept on the floor. It had to be seen that the Lord alone was working at Beit Shalom. There could not be even the slightest effort on Brother John's part or it would allow Satan to undermine the very principle on which he had set out to accomplish the work.

Brother John stayed in that room during most of his time at Beit Shalom. It became the "Holy of Holies" to him. He had many blessed and wonderful experiences with the Lord there. Brother John said later, "It didn't matter that there was no glass in the windows for a time. It didn't matter that there were no carpets on the floor; that there was no sink; that there was no bed. It didn't matter. The Lord was there."

Later on, the bedrooms upstairs were named after the twelve tribes of Israel. The room that Brother John stayed in was named after the tribe of Levi, the priestly room. Later, Shulamith Katznelson, a Jewish friend of Brother John's and the founder and director of a Hebrew language school called Ulpan Akiva, came often to stay at Beit Shalom. She loved to hear about how God was answering prayer there. "Whenever she came to stay," Brother John told us, "she asked to stay in that room. All the other rooms were much nicer, but that was the room she chose whenever she came."

There were times at Beit Shalom when Brother John and those with him were almost down to living on bread and water, but they always had enough. One time, when Brother John left Israel for a short while, the Lord provided enough for him to buy a new car. So he bought a little Peugeot 204 and took it to Beit Shalom. It was the first time Brother John had ever bought a new car. He later recalled that it was his pride and joy. During those early months, though, the Lord placed His hand upon that car. Brother John had a time of devotions at 5:30 each morning. During one of those times, he read a verse from the Scriptures that said, "He that forsaketh not all that he hath cannot be My disciple" (Luke 14:33). Brother John was shocked. He had read this verse many times before, but this time it had great power and force as he read it. He wanted to go and speak to the abbot at the monastery about it. So he went and recited the verse to the abbot and asked him if he remembered it. The abbot responded that he knew the verse, so Brother John asked him what he thought it meant. The abbot replied that it meant exactly what it said. Then Brother John explained that the Lord had placed a burden upon him about the disposing of his car. He explained further that he needed the car, but he also needed some money for the rebuilding of Beit Shalom. He could purchase a lot of tools and materials if he sold the car for 750 pounds sterling, but he couldn't get along without the car.

The abbot said, "Whatever He said to you, you do it." So Brother John made up his mind that the car would be sold.

That week, Brother John received a letter in the mail that had a check in the amount of 750 pounds sterling. John took the letter to the abbot with great glee, thinking that he could now keep his car. He reminded the abbot of what they had talked about and showed him how the Lord had provided the 750 pounds. He wouldn't have to sell his car after all.

The abbot said, "Just a minute, just a minute…what did He tell you?" Brother John said, "All right, you're right," and he sold the car the next day.

For the next six months, Brother John had to travel to Jerusalem by a shared taxi. He would walk more than a mile to the main road to meet the taxi, and he would ride in it, packed with people, for the seventeen-mile drive to the city. He would then shop and pack the heavy bags back into the taxi, ride the seventeen miles back to the road to Beit Shalom, and walk more than a mile to the house, carrying the heavy bags in the heat of an extremely hot Israeli summer. Many times he was so fatigued, he yearned greatly to have a car again.

At the end of these long months, Brother John needed to go back to England, and the Lord supplied the funds for him to go. While he was there, some friends inquired of Rosalie what he was doing in Israel. She replied that he was in charge of a youth center. Without realizing just how difficult Brother John's situation was, they had heard that he was in need of a vehicle. They said they had been burdened and praying about it. Then they gave him the amount of money needed to purchase a van. This was exactly what was needed because he had wanted to purchase several things needed at Beit Shalom while in England. This was the perfect way to get them back to Israel. So Brother John bought the van and literally packed it from floor to ceiling with carpets, stoves, chairs, bedding, even the kitchen sink!

Brother John sent the packed van by boat with his nephew Jim to Israel while he flew down. They met each other at Haifa. The van was the last of seven vehicles to be unloaded from the ship. Brother John watched as the inspector came along and required all the vehicles in front of the van to be emptied completely. Even the seats were taken out and put onto the dock. Every bag and box was opened for inspection. Brother John prayed silently, *Oh, Lord, what am I going to do?* He knew the inspector would open the door to the van and require them to pull all that stuff out. So he told Jim that they needed to pray for the Lord to somehow blind the eyes of the inspector to what was in the van. Brother John watched with great trepidation as the inspector approached. He opened the door, took one look, closed the door, and said, "On you go." Brother John and Jim left that place praising the Lord as all the other people were still having their things inspected on the dock.

But the Lord was not done challenging Brother John with Luke 14:33. He had already challenged him to give up his emergency fund of three hundred pounds sterling and to give up his car. Now the Lord challenged him to leave his job at the Garden Tomb. Brother John not only had been earning wages, but he had also been insured, and some unemployment benefits were available to him. Now the Lord was saying he must give up the work there in order to concentrate on the work at Beit Shalom. This meant there would be no income at all for himself, and any means for insurance would be cut off forever. He would have to rely entirely on the Lord to meet his needs. The Lord said to Brother John, "I'm your insurance. Whatever needs there will be in the future, trust Me." Finally Brother John began to understand more fully what the Lord was getting at in Luke 14:33. It was not that we must necessarily forsake everything to follow Him, but that He *will* provide for us when we depend on Him wholly. He is the Bridegroom, and we are the bride. It is the responsibility of the Bridegroom to see that all the needs of His bride are being met; and it is wonderful how He does just that.

Later on, at a time when there were only seven people at Beit Shalom, they got down to the last of their food and money. They ate what was remaining of the food for breakfast and decided to have a day of prayer and fasting. So each went to his room, and Brother John went to his and made up a list of all the food and supplies they needed. He totaled the amount for the items on the list, and it came to 312 pounds. He divided the list so each person could pray for a part of it, but he did not tell the others the total amount needed. In the middle of the day, Brother John suddenly realized that the Lord had answered their prayers, and he began to praise Him. He rushed from his room and called all the young people together and said, "Let's praise the Lord because He has answered our prayers." They asked how, and Brother John said he didn't know how; he just knew the Lord had answered.

Later that day Brother John went to the monastery to pick up the mail. In it was a letter with a money order for 312 pounds exactly. That letter had taken over a week to get there, and it was there right when it was needed with the exact amount that was needed. Brother John said later, "This was not an isolated incident; this was a regular occurrence. Whatever needs there were, the Lord met those needs."

Up to this point, there was still no electricity at Beit Shalom. Everything after dark had to be done either with lanterns or by candlelight. They had been praying for the Lord to provide them with electricity, but they had no money to buy the supplies needed, nor did they have anyone qualified to install it. A young man from Holland, named Peter, had come to Israel, and while visiting the Garden Tomb he heard about Beit Shalom. So he came out and asked Brother John if he could stay for three days to pray for guidance to understand why the Lord had brought him to Israel. He didn't know why he had come, he only knew that the Lord had sent him. Peter did not know that they had been praying for the funds to install electricity and for a qualified electrician to install it.

At the end of three days, Peter came to John and said, "Brother John, I know what I've got to do now." Brother John asked, "What is that, Peter?" Peter replied that he had to install the electricity in this place. He was a qualified electrician, and he had brought some money with him. He went on to say that he intended to use the money to go back to Holland and buy all the wiring and install all the electricity. For the next three months, that's what Peter did. He spent all his time wiring every room at Beit Shalom. But they still needed a generator.

By this time, the monks at the monastery had become prayer partners with Beit Shalom. Brother John mentioned the need for a generator now that the wiring was installed. The abbot told Brother John that they had just installed one and asked if they could order another for him. Brother John protested, "Just a minute; all I want you to do is pray that the Lord will meet our need because we haven't got the money." He reminded the abbot about the principles at Beit Shalom, one of which was that they wouldn't go into debt. The abbot told him it would cost 750 pounds for a small generator, but he would get the monks to pray that night, and they would pray until the need was met.

The next day, when Brother John got the mail, there was a check in one of the letters for 750 pounds. That check had been sent from England a week earlier. He went back to the monastery immediately and asked if the abbot remembered what they had talked about the day before. The abbot said that he did. Then Brother John asked if he knew the text, "Before they call, I will answer; and while they are yet speaking, I will hear" (Isaiah 65:24). The abbot again said that he did. Brother John said, "There's the answer," and he showed him the check. The abbot clapped his hands and said, "Praise the Lord! Now we must praise Him tonight," and he and the monks joined with Brother John and Beit Shalom in praising the Lord for the way He had provided for the generator. Brother John reflected later on the wonderful spiritual cooperation they constantly enjoyed with the monks.

Brother John always felt that the generator was a wonderful blessing, but when it was first installed, it had to be started with a hand crank. He said there were many times he felt like his arm might fall off! Later, a young man from Canada came and saw how Brother John struggled with the generator. He told Brother John that he needed two batteries to start it, and after they got them from Jerusalem, the young man installed them so all that had to be done to start the generator was to push a button. Brother John said, "What a joy that was."

And not only that, the young man extended the line into the house so they could start or stop the generator from inside. Unfortunately, the starter button was installed in one of the bathrooms. On one occasion they were having a dinner party, and one of the ladies went into the bathroom and pushed the generator button by mistake. All the lights went off. Soon after that, a sign was posted by the button explaining its purpose.

Now that electricity had come to Beit Shalom, Brother John decided to do something about the water situation. There was no running water in the building when the work was started, so they carried buckets of water from a well in the ruins about 150 yards from the house. They did this for about a year until one of the monks happened along and saw how hard they were working for so little water. He told Brother John the monks could bring a tank of water from the monastery and put it behind the building, and they could use the water from the tank. So twice a week the monks brought a tank of water to the back of the building, and the folks staying at Beit Shalom pumped that water to a tank on the roof of the building. Every time they pumped the water it took two-and-a-half hours, and they had to be very careful in the use of that water. You can imagine just how much each person was covered with dust at the end of each day at first, working among the dirt and grime while cleaning and repairing the place. Everyone had to be washed, but they had to be careful not to use too much water.

The monks brought the tank full of water by twice a week for two years. During the first three years, Rosalie committed herself, at Brother John's request, to ardently praying for the water situation.

At one time Brother John decided to put an apparatus on the well so they could pump the water from the well up to the tank on the roof instead of dealing with a second tank. They installed the cables for the electricity and the pipes for the water. Just when they were about to add the pump to the system, Brother John got an official letter from the Israeli authorities stating Beit Shalom would be charged a monthly fee for using the well and another fee for each gallon they pumped. The letter also said that any equipment the people at Beit Shalom attached to the well would have to be left there after they were done using the well.

Brother John was absolutely dumbfounded, so he took the letter over to the abbot and showed it to him. The abbot said, "This is too much. But listen, we supplied that house with water years ago when the British troops were there. There must be a pipeline from the monastery to your place."

So, after three years at Beit Shalom, in the middle of July, Brother John and a young man began digging up that pipeline, finding every place it leaked in the nearly mile and a half from the monastery to Beit Shalom. More than a dozen times, they made a repair and turned the water on, thinking, *Ah, we've finished,* only to discover that another leak had to be dug up and repaired. The heat was terrible, but eventually they managed to repair the entire pipeline. Then they went to the monastery and turned on the water for the last time. Brother John later recalled what a joy it was to have that water flowing from the monastery to the house, up the pipe on the back wall, and pouring into the huge tank they had installed on the roof. They danced for joy when they went up to the roof and saw the water gushing in. It meant they could have a shower every day, even though it was cold water. Later on they installed two solar panels on the roof to heat the water in a hot water tank. They could now take hot showers as long as they limited their shower time to two minutes. Their joy was complete.

Brother John once told me they had to pray for furniture as each room was completed, and it was wonderful to see how the Lord provided. At one point, they had completed several of the bedrooms upstairs but had only twelve beds. Then they got a letter from a group of sixty young people from England who wanted to come and stay for a while. Brother John felt the leading of the Lord to accept them, so he wrote back saying, "Yes, by all means, come." He then told the young people at Beit Shalom that they must pray for God to provide beds.

It just so happened that a nurse from the Church of Scotland hospital in Nazareth had come for a weekend retreat. When she heard of the need for beds, she came to Brother John and said the Lord was permitting her to share that the hospital where she worked had just installed sixty new beds. This meant there were sixty old beds available! Within a week they arrived, and all were ready when the group of young people arrived from England. Later, Rosalie made beautiful little woolen rugs for each of the beds with the Star of David in the center of each one.

At another point, a large room upstairs was completed to serve as a lounge and as a dining room when needed. It just needed one thing: a piano. As Brother John told the story, "Just to show you how the Lord was able to enter into the fun of meeting our needs, I had been praying for a piano for two or three years, but it had to be a particular kind of piano." He didn't want just any piano, he wanted one that would do justice to the Lord and to Beit Shalom. It had to be either a Bechstein, a Steinway, or a Bluthner. They had to seek the best for the Lord.

As Brother John was praying for this need, Shulamith Katznelson came out to see Beit Shalom with her driver and her secretary. While Shulamith's driver was showing the secretary around the building, Shulamith asked John if he would like to join them for a concert in Tel Aviv. Brother John said that he would love to, and he went and dressed for the concert. As they drove toward Tel Aviv, the young secretary mentioned that she had noticed there was no piano at Beit Shalom. Brother John acknowledged they did not have one, and she said they could have hers—a Bluthner.

When the work first began at Beit Shalom, the workers found that all of the doors inside the building had been removed from their frames, and they had to be sorted through to find which door went where. On the bottom floor, the main entrance doors to the room where seminars were eventually held were gone altogether, and the walls around them had to be rebuilt. So they repaired the wall with bricks and formed an opening before they even had doors or a frame for them. Brother John prayed about it, and the Lord put it in his heart to go to a secondhand store in Jerusalem. He had never been inside the place; he had only seen a lot of junk on the outside as he passed by. Still, he had heard from the Lord, so Brother John went in and found two doors and a door frame. Each door had glasswork in just the design Brother John wanted. With some help, he was able to get a truck to load and transport the doors and the frame back to Beit Shalom. When they put the doors and the frame into the opening they had built, they fit exactly.

Later, during a slide presentation of the story of Beit Shalom, Brother John said, "Friends, this is one of the wonders of our God—that He could be so interested in such a simple thing. He guided our minds to the shape, but He knew that we couldn't provide the doors and frame because we didn't have the money to do it. There at the secondhand store were the things ready for us."

The last room to be completed in Beit Shalom was a downstairs office and study for Brother John. On the outside, a fountain was installed in the flower garden in front of the main entrance. The Lord even provided for a young man from Canada to install an electrically powered gate at the entrance so they no longer had to go out to manually open the entrance gate. Now, three years after they had acquired the property, everything was ready for a grand celebration. The building was prepared, and over two hundred guests were invited, including a choir made up of people from all over Israel.

The celebration was planned to start on Friday afternoon at three, but anyone who wanted to do so could stay for the entire weekend. There was only one problem: the only food Brother John had for the event was some packages of flavored gelatin, and the only money he had left after all the preparations was three shillings and sixpence (about three dollars in US currency). Some of the girls there made up the gelatin in little plastic cups and placed them at the corners of the tables for the celebration dinner. That was all they had, but Brother John knew the Lord was going to do something special that day. So he prayed, "Lord, You see the need. I've really gone over the hill, in a sense, in announcing these people could stay, and I haven't got anything to feed them…so You'll have to provide."

Some of the teachers from the Anglican school in Jerusalem and some of the nurses from the Nazareth hospital had come up to help in the preparations for this great feast. Brother John told them to set the tables in the dining room, and they asked about the food. He said he didn't know about it yet and went to welcome the guests at the front door. It was half past two. At five minutes until three o'clock, Brother John went back into the dining room, and the tables were so full of food that there was hardly enough room to sit down and eat! While he had been welcoming the guests at the front door, several people who knew about the celebration had come in through the back door and filled the tables with enough food to feed the more than two hundred guests sumptuously. There was enough left over to feed the eighty people who remained for the entire weekend.

Some of the people also gave gifts during the weekend that totaled one hundred pounds sterling. On Monday, Brother John still had his three shillings and sixpence. After the dinner on Friday, it was only fitting that the choir would sing selections from Mendelssohn's *Elijah* and Handel's *Messiah*, culminating with Handel's "Hallelujah Chorus."

Years later, at one of the last slide presentations of the Beit Shalom story, Brother John summarized what the Lord was really doing at Beit Shalom. After he finished telling the short account of a young man's life-changing experience while at the center, he said, "You see, it wasn't just the material needs the Lord was meeting; it was the inner needs as well of each individual—the transforming of lives—that was the purpose of Beit Shalom. It wasn't the rebuilding of this place at all. It was so that young people from all over would come to know that God could answer prayer; and today, sixteen hundred young people are scattered throughout the world testifying to this very thing. That was the whole reason and purpose for Beit Shalom."

It is to this end—the telling of the transformed lives at Beit Shalom—that the rest of this chapter is dedicated.

※ ※ ※

The first person who came to help Brother John during the first few weeks at Beit Shalom was a young man from Holland named Ari Carpenter. Brother John met Ari at the Garden Tomb, and a deep sense of fellowship in the Lord developed immediately. Ari had come to Israel to learn Hebrew, so he worked with Brother John for a few weeks, living the life of faith. Then he moved into a kibbutz. to learn Hebrew there. Ari was already fluent in Dutch, English, French, and German, and it took him only six months to learn Hebrew. Then the Lord called Ari to work among the Arabs, and he became fluent in Arabic in only nine months. Ari worked with about one hundred deaf boys living at a school for the deaf in a town in Jordan called Salt. So Ari learned their sign language as well. Ari was ordained by the bishop of Jerusalem and put in charge of this home for the deaf. At the school they not only taught the boys academics, but skills and trades so they could earn a living in the world.

Ari became known to the leaders in Jordan as one of the most godly men in the area. They were all Muslim, but they sought out Ari for counsel, and he became known to them as "Brother Andrew." There were also episodes of danger, and at times Ari made amazing escapes to keep from being shot. But he stayed there and worked, full of the joy of the Lord, and witnessed to the power of God in his life.

Brother John recounted how Ari came to visit him for a week several years after the time at Beit Shalom. Brother John said it was "heaven on earth" just to have fellowship with him again. Ari talked about how the Lord had undertaken in his work through the years. Brother John went on to say it was such a thrill to know that Ari was the one who, with Brother John, had first sought to bring Beit Shalom back into the glory of the Lord who had promised.

The principles of Beit Shalom were simple. Anyone who wanted to stay either had to know the Lord or be interested in knowing the Lord. No one was asked to pay anything; their keep was free. If they wanted to give a gift they could, and they were blessed and sent on their way. Brother John told me years later that on one occasion, a man came with a group of people and gave Brother John a sizable gift for their stay. The Lord gave Brother John a check in his spirit and prompted him to return the gift. Even though they needed the money, he obeyed. Later, one of the people from that group intimated to Brother John that the man who had tried to give him the gift was having some difficulties, and his personal finances were in shambles.

Everything that was done at Beit Shalom was done for the glory of God, whether repairing the building, cooking or cleaning, leading a chapel service, or holding a seminar for the young people. All the work anyone did had to be done in such a way that if the Lord suddenly came, He would be honored by their handiwork. The workers received no wages; they paid nothing to stay. All they had to do was enter into the spirit of Beit Shalom, the House of Peace.

On one occasion, a group consisting of three doctors, two matrons, and two nurses came to Beit Shalom for a two-week stay. The first day of their stay, they came to Brother John and said they had not come to Israel just to see sights; they had come to help. Then they asked what they could do. At the time, the downstairs area was still being rebuilt, and all the tiles had been taken up from the floor. They were in a great heap, so Brother John asked if these guests would like to chip and scrape the old grout from the backs and sides of the tiles so they could be relaid properly. There they sat on wooden boxes, doctors and nurses chipping and scraping away for hours at a time. Brother John later recalled that everyone who came to Beit Shalom immediately sensed the Lord's presence. They were willing to do *anything* to help, and they did it graciously and well.

Later, the guiding principles for Beit Shalom were printed on little four-and-a-half-by-six-inch cards and given to those who stayed.

Guiding Principles for
BEIT SHALOM, EMMAUS
Motto: 'To move man, through God, by Prayer alone'
J. HUDSON TAYLOR

1. All sharing the benefits and privileges of the house must love the Lord Jesus or have a sincere desire to know Him and seek His will for their lives. John 10:1–18; 27–30. 'My sheep hear My voice, and I know them, and they follow Me.'

2. There should be a willingness to seek to understand, in a practical way, the work and walk of the life of faith.

3. No one is asked to contribute in any monetary way and no one receives any wages for work done.

4. All labour is done as a practical act of worship and praise to God and is therefore done as perfectly as possible.

5. Acts 2:42 and 4:32 are the guiding principles of the House.

6. The aim and purpose of the House is to prove the complete adequacy of Christ to meet every need. Colossians 1:11–19.

7. The OUTREACH. 'To all who are near, and to all who are afar off.' Acts 2:39

At one point a group was coming to stay at Beit Shalom for a weekend, and they were short a few mattresses. The abbot of the Latrun Monastery had previously told Brother John that if they needed anything at all, they were just to ask. Well, Brother John was feeling a little desperate about the mattresses as the time grew near for the group to arrive, so he went to the monastery to ask if they had any mattresses they could borrow just for the weekend.

He was met by Friar Peter, one of the monks, who was dressed to go into the chapel for a prayer time. Brother John told him why he had come, and Peter replied that he would see to it immediately. John protested and said, "No, Peter, you're about to go into worship." Peter replied, "Brother John, this *is* worship," and he went and got six new mattresses, still in their wrapping, and took them over to the house.

On another occasion, a young man had come who wanted to help, but he didn't have the best work ethic Brother John had ever seen. This young man had decided he wanted to assist a man who was replastering a room that was going to be used for a dormitory. At one point, the man doing the plastering had to be gone for a day or two, and he left the young man to finish the plastering. So he got up onto the scaffolding and plastered a section of the wall, singing as he worked. As he was working, Brother John came into the room. In his words, the plasterwork was as wavy "as the waves of the sea." Brother John asked the young man to come down off the scaffolding and look up. The young man did. "You will be coming to visit this place in years to come," Brother John told him, "and whenever you do, you will look up to this section of the wall and see all the wrinkles and all the waviness in that plaster. Would you like that?" The young man asked where the trowel was and went up and scraped and smoothed the plaster beautifully.

The day began at Beit Shalom at seven in the morning, with breakfast at eight. After breakfast, everyone worked until noon. After an hour for lunch, work resumed until three o'clock in the afternoon. From three until four-thirty there was a Bible study each day, and then preparations were made for the evening service.

All through the years, as Beit Shalom was being rebuilt, Jewish teachers would bring their students out without invitation and would go up onto the balcony to have history lessons about the Valley of Ayalon and the adjacent areas. The view of the valley and the surrounding areas was magnificent, and this afforded Brother John the opportunity to talk about how the work at Beit Shalom was inspired by the Old Testament prophet Haggai, whom they respected deeply. Then Brother John would tell them of all the amazing things the Lord had done through prayer in restoring the building.

Shulamith Katznelson came out to Beit Shalom at least once a week to ask how the Lord had been answering prayer during that week. Shulamith was unique. Brother John often referred to her as a religious Jewess. Shulamith was the daughter of Dr. Reuven Katznelson, the medical superintendent of the entire country of Israel. Her uncle, Zalman Shazar, was the third president of Israel, in office from 1963 to 1973. Her mother, Batsheva Katznelson, was the first female member of the Knesset, the Israeli parliament. Her brother, Shmuel Tamir, was also a member of the Knesset, and he served as the minister of justice under Menachem Begin from 1977 to 1980. It was a tall pedigree, but Shulamith established quite a name for herself also.

In 1951, Shulamith started a language school called Ulpan Akiva in Nahariyya, Israel. She soon moved it to the resort town of Netanya, about twenty miles north of Tel Aviv. Ulpan Akiva was only the third language school in Israel when it started, and it was unique in that both Jews and Arabs learned languages there, often side by side. Some of the Jews would learn the Arabic language and even spent time in Arabic homes. And some of the Arab students would learn Hebrew or Aramaic and spend time in Jewish homes. This work of bringing the Jews and Arabs closer together was so astonishing and highly acclaimed that Shulamith was nominated for the Nobel Peace Prize in 1992 and 1993. She won the 1986 Israel Prize for Life Achievement in Education, Israel's most prestigious award in this arena. Shulamith also won many other national awards in Israel during her life and had a rich history there.

Shulamith became so enthralled with what the Lord was doing at Beth Shalom that she spent a lot of time there and would often take Brother John to different social functions. A close friendship was established between them that lasted for many years. When Brother John served as the pastor at Pendleton Baptist Church from April of 1982 until March or April of 1983, more than once he received a call from Shulamith while we were visiting or discussing the church's ministries in his office. Even from across the room I could hear her through the phone, saying, "Brother John, how are you?" I would take my leave, knowing the conversation would probably be a long one!

Shulamith gave a Hebrew Bible to be placed in the chapel at Beit Shalom with the inscription, "With thanks from the students of Ulpan Akiva. Blessed is the one who offers his hand with fellowship." Because the Lord had spoken through the prophet Haggai to inspire Brother John, she also entered into the spirit of Beit Shalom.

One time when they were having a party at Beit Shalom with a number of Arab boys, Shulamith arrived while they were just sitting down for the evening meal. She came into the kitchen where the meal was being served and saw the Arab boys sitting at the table with their plates of food. She moved one of the boys aside, sat down between two of them, and took food from the plate of one of the boys sitting at her side and ate it. Then she took food from the boy on her other side and ate it too. It was a distinct act of friendship, and they never forgot it.

Shulamith did something else at the ulpan that was highly unusual. A Gentile couple from the United States, by the leading of the Lord, sold everything to come to Israel at seventy years of age, and they went to the Ulpan Akiva to learn Hebrew. After two weeks, they went to Shulamith and apologetically told her they felt they were too old to learn the language. They told Shulamith she could keep the money they had paid to stay at the school. Shulamith asked them what they were going to do, and they said they did not know yet; they only knew that God had called them to Israel. Shulamith then asked them if they would stay on at the ulpan as houseparents. To have Gentile houseparents at a Hebrew language school was unheard of in Israel at that time. But Shulamith was not ordinary.

In this case, Shulamith's instincts were excellent; this was not an ordinary couple! The wife's name was Dorothy, and though she was diminutive in stature, she was a spiritual giant. Dorothy and Walter stayed on at the ulpan as houseparents for seven years, and they continually witnessed for the Lord as they oversaw the young people there. While there, they traveled all over Israel and became known to some of the highest ranking people in the land. They had dinner with the president of Israel and were entertained by some of the members of the Knesset. They were known to everyone as the houseparents of the Ulpan Akiva.

When Dorothy passed away, a wonderful memorial service was held for her at the Garden Tomb. Even though this was a place where Jesus was preached, many Jewish people attended the service for her there. Again, this was something unheard of in Israel. Brother John was one of the pallbearers at the graveside service, and a letter from a prominent rabbi was read which reflected the kind of person Dorothy was. The letter told of an outing taken by some of the people at the Ulpan Akiva to tour the Sinai Desert. Dorothy, Walter, and the rabbi were with them, and at one point the heavy truck on which they were riding became stuck in the wet sand. It was stuck fast, and try as they might, they could not get it unstuck. Even some from the Israeli army tried to pull it out with their large trucks. The rabbi began asking where Dorothy was, and she was found reading her Bible under a tree. He asked her if she would come and pray. Dorothy, without saying anything, got up and raised her hands and asked the Lord to help that truck out of the sand. As she was praying, the truck came out. The rabbi stated in his letter that he firmly believed it was Dorothy's prayer that had caused that truck to move.

Over the years, the influence of Beit Shalom continued to grow. People from different places in the world would send their sons and daughters to Beit Shalom when they came of age, in order to learn the life of faith that was practiced there so eloquently. One such young man was John's nephew Ray. Ray had been studying medicine at St. Andrews University in Scotland when he came to Beit Shalom with his girlfriend for a three-week stay. During those three weeks, the Lord met Ray and dealt with him. Ray accepted the Lord, and Brother John had the joy of baptizing him in front of Beit Shalom. They had found a beautiful marble baptistry in the shape of a cross in the ruins of the fourth-century church and had cleaned it, refilled it, and brought it back into service, and Ray was the first to be baptized in it.

In one case, two sets of parents talked to Brother John about their sons needing the Lord, and they both ended up at Beit Shalom at the same time. By the time they arrived, Brother John had been praying for both of them for over a year. The first young man, Ian, met the Lord after being at Beit Shalom for only two days. Brother John said it was wonderful to see the transformation in him. Ian stayed for three months and then went back to England, where he joined the British navy and became an exceedingly fine cadet. He became one of the chief officers on the large battleship he was assigned to and received the Queen's Award for being the finest officer in the entire Royal Navy. He also started a Bible study on his battleship, the HMS *Ark Royal*, that lasted for years.

The other young man's name was Romney. Romney was a tall Englishman who carried himself in a most dignified and upright way. Brother John always said that Romney was a "proper Englishman," and the first time Shulamith saw him, she said, "Brother John, he looks just like a king!" Romney had spent three weeks at Beit Shalom and had been regularly attending the chapel services. Nothing was ever said about him accepting the Lord until the last day he was there. Brother John met him as he was coming up the stairs; he stood at the top of the stairway and Romney stood two steps down so Brother John could look him in the eye. Brother John exclaimed, "Romney, why don't you surrender to the Lord?" Romney calmly replied, "Right, Brother John, I'll give it a go."

They had a communion service that day, and for the first time Romney came forward to receive the elements. He was the first to come. As Brother John gave Romney communion, he knew that Romney had passed from death to life. Romney went on to marry a medical doctor, and the two of them spent ten years together on the mission field in Africa.

Another young man who came to Beit Shalom was an Arab youth named Yasser. Yasser had helped John with some of the chores at the hospice in Jerusalem. He had been out of work, and he came to Brother John to see about a job. Brother John didn't know Yasser well, but he put him to work painting some of the woodwork in the rooms at Beit Shalom. From time to time Brother John and Yasser would talk, and one day Yasser came to Brother John and said that he wanted to be baptized. Brother John felt that this was an unusual request, and it could be dangerous for Yasser, as a Muslim. So he asked Yasser if he knew what it meant. He told him he had to know the Lord and believe in God, and Yasser assured him that he did. Brother John asked him when this had happened, and Yasser told him it was when they were working together at the hospice on the Mount of Olives. Brother John said that Yasser had never told him about it, and he said that Brother John had never asked. It was a difficult situation, so Brother John asked Yasser to wait and pray about it for a week.

After the week, Yasser came back and again asked if Brother John would baptize him. Brother John still wasn't sure what to do, because he knew that to baptize a Muslim would mean cutting him off from the Muslim religion in a most definite way, and Yasser would be in violent opposition to everyone he knew, including his family. So he asked Yasser to wait another week. After yet a third week of waiting, Yasser came to Brother John and said that if he would not baptize him, he would get someone else to do it. Brother John knew then that Yasser was absolutely serious about being baptized. So they went to a hospice in Galilee one evening and got up at half past five the next morning. They went to the place where the Sea of Galilee runs into the Jordan River, and there, with only the birds to witness it, Brother John baptized Yasser.

When Yasser came up out of the water he told Brother John that he understood that when people were baptized, they were given a new name. Brother John asked him what name he would like to be given, and Yasser replied that he wanted to be called John. So they called him "Johnny" from that point on.

Johnny went on to marry; he became an architect in Bethany and has a beautiful family. His favorite hymn is "Thine Be the Glory, Risen Conquering Son," and Brother John said that to hear him sing it was pure joy.

On one occasion Brother John received a letter from England from a woman asking if she and seven of her friends could come to stay. Brother John didn't know at the time that two of her friends were Sir Horace, admiral of the British fleet, and his wife. They had both been knighted by the queen of England and were known as lords of the commons. When Brother John found this out, he was astounded to have people of this caliber coming to Beit Shalom and wondered how he should treat them. Despite his reservations, Brother John said they were the most gracious couple he had ever met. They knew the Lord, and that made all the difference.

Sir Horace would come down to the kitchen early in the morning and ask Brother John to tell him what he could do to help in the kitchen or in the dining room. He would help peeling the potatoes or preparing the breakfast, or he would set the table, and so on. His wife would go out and help with all the washing up, assisting with the laundry, or anything else she could find to do. Brother John said it was so beautiful to see the spirit and humility with which these two entered into the work.

Then there was Friar Peter. He would think of any excuse to come over from the monastery to Beit Shalom almost every day. He always managed to arrive about the time when they were making scones and would come in when they were piping hot. So whoever was in the kitchen always scraped up enough dough to make an extra big scone for Friar Peter. Friar Peter was a wonderful fellow. He was always happy, always laughing, always joking.

The monks at the monastery had taken a vow of silence, but they could not keep silent when the people from Beit Shalom were around. John said that by the time the work was completed at Beit Shalom, the monks were chatting it up with anyone they could find. They had wonderful fellowship together.

As the fame of what God was doing at Beit Shalom grew, people of note began to come even more. They held concerts almost every week by people from all over Israel and from other countries too. At various times, musicians from the Israeli Philharmonic Orchestra would come to give concerts of chamber music. All the members of the orchestra were Jewish, of course, and the first time they played there, one of the young men came to Brother John and asked him if there was a place where he and four others could pray to ask God's blessing before they started the concert. It overwhelmed Brother John when he realized there were some who knew and loved the Lord and sought to serve Him even in the Israeli orchestra. It made the concerts all the more delightful.

Another group of musicians of note who came to Beit Shalom were Peter van Woerden and his family from Holland. Peter and his family were noted for two reasons. First, they were fluent in Hebrew and gave concerts all over Israel, as well as recording in Hebrew. Second, Peter was the nephew of Corrie ten Boom, whose life story was made famous through her books *The Hiding Place* and *Tramp for the Lord* and a subsequent movie also titled *The Hiding Place*. *The Hiding Place* gives an account of when Peter was playing the organ for a church in Holland at the beginning of World War II. Peter was only seventeen or eighteen years old, and the Nazis had occupied Holland. At the end of a service in a large church where he had recently been chosen as the organist, he suddenly began playing the Dutch national anthem. All of the people rose to their feet and loudly sang the anthem. A few days later Peter was arrested, and they took him off to prison for two months.

Corrie herself came to Beit Shalom and ministered at a conference there that lasted for a week, attended by about three hundred people. Brother John said they had a wonderful time of fellowship during the conference. Peter and his family went on to give Christian concerts all over Europe and produced and sold recordings there as well. My wife Debbie and I had the blessing and joy of meeting Peter's son and daughter-in-law, Danilo and Barbara van Woerden, while traveling with Brother John through Israel in August of 1983.

Another person of distinction who visited Beit Shalom was Moshe Dayan's mother, Devorah Dayan. She had heard about Beit Shalom and subsequently came out one day. For three hours Brother John related the account of Beit Shalom to her. When she got back to Jerusalem, she sent him a parcel containing photographs of etchings of musicians through the centuries to be placed in the music room specially at her request.

Brother John said that some of the most blessed times they had at Beit Shalom were the Shabbat (Sabbath) meals every Friday evening on the balcony as the sun went down. Shabbat was very much observed throughout the land when Brother John was in Israel, and everything was still. There would be no traffic at all on any of the roads or highways, and the beautiful stillness he felt was one of the great features of Israel.

Along with the people of note who came to Beit Shalom, many Christian groups from all over Israel and other countries would come to spend weekends and hold retreats there. One of the most wonderful times was when fifteen young people came, and they decided to have a time of prayer, fasting, and silence for two days. One of the young ladies from the group was a nurse from Scotland. She came to Brother John and said she could appreciate the prayer and fasting, but to not talk—she didn't know how she was going to exist! At the end of the two days, this same young lady told Brother John that she thanked God for the opportunity to be quiet for two days so the Lord could speak to her.

In the last few years that Beit Shalom existed as a youth ministry, Larry Gordon came to stay for a season while he was learning Hebrew at the Ulpan Akiva. Larry fit well with the spirit at Beit Shalom. On one occasion, a group of young people came to stay while Larry was there. One of the young men in the group was exceptionally argumentative, especially during their afternoon Bible studies. Whatever point the group or an individual was discussing, he would argue the opposite point of view. Larry would not enter into these discussions but would just sit there quietly. At one point, when the argumentative young man was promoting his point, he turned to Larry and asked what he thought about the subject being discussed. Without saying a word, Larry left the room and came back a short while later with a basin of water, some soap, and a towel. He took the shoes and socks off of the disagreeable young man and washed his feet. The young man's heart melted, and he immediately apologized to the group for his discordant spirit. The impression of this act was so deep upon the group that Larry was up until the early hours of the next morning listening to the young people as they poured out their hearts to him. He also shared his heart about the Lord with them.

On another occasion, a young man came to Beit Shalom who hadn't been trained very well in his home. He was an only child, and he had become very selfish. When he came, he was accustomed to having the best and most of everything. He would take very large portions at mealtimes, and the others who were there were upset at him. They came to Brother John and asked him to do something about it, saying that what he was doing wasn't right. Brother John told them that he could do what they asked, but if he did, it would create an invisible barrier between the young man and himself. He went on to say that if they said anything to him, the same thing would happen between them and the young man. So Brother John challenged them to commit it to the Lord, asking Him, by His Holy Spirit, to touch the young man.

The next day that young man came to Brother John and said that he wanted to apologize for the way he had been acting since he had been there. He continued, saying the Lord had convicted him about his greed and selfishness. Then he apologized to the entire group.

"Believers," Brother John told us many years later, "you see the power we have. Let's use it to bring glory to Him and to help us to live more consecrated lives for Him."

Chapter 6

THE CHALLENGE OF BEIT SHALOM

The ministry of the youth center at Beit Shalom lasted for about eight-and-a-half years. To the best of my knowledge, it started in 1969 or 1970 and ended sometime in 1978. It was in October of 1980 that Brother John Samson first arrived in the parking lot of Pendleton Baptist Church. Even some of those very close to Brother John did not understand why he had God's peace regarding the end of the youth ministry at Beit Shalom, but he could see that it was all in God's plan and timing. He shared a few factors with me while he was in Pendleton.

In the last year of the youth ministry, the Israeli government began to build a major highway from Tel Aviv to Jerusalem that ran right through the Valley of Ayalon only about a hundred yards from the front of the building. As Brother John showed the slides of the building of the highway, he would say that the prophecy of Isaiah was unfolding right before their eyes: "I will make all My mountains a road, and My highways will be raised up" (Isaiah 49:11, NASB). Many large trucks used that highway and vibrated the building. Cracks began growing in the foundation. Then a French geological organization wanted to use the building for a geological center. They agreed to fix the cracks in the foundation when they took possession of the building. Between these two coinciding events and the peace that Brother John felt, he knew it was time to end the ministry. He could see the fingerprints of God, so the building was turned over to the French geological organization.

In reflecting upon his experience at Beit Shalom, Brother John was reminded of a text from the Scriptures that he had known from his youth: "There is no one who has left house or brothers or sisters or mother or father or children or farms, for My sake and the gospel's sake, but that he shall receive a hundred times as much now in the present age, houses and brothers and sisters and mothers and children and farms, along with persecutions; and in the age to come, eternal life" (Mark 10:29–30, NASB). Brother John often said at the slide presentations of Beit Shalom that he did not receive the hundredfold—"It's been a thousandfold." At one presentation, he said, "I've met people throughout the world that I would never have come upon yet. I have homes galore. I have people who looked upon me as their son; I have young people who looked upon me as their father. So, literally, the Word has been absolutely met by God's promise. This is why I insist: believe what the Word says, and act on it."

This is the core of the Beit Shalom challenge. We must *really* believe God's Word, and we show that we really believe it by acting upon it. We must step out in faith beyond our perceptions and experiences. We must not only believe that God's Word is true, but that it is there for us to act upon in faith *now*. It is not for later; it is not just for the Brother John Samsons and Hudson Taylors of the world. It is for each one of us.

My Beit Shalom challenge had come through the horrific death of my best friend. It was now unfolding before my eyes. All I had to do was walk over the threshold and have the patience to follow God's quiet leading.

Brother John came to Pendleton in October of 1980, a few weeks after Larry's death, and stayed for two weeks. It was then God began to reveal the beginning of the "wait and see" to me and to many others. Soon after, I began to understand the challenge of Beit Shalom for myself.

Brother John came back to Pendleton in April of 1981 and stayed for more than two weeks. Rob Nichols flew in from his home in Vermont a few days after John arrived. Early in 1980, Rob Nichols had a chance to see Beit Shalom while he was in Israel to visit Brother John and Larry. By then it was no longer operating as a youth center, but Rob shared with me that he had a great experience walking from Beit Shalom to Jerusalem, singing and praising the Lord. While getting to know Brother John and Rob, I was becoming aware of what great souls they had. They reminded me very much of Larry Gordon. This was not only comforting after the loss of Larry, but it challenged me to a greater and deeper walk with the Lord.

During this visit, about a dozen of us from the Pendleton church viewed the slide presentation of Beit Shalom for the first time one evening after a dinner gathering. It would be modest to say we were awed by what we saw and heard. The "oohs" and "aahs" were multitudinous, but more importantly, there was an unspoken and growing sense of destiny at the end of our time together.

As Debbie and I headed out the door to go home after such a wonderful evening, I felt a compulsion to go back inside to speak briefly with Brother John. I couldn't really explain why, so I just asked Debbie to wait in the car for a few minutes. When I went inside, Brother John was alone by the breakfast bar as if he was expecting me. He asked me what I thought the Lord was doing in my life. I told him I wasn't sure, but I felt like I was standing on the threshold of a doorway, and the Lord was encouraging me to step forward into a larger future with Himself. Brother John encouraged me to follow the Lord with all my heart, without hesitation or reservation.

When the time came for Brother John and Rob to leave, they took the train to Cutbank, Montana, to retrace Larry's last days on this earth. I can remember feeling a deep longing to accompany them on that train, and I expressed it to Brother John as they were about to board. He replied in a most welcoming way that I could come with them if I wanted. I did not have the faith to believe there was any way for something like that to possibly work out. It was some time later before I began to understand what John was really getting at with his invitation.

Brother John came for a third two-week visit to Pendleton in October of 1981, just over a year after Larry's death. The Lord had challenged me to grow spiritually during that year. It was a struggle, and I experienced frustration in the process—so much so that I felt some resentment toward Brother John when he burst through the door and hugged me ever so tightly in the kitchen of our modest little home. I almost resisted his hug. Later, I mused at how odd it was that I felt that way. Somehow, it seemed as if he was the source of my frustration, when it should have been directed at my own failure to yield more fully to Christ.

When we learned that Brother John was coming for this visit, we asked him to give his slide presentation of Beit Shalom again. He agreed, and we planned for it to be shown at the church. We invited some youth groups and other churches from around the Pendleton area to come and see this remarkable account with us. When the night came, we had to jam over 250 people into a sanctuary that was made to comfortably fit only about 200. Even though it was pretty warm during the two-hour presentation, not one person budged from his seat. All were riveted on the incredible things our eyes were seeing and our ears were hearing. The hunger in our hearts for a deeper walk of faith was being stirred and fed. It created quite a buzz of excitement and hope.

Six months later, in April of 1982, Brother John came for a fourth visit to Pendleton. This time he said something very unusual; he related that he didn't know why the Lord had brought him, but he was going to stay until he found out. This thrilled me. Little did I know just how much longer this would mean!

When Brother John arrived, our pastor, Charlie Wasson, was on vacation, or so we thought. Three days after Brother John's arrival, Charlie and his family returned from their trip. A few days later, Charlie announced that he had been candidating for the pastoral position in a church in a town called Anthony, right on the border between Texas and New Mexico. Within two weeks we helped Charlie and his family pack up all their belongings, and they were gone. Charlie and I had become pretty close, so close that Charlie and his wife had named Debbie and me as godparents for their children, so I was sad to see him go. But the church had struggled under Charlie's leadership for the past few months. This did not seem like a fitting end to his time as the pastor of our little church, but the Lord always knows how to bring beauty from ashes.

A few days after Charlie and his family left, we held a church meeting to discuss searching for a pastor to fill the vacancy. Even though I was only twenty-eight at the time, I had been chairmen of the deacons for about a year, the next highest position to the pastorate in the church. As the meeting began, I started to explain to the congregation the procedure the church had traditionally followed in circumstances like these—forming a pulpit committee to search for candidates and so on. Before I got very far, Tommy Burton spoke up and said that we had an unusual set of circumstances, and he nominated John Samson to be our pastor.

I was a bit stunned by this motion, but I began to piece it together with Brother John's unusual statement about staying until he discovered God's purpose for his being here. It was happening right in front of me. So I responded by commenting on how out-of-the-ordinary the motion was, and I asked if there was a second. Someone quickly gave a second to the motion, so we asked if Brother John would mind exiting the room for a few moments. John graciously left, and I asked if there was any discussion regarding the motion. The silence was almost deafening, so I brought the motion to a vote. It was passed unanimously.

Brother John immediately accepted the offer. In the less than forty-eight hours since Pastor Charlie had left town, we had a new pastor. I have never seen a motion that serious pass so quickly and smoothly in our church, or in any church, before or since that night. And I do not remember anything passing by a unanimous vote in our church before or since that vote. It was becoming abundantly clear why the Lord had brought Brother John to Pendleton.

Under Brother John's leadership, the church began to grow, spiritually and numerically. I spent an hour or more each day after school in his office, talking with him about the school and church and spiritual matters in general. Sometimes we engaged in casual conversation or just joked around. We also went on occasional weekend retreats into the wilderness just to get away and spend time together in the Lord.

I grew much under Brother John's mentoring and leadership at the church. He had an intimate knowledge of God's Word such as I had never been exposed to before. I soaked it up as much as I could. His relationship to the Lord was so real and so alive, and I was learning to practice my faith daily in the small things as well as the great. He taught me how to lead people in ministry with grace and love. And in the spirit of Beit Shalom, I was learning how to pray.

Before long, a morning prayer time had begun with Brother John, myself, and Bill Oleen, who attended the church. We invited others to join us, but in the end it was just us three. We called ourselves "the threefold cord" based on Ecclesiastes 4:9–12 ("Two are better than one; because they have a good reward for their labor. For if they fall, the one will lift up his fellow: but woe to him that is alone when he falleth; for he hath not another to help him up. Again, if two lie together, then they have heat: but how can one be warm alone? And if one prevail against him, two shall withstand him; and a threefold cord is not quickly broken"). We prayed every morning for about an hour, seven days a week, and we began to see some incredible and dramatic answers to our prayers. We also formed a bond in friendship, love, and spirit that would not be quickly broken.

One morning we were praying for a difficult situation a friend was experiencing, and he called right while we were praying and told us how the Lord had just resolved the situation. Another time, we were praying for a man's salvation, and while we were praying, he knocked on the door. He explained to us that his daughter, who attended our Christian school, was displaying some serious rebellion at home. He wondered if we could somehow help. This afforded me the opportunity, as administrator of the school, to not only address the difficulty with his daughter, but to share with him his greater need of the Savior.

On another morning, we prayed for a man we knew. After praying, we decided that we needed to talk to him. However, we hadn't seen him for some time and didn't know how to contact him. We were feeling a bit helpless when we heard some noise just outside Brother John's office. We looked out the window to see what the racket might be and saw the very man we were hoping to meet chopping some wood for the school's woodstoves! This is how our prayer times often went as long as we continued that ministry.

Brother John also spent many times of sweet fellowship in our home with one or two of our friends or just with us. On one occasion with just the three of us, Debbie made a pan of *aebleskivers,* a traditional Danish treat described as a spherical cross between a pancake and a popover filled with sweet applesauce. While Debbie was busy preparing a second pan to put in the oven, Brother John and I were busy finishing off the first. We graciously gave her a generous portion of the second pan.

During the time Brother John was our pastor, we showed the Beit Shalom slide presentation around the area two or three more times. A sense of the challenge of Beit Shalom was beginning to take root in the congregation of the Pendleton Baptist Church.

A few months later, a large public school campus was put up for auction because a new school had been built in the area. The campus included a large main building with several large classrooms, a few offices and storage rooms, a small gymnasium, a cafeteria, an annex building with more large classrooms and a large shop room, some old tennis courts to one side, and an entire football field in the back. The campus covered more than two large city blocks and was fairly centrally located in Pendleton atop the South Hill section of town.

Some of us in the church began to discuss with Brother John how this campus might make a wonderful youth center. Then it began to dawn on us: if we could purchase this campus, we could turn it into another Beit Shalom. We decided that, if this ministry came into being, we would call it Beit Shalom Pendleton. But how could we do such a thing? We were a fairly small church, we had no building fund or savings, and we barely covered our expenses each month.

We held a church-wide meeting shortly after the idea began to take hold, and the people of the church got really excited about the possibility of purchasing the campus and turning it into a youth center. The Beit Shalom challenge was beginning to form in our modest congregation. So it was decided that we would have an all-night prayer meeting to ask the Lord to show us how we could acquire the funds and staff for such a venture. I sensed a strong presence of the Lord during this first discussion, and the whole thing reminded me of the saints meeting in the upper room after the resurrection of the Lord (Acts 1:13–14).

Within two weeks, we held the prayer meeting on a Friday night, with about thirty people in attendance. We held the meeting in a good-sized room in the daylight basement of the church. We started about seven o'clock in the evening and began praying after a short introduction by Brother John. Some people sat in chairs as we prayed, and others got down on their knees. Some people moved in and out of the room to have discussions about how the Lord was leading them. About one-thirty in the morning, the meeting began to break up, and several people stayed for a while and talked in the kitchen area next to the room where we had prayed. I thought we were just taking a break, so I joined them. After about half an hour of conversation over some hot tea and snacks, I asked if we were going to go back into the large room to continue praying. Brother John told me that the meeting was over, that we didn't need to pray anymore. I was surprised by his statement, but I was unaware of what

The Challenge of Beit Shalom

had transpired during our prayer time in the discussions outside the prayer room.

I soon learned that the Lord had moved in some amazing ways in people's hearts during the meeting. Brother John; the church's secretary, Myrna; and a married couple had felt the leading of the Lord to move into the youth center and become houseparents. The couple also felt the leading of the Lord to sell their house and property to finance the purchase of the campus. Debbie and I also agreed to move into the building, and several others committed to help with the finances or the work of the ministry or both. It seemed as if Beit Shalom Pendleton was going to become a reality, and the prospect thrilled me to the very core of my being. The thought of living what I had seen and heard of the Beit Shalom story—the thrilling answers to prayer and lives being radically changed for the Lord—was more than I had imagined possible. All of this here, now, with Brother John at the helm.

Based on the commitments made at the prayer meeting, we made a bid for the school campus and turned it in at the school district's office. The district decided to auction the property by sealed bids and determined they would receive the bids until a certain date. Then they would announce to the public who had won. Those who submitted the winning bid would take possession of the property upon payment.

A few weeks after turning in our bid, the winning bid was announced. Our hearts burned with anticipation and hope as we waited for this moment, but our hopes were dashed when we found out that we had not won. We didn't even come in second place. I think our bid was the third highest, so there was little hope that the two groups who outbid us would both default on claiming it. I was greatly disappointed and confused. It seemed as if the hand of God had certainly been guiding us thus far. What could have possibly gone wrong? Had we made some kind of mistake or completely misread God's intentions for us?

The Lord had closed the door to the possibility of Beit Shalom Pendleton, and it would not be reopened. It was a hard pill to swallow. My confusion on the matter was great, but there were lessons yet to be learned, more maturity needed, and soon after this, I began to sense God's call elsewhere.

When things don't work out the way we think or desire, we are tempted to blame something we or others did as the source of the disappointment, but God's grace is bigger than this. While the turn of events could be the result of our own sinful actions or lack of action, it often is not. Sometimes the Lord sees things that we cannot see. Later I came to understand that we simply were not ready in our walk with the Lord, as a congregation or as individuals, to take on such a large undertaking. The seeds of destruction were among us.

In the next few months, the enemy of our souls began to attack individuals within our congregation, and we were not very successful in fending off the attacks. Sin and disagreements began to arise among us, and they caused some divisions and disunity to the point that some people left the church. There were even personal attacks against Brother John and some of the other leaders. It grew so bad at times that Brother John began to sense that his time as pastor of the church was coming to an end. He mentioned this to me more than once, and he told me he felt that we needed a younger man to take over leadership. I refused to even entertain such a thought.

While Brother John pastored our church, Rosalie was not able to join him. She stayed back in England because her sister, Mabel, was experiencing some poor health. Rosalie felt she could not leave her alone under these circumstances. Brother John went back to England for two or three long periods during the year to be with Rosalie. As the attacks and disagreements continued in the church in Pendleton, Mabel's health took a turn for the worse, and Rosalie told Brother John that she needed his help. To him, this was the Lord's confirmation that it was time for him to resign the pastorate at the Pendleton Baptist Church and go home to England.

In late March of 1983, almost a year after coming to Pendleton, Brother John boarded an airplane at the Portland International Airport and flew back to England. It seemed more than I could stand to watch him board the plane and fly away for what I thought could be forever. It was like another death. All the promise of the future seemed to be crashing down. Where would I go from here?

Before Brother John left, he told Debbie and I that if we came to England to visit him sometime, he would take us to Israel. I had a growing sense that God was calling me to help start a church and school somewhere, but first I needed to get more training in school. This sense of God's calling had grown so strong that I resigned my position at the Christian school in Pendleton a few months before Brother John left. I had finished three years of college, but not my bachelor's degree. Brother John and I had talked about me attending the Bible College of Wales after reading a book together about Rees Howells, the founder of the college. All this seemed entirely impossible to me, as I had barely been outside the borders of the United States. But the Beit Shalom challenge had not disappeared with the failure to get Beit Shalom Pendleton off the ground.

In fact, I soon found that the seed of the Beit Shalom challenge had begun to germinate in my heart and in the hearts of others, too, not just in Pendleton.

Chapter 7

My Personal Beit Shalom Challenge

As I said earlier, Brother John once said that the most important thing about Beit Shalom wasn't the rebuilding of the place, but the lives that were transformed. That was also the Beit Shalom challenge—that God could and would transform the life of anyone who would walk by faith in Him.

While Brother John was in Pendleton, both during his visits and while he was pastor at the church, he ministered to people in and out of the town. When he first arrived, he reached out to Larry Gordon's father, Max, and stepmother, Jean, who lived in the southeastern part of Portland. John made several trips from Pendleton to Max Gordon's house. Max came into the kingdom just two months before he slipped into a coma from cirrhosis of the liver and died a few weeks later. Jean also assured Brother John that she had become a child of the King just after Max's death. Max had spent most of his adult life as an alcoholic and had strained relationships with everyone in the family until Larry came through Portland just before he settled in Pendleton. Larry had spent two weeks with his dad, and it was the best time they'd ever had together in his adult life. Larry said when they parted, they hugged each other with a long, deep embrace. Larry was touched deeply by that hug. It was the last time they saw each other this side of heaven.

Brother John had also spent time with Larry's mother in Tyler, Texas, before coming to Pendleton, and she came and spent time at Tommy and Clara Burton's house. She also came into the kingdom before she died of cancer a few months after those visits. In a little over a year, Larry and his dad and his mother were together in heaven. What a reunion!

My personal Beit Shalom challenge was coming to the understanding that God could and would do mighty and great things through anyone who turned to Him in faith, no matter how weak that faith was. He would not only do this through the great saints of the world, but He would do it for anyone who simply trusted in Him enough to act upon their faith. I had always thought that God blessed only certain men and women who had great faith through some kind of special relationship with God. It is true that we can only have a relationship with God through faith in Jesus

Christ (see John 14:6, Acts 4:8–12, Romans 10:9–13, etc.), but every relationship to God is special, and He desires to greatly bless every one of us if we will simply abide in Him (John 15:1–16). The greatest saints in the history of the world were not extraordinary people; they were ordinary people who came to realize they had an extraordinary God. And God has gone to extraordinary lengths to help us understand this.

During the first few weeks after Brother John left for England, this challenge began to grow in me. I couldn't get his invitation to come visit him in England out of my mind, so Debbie and I began to pray about it. We asked that if the Lord wanted us to go to England, He would provide the way. Even though going on a trip like that was still beyond my wildest dreams, what I had learned from Beit Shalom had begun to grow the seed of faith in my heart and soul.

There was no way that Debbie and I could afford such a trip through the modest salaries we received at the school. We lived comfortably, but we usually had little or nothing extra. Then, about two weeks after we began praying for the Lord to provide for a trip to England, Debbie got a most unusual phone call from her father. He bluntly asked her what she would do if she had a thousand dollars she didn't expect. He explained to her that he had inherited some stocks from a distant relative a few years ago, and the stocks hadn't increased or decreased in value during that time, so he had decided to sell them. He wanted to divide the money from the sale between Debbie and her sister. Surprised, Debbie said she supposed she would use the money to finish some remodeling work in our house. By this time, I had gathered the gist of the conversation, and I knew instantly the Lord was beginning to provide for our trip to England. When Debbie got off the phone, we talked about it and quickly agreed to set the money aside for the beginning of a fund for our trip.

Just a few days later, we were informed that there was going to be a shortfall in the school finances during the month of April. Some of the families were having financial difficulties and were not able to keep up on their tuition payments. We were ordinarily paid twice a month, and we were told that we would probably not be receiving our second paychecks that month. We paid the entire month's bills with our first paychecks and hoped that we could get by without the second. When the time to receive our second paychecks came, we were told that one of the families had caught up on their payments unexpectedly—so we ended up getting our second paychecks in April after all. We had made it through the month, so now we each had a paycheck with no bills to pay. The amount of money in those checks plus the thousand dollars from Debbie's father totaled exactly enough for us to purchase two round-trip tickets to England. By faith, at our first opportunity, we went down to a travel agency and purchased tickets from Portland, Oregon, to London, England. Even though we had no other funds for the trip, we knew it was quickly becoming a reality, and we were delirious with joy. It all seamed so unreal.

Over the next few months, the Lord provided the funds to not only go on the trip, but to meet all the financial obligations at home while we were gone. And He did it in some very unusual ways. After the gift from Debbie's dad and the unexpected paychecks, we also received an unexpected amount of profit from an old apartment building that Tommy Burton had virtually given us. The apartments usually provided little to no income each month. We also received a much larger than usual tax refund. On top of that, Debbie had had some work done on her jaw by a dentist which we had paid for because we had no dental insurance. Suddenly, all that we had been paying on that for months was completely refunded. It was decided that her condition was a medical condition, and we did have medical insurance. Then we received some funds unexpectedly from an estate, and friends and relatives gave us some monetary gifts when the news got out that we were going on the trip of a lifetime.

Since going to England was becoming a reality, I sent in an application and was accepted to attend the Bible College of Wales. Brother John and I planned to take a trip over to Wales while we were in Britain to finalize the arrangements for my attendance.

As the time for the trip grew closer, I had a lapse of faith and borrowed some money from a relative, but the Lord was gracious even in this. Later, when we started paying back the loan, that relative generously forgave the debt well before it was paid off. Even in our weaknesses, God is gracious, "For He knows our frame; He remembers that we are dust" (Psalm 103:14, NKJV).

As the time for the trip neared, our excitement grew immensely. On August 2, 1983, Debbie and I left Pendleton and stayed the night with Debbie's mother in a suburb of Portland. We spent the day of August 3 with many longtime, close friends around the Portland area. A little after 11 a.m. on August 4, we boarded a jet at the Portland International Airport and headed east. After a three-hour layover in Minneapolis, we flew our final leg to Gatwick Airport in London, England. We didn't sleep much during our short night on the plane, and we looked down with amazement at the fields and hedgerows of the English countryside as we made our final approach to the Gatwick runway. It hardly seemed real, but it was—very real.

After some confusion about how to proceed after landing, we exited the international landing lounge and found Brother John smiling as he awaited our arrival along the corridor. What a wonderful sight it was to see him again, and we embraced tightly for a long while. After collecting our baggage, we made our way to the parking lot and got into Brother John's car. As a passenger, it felt very unusual getting into what was, to Americans, the driver's seat. It also took some getting used to driving on the left side of the road! Regardless, we drove to the north side of London to the Crawley area and stayed in a three-hundred-year-old farmhouse called Water Hall, which had been made into a bed-and-breakfast.

After getting settled into Water Hall, Brother John and I took a short walk down the narrow road that ran alongside the bed-and-breakfast. The day was sunny and warm. It was pretty humid, and the countryside was lush and green. I was drinking in as much as I could, still in great wonderment that we were actually in England. I felt as if anything was possible with God at that moment.

We visited and rested for the remainder of the day before turning in at ten o'clock for a short, noisy night's sleep. It felt like Water Hall was right at the end of Gatwick Airport's main runway. We were up at 4 a.m., and after a large breakfast, we were headed north on one of Britain's main "motorways" for a ten-hour drive along the North Sea, headed for Edinburgh, Scotland.

Our eventual destination was the city of Inverness, one of the northernmost cities in Scotland. Brother John had been a pastor in a church there many years before. In a little town called Kingussie, we stayed with Rob Keltie, an old friend of Brother John's. Rob's son, Rob Jr., had spent some time at Beit Shalom and later married and came to the United States to attend Bible college. He and his wife had spent about two months in Pendleton with Brother John.

Rob Keltie Sr. was a large and imposing Scotsman with a gentle, humble spirit. He had a great sense of humor and personality that captivated those around him. When we arrived at his house, Brother John twice tried to drive up the steep driveway before spinning to a halt halfway up each time. As Brother John backed down and readied for a third attempt, Rob called out, "Put your foot doon, John, and make a run for it!" in his deep Scottish brogue. So Brother John hit the gas pedal hard and sped up to the house before skidding to a halt uncomfortably close to the garage. We quickly exited and were at once receiving warm hugs that made us feel as if we were old friends.

Rob had begun his professional career as a preacher in the Church of Scotland years before. The denomination, in general, had eroded much from the great faith of her founder John Knox and the days of the Covenanters. Rob was caught up in this lukewarmness even though he had spent time on the mission field in Africa with his wife and his four young children. He had a very close relationship with his eldest daughter Margaret in those days. On one occasion, Margaret came home after having been on a mission trip with a group of believers. She told her father that she had received Jesus Christ as her Lord and Savior and had been born again. He thought it was foolishness until she explained that she wanted to be baptized by total immersion. She had already been baptized by sprinkling as an infant, which was strictly all that the Church of Scotland allowed. To be baptized by immersion was unthinkable to Rob. He told Margaret that if she followed through with it, he would disown her. Margaret painfully chose her Lord over her beloved father and went through with the baptism. Rob disowned her, but as time wore on, Margaret's extreme act of devotion, her prayers, and Rob's deep love for his daughter had a pronounced effect on him. In time, Rob accepted the Lord Jesus as his Savior, and his entire family followed him in faith and most in baptism by total immersion.

Later, at a denominational conference, Rob and other leaders in his church were discussing the content of their teaching for the next year or so. When Rob saw that the others were considering teachings devoid of his newly found faith, he suggested that they teach a saving personal relationship to Jesus. He was told that they would have none of that. Rob quickly understood that his time with the Church of Scotland had come to an end. He resigned his position. In doing so, he lost his retirement, his insurance, and his parsonage home, as well as his income. But Rob's faith in the Lord was strong, and the Lord provided him with a new congregation and a home. The little church group of forty or fifty believers met for services in the large, old, and very homey stone house with walls two feet thick where we were now staying.

Over the years, Rob's first wife died of cancer, and he remarried. He and his new wife added two more sweet little girls to the family, Mary and Katie. So when we arrived at the Keltie home, it was occupied by Rob, his wife, Helen, and his five daughters, Margaret, Jean, Kirsty, Mary, and "Wee Katie." They also were boarding a young lady who was training to be a nurse. We were welcomed into a home which was warmly saturated with God's love.

I was amazed at the thought of Rob risking so much to follow the Lord. Yet here I was in the midst of God honoring His Word, providing homes and lands and children to those who had given up much for Him. It challenged me deeply; I could see that He truly does honor those who honor Him (1 Samuel 2:30).

We stayed the night at Rob's house and visited as Rob and Brother John caught up on each other's affairs. In the morning after some more fellowship over a great breakfast, we went up to Inverness and saw the church where Brother John had held his first pastorate and enjoyed that beautiful city for the day. When we returned to the Kelties for the evening, we enjoyed a stunningly glorious night of singing and fellowship. The Kelties had invited several friends from the congregation that met each week in their house.

The next morning we left the gracious Keltie home and headed south. We drove as far as Keswick, the home of many great writers (Robert Louis Stevenson, Sir Walter Scott, Robert Browning, Percy Bysshe Shelley, etc.). It is where the Keswick Holiness Movement started over one hundred years before. The Keswick Convention is still held for two weeks every summer in honor of this historic event, and hundreds of people come from all over the world to attend. We spent the night in a cozy little inn, and the next day we drove the rest of the way back to London.

After we returned our rental car at the airport, Debbie and I rode with Brother John to St. Albans, just a few miles north of London, and stayed in the home of Howard and Lynn Roberts. Howard and Lynn were a very delightful couple who treated us royally. Howard was doing research and giving seminars on the ancient Roman ruins in the area. On the humorous side, when we first arrived at their home, Debbie asked if she could use the restroom. Lynn quickly responded, asking Debbie if she was "tired." I informed Lynn that Debbie was really asking for the water closet, the British term for *rest*room.

While we stayed with Howard and Lynn, we went on a tour of St. Albans Cathedral. Alban was the first known Christian martyr in Great Britain. He is thought to have been martyred by the Romans, in what was called Verulamium, in AD 283 or AD 209. The original abbey to this magnificent cathedral in his honor began to be built as early as the seventh or eighth century, but the current cathedral was started in the eleventh century. There have been many additions through the centuries, and it boasts the longest nave in England. It is the second largest cathedral in all of the United Kingdom.

Upon entering the nave, I was astounded by its immensity as I looked upward at its incredible beauty and majesty. Brother John asked me what I felt as we entered together, and I told him I was awestruck by the vastness of God. He told me that all the cathedrals of the Church of England were built in the shape of a cross and were intentionally designed to cause all who entered to looked upward toward heaven. I wondered at such a great thought.

The next day we went into London early and attended a communion service and then a church service at All Souls Church, Langham Place. The church was pastored by John Stott at the time. The services were very personal, and in the afternoon we toured St. Margaret's Cathedral, Westminster Abbey, and the incredible St. Paul's Cathedral. The beauty and majesty of these places were overwhelming, and they impressed upon me the unfathomable depth of God.

The following day we went back for one more look at St. Albans Cathedral before heading south to Hove to New Orleans, the house of John and Rosalie Samson. We would finally meet the great prayer warrior and famed former leader of the Girls' Guild troops.

Rosalie was fairly diminutive and frail in her appearance. She had a gentle spirit that all but veiled the mountain of godly strength that presented itself in appropriate measure any occasion might require. There was also a fair amount of good-natured mischief and fun in the mix. In a short time, I would see what a rock she was to Brother John, representing so well the Rock of Ages.

Brother John and Rosalie occupied the main floor of the house, while Rosalie's sister, Mabel Cole, resided on the second floor. The third floor had only two rooms, a large room for guests and a storage room off to its side. The large room was known as the Prophet's Chamber, based on 2 Kings 4:8–10, and Brother John shared about several of the special guests who had stayed there throughout the years, including Larry Gordon.

The room was decorated with brightly colored wallpaper with several pictures on the walls, one of them a painting done by Larry. From then on, every time we came, we stayed in the Prophet's Chamber, but it was during that first night that I strongly sensed the presence of Larry Gordon. This trip had greatly enlarged the boundaries of my faith, visiting distant lands and meeting some amazing people from Brother John's life. Now in the quiet of the storied Prophet's Chamber in this home, the largeness of Larry's life was once again making its impression upon me. He had been here, in this room; his painting was there on the wall. In so many ways, he was here.

Tomorrow we would be flying to the Holy Land, the very place where our Lord Jesus had lived. I could hardly contain myself at the thought. And Beit Shalom; we were going to see the halls and rooms where so many miracles had taken place not so long ago! My anticipation was immense; my soul thrilled to it all.

The next evening, we took a train back to Gatwick Airport to fly to Israel, the Holy Land. What a joy it was to think that we were going to walk the very land that our Lord and Savior walked! I could hardly believe the reality of it was upon us.

The plane was supposed to take off a little after nine, but it was nearly nine when they opened the ticket counters to start processing the passengers. As a result, our flight was very late in taking off, and we didn't get to Tel Aviv until three in the morning. We were met at the airport by a big Minnesota farmer named Quinten Erickson, whom Brother John had known well from his years in Israel.

Years earlier, Quinten had felt God calling him to come to Israel. So he sold his farm and possessions and moved his wife Patricia, known as Sister Patty, and his five children to Israel. They lived in a modest two-room apartment in Netanya while Quinten was looking for work. A few months passed, and he had found nothing. However, each morning Quinten noticed young Israeli schoolchildren trying to cross the busy street in front of the apartment building to get to school. So he went down to the street and raised his large farmer's hand to stop the traffic, and the children crossed safely.

The owner of a food processing plant across the way from Quinten's apartment took note of this daily routine, and one day he pointed out the scene to his assistant and said he wanted that man in his office right away. Quinten entered the man's office unemployed and left as the plant supervisor. Now he and Sister Patty were living in their own large home with twelve of their thirteen children and a fourteenth on the way. Their oldest son, Boaz, was married and living in Jerusalem, and an Armenian girl had come to board with the Ericksons while attending a college nearby. It was both inspiring and challenging to meet and get to know so many people with such amazing faith in one trip. In the not-too-distant future, I knew the Lord was preparing Debbie and I to make some steps of faith of our own.

By the time we got to Quinten's home and went to bed, it was four o'clock in the morning. Debbie and I slept on a couch that folded down into a bed in a room that looked like a family room. We knew we were in a very different climate as we noticed a greenish lizard on the outside of one of the window screens. About seven in the morning, we awakened to five sets of eyes in perfect stair-step fashion shyly peeking over the edge of our blankets at us. After I mumbled some sort of greeting, the children giggled as they tumbled out of the room.

It was mild and somewhat humid as we awoke, but our first day in Israel had all the promise to be a beautiful one, and it did not let us down. After a big Midwest breakfast at a very long wooden table with benches, each of the children sprang to his or her cleanup chore without a word from Quinten or Patty. The attitude toward their work gave the house a pleasant atmosphere of joy and peace.

Since we were already in Netanya, we drove to the Ulpan Akiva, where Debbie and I met Shulamith Katznelson. Shulamith was slightly stocky but pleasant in appearance, with short, graying, slightly curled brown hair. She was delighted to see Brother John again, and upon introduction she greeted Debbie and I with a slight but warm smile and a humble nod of her head. She turned and engaged in lively conversation with Brother John after we sat with her at a large cafeteria-style table. Debbie and I sat quietly and enjoyed this happy reunion as people around us were fully engaged with each other in various conversations and activities. I was amazed as I watched Jews and Arabs and people from various other nations and cultures interacting with such friendliness toward each other. Considering the recent and historic hostilities that some of these people groups had shown toward each other, this scene seemed nothing short of miraculous. It was a phenomenon that many in the world would not believe was possible to achieve, yet here it was right before us.

After this warm reunion of old friends, we drove back to the Ericksons' home in the van that Quinten had loaned us. In the daylight, we saw a number of holes in the side and front of the van that looked like bullet holes, and they didn't seem very old. After we arrived at the Ericksons' house, we questioned Quinten about the holes in the van. The story he told us was a harrowing one. He and his oldest daughter Elisheva were driving the van about two weeks prior when they came upon an Israeli soldier hitchhiking. It was a common courtesy in Israel to pick up soldiers, so they stopped to give him a ride. He was trying to get back to the military outpost where his unit was staying in the area, so Quinten and Elisheva followed his directions. When they arrived at the front gate to let him off, the guard opened fire at them with his automatic weapon. Several bullets hit the van, shot through some of the windows and tires, and pockmarked the body of the van. One bullet even slightly grazed Elisheva's cheek.

Through the immediate ensuing investigation, they found out that a very similar van had approached that same gate just the night before, and someone in the van had thrown a bomb at the gate. If the soldier had not been with Quinten and Elisheva, they would have had a very difficult time convincing the authorities they were not the same people who had thrown the bomb. Even with the soldier testifying on their behalf, they were not easily convinced. This account helped us understand clearly the dangers the people of Israel faced daily. We also took note of the miraculous protection of God upon Quinten and his daughter and the soldier.

We stayed that night with the Ericksons, singing hymns and choruses and visiting well into the night. To have such oneness of spirit so far from home with people we barely knew was a testimony of the unique working of the same Spirit of God within each of us. In the morning, we rented a car for touring the country and headed for Jerusalem. The ascent up to Jerusalem was fascinating, with several battle memorials commemorating the capturing of the city by the Israeli army along the way.

We entered the Holy City at 9:45 a.m. on August 18, 1983. I was nearly overwhelmed with amazement at the thought of being in the City of David. Our Lord had spent so much of His time on earth here, and it was outside Jerusalem that He was eventually crucified.

Brother John guided us through a myriad of streets until we found the apartment where Boaz Erickson lived with his wife and two daughters. We then made our way through the narrow roads of one of the older parts of Jerusalem to the apartment of Danilo and Barbara van Woerden. Danilo is the son of Peter van Woerden, the nephew of Corrie ten Boom. Danilo and Barbara were in Jerusalem trying to bring several of the world's Christian church denominations together, some which had not met together in any formal way for many decades, possibly even centuries, for a gathering that would come to be called Jerusalem '84.

Brother John wanted to bring something for our lunch with the van Woerdens, so we haggled with an Arab street vendor for a small loaf of pita bread. Barbara mildly chastised us when she found out what we paid for the bread, even though we paid only about twenty cents (US) for it. We spent the afternoon talking with Danilo and Barbara about the work they were doing in Jerusalem. Danilo and Barbara were about the same age as Debbie and me. I was amazed at the immensity of the challenge they were taking on. Even if Danilo was a relative of the great Corrie ten Boom, could this really be accomplished? Again my faith was challenged to accept just how powerful our God is, and that we just need to catch His vision and get busy.

We heard later that they had a lot of success with Jerusalem '84. Over one thousand participants from all over the world gathered for prayer and sharing. After this success, Danilo and Barbara started a company called Agape Tours in 1985, with the goal of promoting Christian contacts throughout the world. I was continually amazed at the caliber of people Brother John had come to know during his time at Beit Shalom. Hearing about them during our many conversations and slide presentations was inspiring, but meeting and talking with them in the flesh challenged my faith even further. These were no longer just stories about people of great faith; here they were right before me testifying to the reality that God honors those who trust Him wholly.

After our time with the van Woerdens, we walked through the streets of the Old City of Jerusalem. It was like going back many centuries in time with its crowded streets of donkey carts and vendors shouting out their interesting and sometimes unusual wares. Many people wore the same style of clothing that had been worn for centuries, just like those I had seen depicted in biblical pictures from the time of Jesus.

We treated ourselves to some delicious, freshly made baklava and bought some figurines carved from olive wood. We also went to a fruit shop that seemed to have every fruit in existence, all grown right in Israel. We looked at a beautifully embroidered blouse in another shop. The owner claimed it was handmade in Israel, even though its tag said "Made in India." Its price was twenty-six dollars, which was pretty expensive for that time. The shop owner told us we could have it for a special price just for us. We declined and kept declining as he continued lowering the price. We turned from him one final time, walking away a block from the shop as he shouted, "Six dollars!"

We left the Old City of Jerusalem with wonderment, thinking that Jesus had walked streets just like these. Then we went to the Garden Tomb, where Brother John had worked during the early years of Beit Shalom. Even if it wasn't the exact location of Jesus' death and resurrection, it stirred us to see a similar tomb from the same era. I was particularly moved when we turned to exit the tomb and read the words from Mark 16:6 on a plaque hanging on its rock wall: "He is risen; He is not here."

The place had a personal connection as well; I felt privileged to see the very place where Brother John had worked for two years while beginning the work at Beit Shalom. I felt we were more a part of his personal history as we left the Garden Tomb and headed toward Bethlehem to see the Church of the Nativity. There were two churches, side by side, one a Greek Orthodox church and the other the Catholic Church of the Nativity. They were both incredibly adorned with many beautiful religious objects, altars, and structures, and of course, the supposed site of Jesus's birth in the Church of the Nativity. I wondered if this really was the exact location where the shepherds had met our Lord so many years ago. Even if it was not, I knew that meeting had happened in this vicinity, and I felt a great sense of awe. I stood there for a moment looking at the ordinary people around me. It seemed so unbelievable that God became a man and walked among us, but He did. At this moment, I couldn't imagine what it would be like to be face-to-face with Jesus in the body of an ordinary human.

From there we drove to the home of Sister Nellie and her friend Mary. Sister Nellie was Patty Erickson's mother, and after a very warm time of visiting, as we stood on the porch for a final farewell, they broke out singing Squire Parsons' "Sweet

Beulah Land" in stunning two-part harmony. It felt as if we were already there.

It was late in the afternoon on Friday, so we hurried back to Jerusalem to join the celebration welcoming Shabbat at the Wailing Wall. People thronged the many concrete stairways that led down to the wall, anticipating the men who would come down one of the stairways singing and dancing at the arrival of the first star, signifying the beginning of the Sabbath. We stood halfway down one of the stairways, wondering if we would be able to see them. Then we heard the singing not too far away. They appeared and were coming right down our stairway. They were so full of joy as they danced their way by us; what a glorious celebration!

After a restful night's sleep and an outstanding breakfast, we drove north to a village of Druze Muslims to find a friend of Brother John's whose family name was Daboer. As we entered the village, we began to ask people for guidance to the Daboer home, as John did not know where his friend lived. We did not know any Arab words, so we simply said "Daboer" to all we accosted for help. One after another stared at us incredulously while shrugging his or her shoulders helplessly. We couldn't understand why no one in this small village seemed to know where the Daboer family lived. Suddenly it occurred to John to say "Salmon Daboer," the full name of his friend, to a man walking by the road. We were showered with a multitude of unintelligible words, along with several waves of his arms motioning the direction to the house of Salmon Daboer. We felt we understood the arm gestures well enough to venture forth, and as we did John explained to us that Salmon's family had lived in this village for over six hundred years. Probably two-thirds of the six or seven hundred people who lived in this village had the last name of Daboer. We laughed for most of the trip to Salmon's house as we now understood why no one could explain to us where "Daboer" lived!

That night, we stayed at the Scots Hotel in Tiberias on the Sea of Galilee. It was a very hot and humid night, and sleep did not come easily even with a ceiling fan blowing a gentle breeze on us. We were in the lowest inhabited place on earth (about 650 feet below sea level), and the air, heavy with humidity, was not moving at all in the city.

After a fitful night of sleep and a good breakfast, we left Tiberias and began a long, thrilling day's journey circling the Sea of Galilee. We stopped at the Mount of Beatitudes and the Capernaum ruins and took a side trip through the Golan Heights. The Golan Heights were full of soldiers and military encampments. We learned later that those troops invaded Lebanon just a short while after we were there.

The next day we visited a church at the top of Mount Tabor, one of the supposed sights of the Mount of Transfiguration, and stopped again in Nazareth to get some lunch. Brother John went into a fruit market to buy some bananas, and as the shopkeeper weighed them on the scales, Debbie noticed he was pushing down on the scales with his finger. She motioned for him to stop that, so he put the bananas into a heavy iron pot and weighed them again. Before Debbie could stop this chicanery, Brother John had already given the man the money to pay for the weight of the bananas and the pot. When Debbie informed Brother John of this latest dishonesty, he was so flustered by the whole affair that he didn't want to bother with trying to straighten it out. The bananas were a nice addition to our lunch, even though they were a bit expensive.

We got back to the hotel in time to see a beautiful rising of the moon over the peaceful Sea of Galilee. At a moment like this, it was easy to understand why the Lord spent so much time here. The sense of His presence was very strong. The Lord had brought us here to this serene moment in the Holy Land. It was all so remarkable; my faith was being enlarged with each step of the trip, and Beit Shalom was yet to come.

On the following day, we went to the Mosque of Omar (the Dome of the Rock), the oldest existing Islamic structure in the world. It is built on the Temple Mount right over the site of the Second Jewish Temple, which was destroyed in AD 70 during the Roman siege of Jerusalem. The outside of the Mosque of Omar is covered with small, nearly five-hundred-year-old Iznik tiles, and the huge dome is gold-plated on the outside. It is the third holiest site of all Islam (only Mecca and Medina are considered more holy), but it is *the* holiest site in all of Judaism. The dome is set right over the Foundation Stone, which some believe is the location of the Holiest of Holies, and it is also thought to be the site where Abraham nearly sacrificed Isaac on the mountain in the land of Moriah. The Muslims also believe it to be the spot where Muhammad ascended to heaven attended by the angel Gabriel. As the Muslim authorities do not permit Jewish prayer in the Temple Mount area, the Jewish people now pray at the Wailing Wall, the site nearest to the Foundation Stone that they are allowed to pray.

As we went inside, we saw walls covered with mosaics, marble, and other fine materials, and the floors were covered with costly Persian rugs. An ornately carved, elevated wooden case claimed to hold three hairs plucked from Muhammad's beard as he ascended to heaven. We also walked in a corridor that surrounded the Foundation Stone. There were rivulets carved into the whitish stone that some believe were for draining the blood of the sacrifices made at the Jewish Temple. There was an atmosphere of deep reverence as people observed the artifacts and the incredible beauty inside the mosque. To be present near, possibly *in*, the Holy of Holies was a remarkable thought. The Lord had indeed opened the way to Himself (Hebrews 10:19–22), and we were witnessing this in a very tangible sort of way. The Lord seemed to be taking me through multiple ascensions of faith that would become more evident in the following days, months, and years. More was still to come.

After our tour of the Dome of the Rock, we drove the seventeen miles from Jerusalem out to Emmaus to see the French geological center that had once been Beit Shalom. It was impressive and thrilling as we approached the ancient ruins in front of the majestic white stone structure with its beautifully arched balcony. I remembered the accounts of the Bible studies and baptisms that had occurred in the ruins as we drove past them. As we pulled up to the front of the building, I thought about the slides showing the transformation of the ornate front door as we passed through it into the foyer. The inside was much more austere than what I had seen in the slides, but it still looked familiar. It was now only a semblance of its former glory, with most of the rooms lined with shelves filled with antiquities. Yet, I still marveled that I was actually standing inside the storied structure.

Brother John briefly spoke with those who were now in charge of the building before giving us a room-by-room tour. He showed us the rooms of the ground floor and grieved that some of the etchings in what had been the beloved music room had been callously painted over. I tried to visualize how I had seen it in the slide presentations and recall all of the memorable events that had taken place there involving so many special people.

We went up to the balcony on the second floor and sat on the ledge as we viewed the panorama of the historic Valley of Ayalon. I felt a great sense of history, both ancient and recent, as we reposed momentarily in reverent silence. Brother John and I sensed that the Lord still had His eye on Beit Shalom for a special purpose in the future, possibly even in His Millennial Kingdom. If that comes to fruition, how I long to be a part of it!

Brother John showed us what had been the immense kitchen, the beautiful chapel, the Levi room, and the rest of the rooms before we began the short journey back to Jerusalem. Having now seen Beit Shalom, I sensed more than ever the greatness of God and His willingness and desire to use ordinary men and women, even me, in His extraordinary ventures.

Over the last few days in Israel, Brother John began to sense from the Lord that he was needed at home in England, so he managed to make an international call to

Rosalie. Rosalie confirmed that she had been yearning very much for John to come home, as she had not been feeling well. So we went back to the Ericksons' house and rested before going to the airport in Tel Aviv to try to get standby tickets back to England. We finally departed on a flight out of Israel at three o'clock in the morning. We arrived at Gatwick at 9:15 a.m., London time, and drove to Brother John's house. Rosalie was greatly relieved to have her husband home and began to feel much better immediately.

That evening we rejoiced together, singing hymns, and we spent the following day, Saturday, roaming around Brighton. Brother John encouraged us to try our wings in making a little foray into France. Traveling into yet another country on our own made us a little nervous, but it proved to be a good gamble (though there is no gamble at all if the Lord is truly in charge).

On Monday morning, Debbie and I set out on a large ferry for a four-hour voyage across the English Channel to Dieppe, France, on the coast of Normandy. It was a place rich with history. On August 19, 1942, the allied forces made a raid on Dieppe in an attempt to find the best location for the D-Day invasion. They suffered heavy casualties. Dieppe was heavily fortified by the Germans, so they decided to establish a beachhead elsewhere. Now it was a quiet little town that received as many as four ferries a day with as many as four hundred passengers on each. Dieppe hardly seemed to notice this large daily influx of mostly tourists and remained a slow, peaceful town. We foraged through some restaurants, shopped in a few unique little emporiums, and did some sightseeing before settling into our hotel for the night, all with a French vocabulary of less than a dozen words. Sometimes it was quite humorous. After disembarking from the ferry and enduring a fairly long train ride, we arrived back at John and Rosalie's home in the early evening for another night in the Prophet's Chamber.

That night, we opened the skylight in the chamber and stood on one of the beds on our tiptoes to look out over the amply lighted city of Hove as large, silent ships drifted in the twilight background on the English Channel. We felt so childlike and free as we enjoyed the spectacle before us. After we got back into our beds, we anticipated the next day's trip to the Bible College of Wales in Swansea, the capital. The college had no residential provision for couples, so we planned to have Debbie stay with Brother John and Rosalie while I attended classes during the week over a two-year period. I would come to stay at Brother John's every weekend that I was able. But tonight, as we discussed this arrangement, Debbie expressed great discomfort with being over four hundred miles away from me for the next year. I was quite taken aback by this revelation, but we decided after much more discussion and some prayer that I would attend a college much nearer our home in Oregon.

After discussing the change of plans with Brother John in the morning, we decided to go visit the college anyway as we felt it would be best to explain the situation in person. Brother John also planned on stopping at Torquay, England, on the way back to visit his nephew Ray, who had committed his life to Christ while staying at Beit Shalom. We left late in the morning and drove through Bristol, England (where the buildings from George Müeller's famous orphanage still stood), and survived many roundabouts before spending the night in Newport, Wales. The next morning we drove to Swansea and met with Richard Maton, the headmaster of the Bible college, and explained our change in plans. He graciously gave us an extensive tour of the college before we left.

I spoke at a youth meeting at a Methodist church on our last evening in England. The meeting was led by a friend of Brother John's named John Chambers. John Chambers had come to stay with Brother John for five weeks while he pastored in Pendleton. John didn't seem to know the Lord when he first came to Oregon, but he certainly did after he left. He had since married his longtime girlfriend, Wendy. Debbie and I spent the rest of evening with them after the youth meeting ended, getting to know Wendy and renewing our friendship with John.

The following day, Brother John drove us to the Gatwick Airport where we began our long journey home after a sorrowful yet joyful parting. Two flights and many hours later we arrived in Portland, Oregon, where we relaxed the rest of the day and stayed the night. We drove the two hundred miles back to Pendleton the following day and thanked the Lord for a safe arrival after an incredible forty-day journey.

We had finished the trip of a lifetime. We had met many amazing people while touring parts of five countries. We had also seen some marvelous sights. But what did it all mean? What was the Lord's purpose in this incredible blessing and experience? We would soon learn that our trip was but the beginning of the Beit Shalom challenge for us. We had much more to learn and experience while continuing the spiritual journey we had set out on when the Lord whispered "wait and see" in His quiet leading.

Chapter 8

A SWIFTLY CHANGING LIFE

When God begins to take us more deeply into His purposes, things change dramatically—on the outside and on the inside, and He is much more interested on what is going on inside, in our hearts. He also blesses us incredibly, especially in the initial stages of the change. Since Larry's death, our lives had changed much, and they were about to change even more.

After I resigned my position at the Pendleton Christian School and decided not to attend the Bible College of Wales, we really didn't know what we were going to do to make a living. We knew by this time that I was going to go to Eastern Oregon State College (now Eastern Oregon State University) to finish my bachelor's degree in education. We didn't have any idea how we were going to eat or pay our bills, but we weren't especially worried about it. After seeing the Lord provide so bountifully for our trip to England and Israel, we sensed that somehow He was going to take care of it all. We hadn't planned things this way, and we strongly sensed that the Lord was in charge of it all.

We returned to Pendleton on Saturday, September 10, 1983, and that evening the Burtons invited us to come to their house for dinner and an evening together. We had barely gotten started into the evening when Tommy informed us that they were ready for us to come back to the Christian school and take over our responsibilities there again. We were a bit taken aback by this announcement, but it really was what we needed. The school year had already begun the week before we returned, and Tommy had held down the fort waiting for us. He was more than ready for us to come back. He had left off his own work as a contractor and had maintained the school well, but they needed someone to take over the responsibilities, and we needed some income. Since we still had no children, together we arranged for Debbie to work at the school full-time, and I would work there part-time while going to college.

It all worked out very well, even though it turned out to be the busiest year of my life up to that point. I took fifty-eight hours of credit during the three terms of the 1983–1984 school year while driving one hundred miles round-trip to the college each day. I worked at the Christian school when I had time off from classes. During the winter term, the Lord worked it out so that I was able to take all of my classes by extension at the community college right there in Pendleton. Because of that, I only had to drive over the treacherous pass to La Grande three times during the entire winter term. I still almost got stuck in the deep snow during an ice storm on one of those trips, and another time I was so tired that I actually fell asleep at the wheel coming back. But the Lord put a semi right next to me, and the driver blasted his horn right into my ear as I began to drift into his lane. I was then very wide awake!

On another trip, I was headed to La Grande to take a major midterm test in a critical class. I had been so busy that I had not had enough time to study properly for the test. I had highlighted some of the lines and sections from my class notes, and I set the notebook open on the seat next to me as I drove. I asked the Lord to help me see the notes to the material that would be on the test, glancing down at the notebook and flipping pages as I drove. The Lord is always faithful, even when we are a bit maniacal; I got the highest grade in the class of over eighty students.

During the last week of school in the spring, it worked out that I had to take no finals at all that term. That really helped, as I had so many papers and projects to finish that Debbie and I spent the entire final week in the library at the college. We were there from nine in the morning until nine o'clock at night, besides the hundred-mile round-trip each day. On the very last day, I finished several papers and projects for one class and put them into a self-addressed envelope so the professor could mail them back to me after he graded them. The librarian kindly volunteered to give them to the professor the next day, when they were all due, since the professor was long gone by this time of the night. I sternly warned her to make sure he got them on time as I would be penalized pretty heavily for having that many papers and projects late. She slyly joked with me about possibly getting confused and dropping them in the mail instead. I wasn't tremendously amused and was somewhat unsettled when I received the large envelope back at our house in Pendleton just two days later. My disturbed feeling began to turn into a slight panic as I thumbed through the pages of the first paper I pulled out of the envelope. I saw no markings of correction anywhere. I was sure I had not done the paper that perfectly, so I scrambled to the end of the paper. A huge sigh of relief escaped me as I saw a single "A" marked in red at the bottom of the last page. Praise the Lord. I was done. I had finished my bachelor's degree almost twelve years after I started it. It felt like a huge weight rolling off of me.

A few days later I received my diploma, with Debbie, my faithful mother, the Burtons, and two students from the Christian school cheering for me among the hundreds in attendance at the graduation ceremony. My mother could not hide her smile afterward. She had promised my father, before he died, that she would get all four of us kids through college. The promise was now fulfilled. I still regret that I put my mother through the turmoil of quitting college. At that moment, however, my earlier rebellion was swallowed up in the joy of the accomplishment the Lord had helped me to achieve.

That summer I worked with Tommy Burton, doing construction jobs that involved a lot of digging. I teased my mom about the way she used to say that if I didn't finish college, I would end up "digging a ditch" for a living. Well, here I was a college graduate, and I was digging a ditch. She got a kick out of that.

During that summer, Debbie and I scrimped and saved all the money we could. I felt strongly that the Lord wanted me to go to a Christian college in the fall to get a master's degree in theology in one year. Then I was to help start a nondenominational church and Christian school somewhere. It was not that I thought denominations were wrong, I just felt the Lord was leading me to be part of a ministry that was free from any constraints, as was Beit Shalom. I believed this would give the Lord greater freedom to help Himself to the lives of those involved and to any projects that might be undertaken. I don't know why, but I also felt strongly that one year was the time limit the Lord had set. Debbie and I sensed strongly that the Lord someday wanted a children's home to be a part of the ministry as well. We still were not able to have children, yet we felt they would one day be a big part of our lives.

I found two Christian colleges that offered a one-year master's degree in theology. One was in the middle of Alberta, Canada, and the other was in Pensacola, Florida. Both programs looked good, so the deciding factor became where I wanted to spend the winter. It didn't seem very spiritual, but Florida won the debate.

I applied to the college in Florida and was accepted, and Debbie and I began the difficult process of selling most of our furniture and things we would not need. We stored some things in a storage room at my mother's house. We also bought a covered utility trailer to haul all that we could pack into it and our little Mazda station wagon.

We were about finished getting ready to start the long drive to Florida when we got a very unusual phone call. It came two days before we were to leave and one day before we disconnected our phone. A dear friend and former pastor of ours called and asked us if we wanted to adopt a baby! Another family in his church had been planning on doing so but had backed out only two weeks before the baby was expected to be born. He knew Debbie and I had been trying to have a baby but were not able to do so yet, so he thought we would be good candidates. We were stunned, to say the least. Debbie started to cry because she really wanted to adopt the baby but thought it impossible in our current circumstances. She also thought I would not want to do it because of our situation. I assured her that I did want to try, and I encouraged her (and myself) to see what the Lord could do.

We received the call on a Friday, so we delayed our departure and talked to the birth mother by phone on Sunday. She gave us permission to adopt if the baby was a boy, but she wanted to keep the child if it was a girl. On Monday, we called a lawyer and were able to see him that day. When we met at his office, he tried to fill out a long legal form to get the proceeding underway. He wanted to know where we were going to live when we got to Florida. We didn't know; we were going to find a place when we got there. He wanted to know what work we were going to be doing when we got to Florida. We didn't know; I planned on finding a part-time job, and Debbie was planning to find full-time work when we got there. So it proceeded through almost the entire form.

By the time he had asked all the questions to fill in every blank on the form, we had only answered one. That, surprisingly, was what we wanted to name the baby. We said his name was to be John Michael Winters. He raised his eyebrows and said he didn't know how we were going to do this, but he would try. We agreed to keep in close contact as things developed.

We left Pendleton the next day from my mother's house after a teary good-bye to my mother, my brother, Phil, and his wife, Jo Ann. We headed east on Interstate 84 and made it all the way to Logan, Utah, where we spent the night with a friend who had served as the interim pastor in the Pendleton church just after John Samson left.

From there, we drove south and stayed in a motel in Williams, Arizona. In the morning, we drove north on Highway 64 and followed it along the south rim of the Grand Canyon. Then we drove east on Interstate 40 across the rest of Arizona and all the way across New Mexico. We pulled into a motel at two-thirty in the morning, just on the other side of the Texas border.

We covered over 850 miles that day, even though we toured the Grand Canyon for most of the morning. We pushed ourselves so that we could make it to the airport in Dallas, Texas, by the next evening. Brother John was flying in from England to spend time with mutual friends, the Weavers. We got up at five-thirty in the morning, after three hours of sleep, and drove all day across Texas. We arrived just in time to reach the gate where Brother John's plane arrived a few minutes later. Together, we spent four very hot and humid days visiting, dining, and singing hymns and choruses together in the Weavers' air-conditioned home.

Next, Brother John, Debbie, and I headed south to Galveston to the home of Harold and Judy West. Harold was the pilot who led Larry Gordon to the Lord about seven years earlier. As we drove into the outskirts of Houston, it began to rain. We were surprised to see cars pulling off to the side of the road. I thought the other drivers were being too extreme in their cautions and drove on. Less than two minutes later, it was raining so hard I could hardly see the end of our car's hood. I blindly found my way to the side of the road, and we waited fifteen minutes for this torrential downpour to stop. After we continued driving, we saw a car overturned from hydroplaning on a large pool of water that had aggregated on the road. That was my first lesson with the sudden intense downpours of the southeastern part of our country.

When we arrived at the Wests, Judy met us at the door. Harold was gone on a flying trip. We spent many hours over the next two days reminiscing about Larry with Judy and her two sweet but shy children. Judy related a time when she had invested a lot of time trying to bring a Jewish friend to the Lord. She said she had been prayerfully taking things slow and easy, not wanting to offend her friend. One day, Larry approached Judy's friend, put his hands on her shoulders, and asked her if she knew how much Jesus loved her. Judy recalled feeling very apprehensive as Larry spoke, but her fear was allayed as her friend received Larry's gesture with great warmth.

At the end of the two days, Debbie and I headed east for Pensacola while Brother John stayed behind. Brother John wanted to spend his last few weeks with Harold and Judy and with Rob Nichols in Vermont before returning to England. Debbie and I were sorry we did not get to meet Harold, but we had an appointment at the college that made it impossible to stay any longer. We were saddened to be separated from Brother John, but we strongly sensed that we would see him many more times in the future. To our great delight, our premonition became utterly true.

To some our future would have seemed daunting. We were headed off to graduate school over three thousand miles from home. We were about to adopt a baby. Where would we live? How would we do all of this? Somehow, we were not overwhelmed. Rather, I had a sense of adventure about all of it. There would be some challenging moments, but after the Lord had taken us on the trip to Europe and Israel and helped me finish my bachelor's degree, it seemed like nothing was impossible. I had much to learn yet, and the Lord would test me, but He had stretched me enough to know that ultimately everything would work out. The further we stepped out in our faith, the bigger our God seemed to be.

Chapter 9

FAITH BUILDING IN PENSACOLA

After the long drive from Galveston, we arrived in Pensacola toward the end of a hot summer day in late August. We found a motel room close to the college I was to attend, and the cool, air-conditioned room was appreciated immensely. After settling into our room, I dressed in some slacks, a dress shirt, and a tie, and we found our way to the admissions building. We checked in and started the search for a place to live from the list of rentals the college provided as satisfactory residences for off-campus students. We were looking for something clean with at least two bedrooms, one for us and one for a baby. We strongly sensed that the Lord really was going to bring us a baby boy.

After a short search we found a furnished, two-bedroom mobile home ten feet wide and sixty feet long. It was behind the home of Harvey and Neva Bowen, a wonderful Christian couple who would be our landlords and friends for the next four-and-a-half months. Harvey and Neva owned four other rentals. Three were near our mobile home, and one was across the street. All were rented to students or employees of the college. Together with Harvey and Neva, this became a splendid little neighborhood of close friends.

Our cozy little community was located at the end of a short, picturesque, dead-end road called Oleander Drive, about a half-mile from the college campus. The narrow lane was lined on each side with majestic old oak trees which arched beautifully over the road, their branches overlapping its center. Harvey and Neva's property was sprinkled with many mature pecan trees, which provided us with tasty snacks throughout the fall as the ripened nuts descended to the lawn.

We had been settled just two days in our comfortable little abode, and we did not yet have a phone installed when Harvey excitedly came to our door. We had a phone call from Oregon. A baby boy had been born in Portland! John Michael Winters came into this world a week later than predicted at eight o'clock in the morning on August 31, 1984. He weighed seven pounds thirteen ounces and was twenty and one-fourth inches long, with a head full of dark brown hair. The delay in John's birth gave us just enough time to set up our new home and put a changing table and bassinet in his nursery.

Two days later, Debbie was on a jet to Portland to pick up our precious little bundle. We scrambled to get airfare for her back to Portland on short notice. I did not accompany Debbie on the trip as I didn't have the faith to believe that we both could go.

It was a difficult trip for Debbie, as she had to meet with the birth mother and her family and adjust fairly suddenly to the revelation that she was now the mother of a newborn baby. Debbie's mother, Dorothy Stone, picked her up at the airport, and together they went to our former pastor's house. There she met our son John for the first time at the ripe old age of two days and seven hours. After an hour of getting acquainted, Debbie and her mother went to a store to get diapers, formula, and all the things they would need for John. Then they went to Dorothy's house for two days of continuous visits from well-wishing friends and relatives.

On the following day, Debbie drove her grandmother and John to Pendleton for a busy three-day stay that included a shower given by the Pendleton Baptist Church. It was attended by more than fifty friends and relatives. Two days after returning to Portland, Debbie and John boarded a plane at the Portland International Airport to head back to Pensacola. Nine hours later, I met a very tired and anxious mother and my nine-and-a-half-day-old son. What a thrill! What an incredible thought that we were the parents of this precious little child lying right in front of us. I would need so much wisdom from the Lord to bring up little John in God's ways. I would be stretched in my faith in many ways to lead our fledgling family.

While Debbie was gone, I started my courses at the college. I realized immediately that I would not be able to hold even a part-time job with the amount of work and study required. I had already found a job, so I called the man who had hired me and apologized, explaining that I would not be able to accept the position.

Then I became greatly alarmed when I realized that Debbie would not be able to work at all with the responsibilities of a newborn baby, and we had spent a large portion of the funds we'd brought with us on the costs of the adoption. How would we be able to pay the rent and bills, not to mention pay for graduate school, with no income and our funds rapidly disappearing?

I went to the Lord instantly with my panic prayers, and almost immediately I heard the quiet leading of the Father inside me saying, "I will take care of you." I reacted as if I had heard nothing and continued with my panic prayers. He repeated with the same calmness, "I will take care of you." Again I ignored Him, and this went on for days, as often as I prayed. Finally, after four days, I became weary of my fears and started to hear and believe the Father's words of assurance.

After giving Debbie a couple of days to settle in with our new addition, I told her about turning down the part-time job. She asked me what we were going to do to meet our financial obligations. She knew her availability to go out and work was not plentiful with a new baby to care for. I told her, "The Lord will take care of us." She looked at me, unassured by my words, but said nothing. I had grown so confident in the idea of the Lord taking care of us that I began to imagine how He was going to do it. I thought I had it figured out pretty well, but the Lord is always much more creative than we can imagine.

During the next few weeks, word of our adoption spread to many corners of the campus. About a dozen ladies who were wives of students and staff gave a lovely and generous surprise baby shower, complete with refreshments and gifts. Many of these ladies would become my wife's best friends during our stay at Pensacola. Helen LaPointe and her husband, Buddy, became our closest friends and kept in contact with us for many years after our time at Pensacola. Brother John also came down from his visit with Rob Nichols in Vermont and stayed with us for almost a week to see the young lad who was his namesake. The fellowship we shared was filled with laughter and joy. The presence of Brother John and little John gave us a sense of assurance that the Lord was indeed with us in our new role as parents.

We had Brother John sleep in little John's room while we put our son in his bassinet in the living room. One night Brother John had a terrible nightmare. Debbie and I were awakened by loud shouts and a powerful crash as something hit the wall separating our rooms. We rushed into Brother John's room and turned on the light, expecting who knows what. We found a very sheepish-looking Brother John and an empty diaper pail at the foot of the wall with its contents all over the wall and half the nursery. We laughed uproariously about it for days, and we still laugh about it.

About a week after Brother John, left, I was balancing our checkbook one evening. When I finished, I saw that we only had one hundred and twenty-five dollars left. We had over four hundred dollars in rent, tuition, and other bills coming due within the next ten days. I found Debbie and shared the news with her, and she asked, "What are we going to do?" Without missing a beat, the most absurd thought popped into my head and was out of my mouth before I had time to think. I said, "Let's go to Po' Folks," a nice seafood restaurant in Pensacola. Even I was surprised at the words I had just spoken.

We exchanged looks of surprise but decided it really wouldn't make that much difference whether we went or not. So we went out and had a very nice dinner before coming home for a quiet evening. After Debbie went to bed, I went into my panic prayers once more. This time I screamed at the Lord in my spirit for only about three hours before I heard His quiet leading once more. He said, "I'm going to take care of this *tomorrow*."

This time I believed the Lord more readily, and I went into the bedroom immediately to tell Debbie what He had said. She pacified me with a sleepy "Uh-huh" before falling back into a sound sleep. My mind began to race. How was the Lord going to take care of this tomorrow? We were over three thousand miles from home. I couldn't imagine how He was going to do it, but I felt sure that He would.

The next morning as I was getting ready for the day's classes, I still wondered how the Lord was going to solve our financial crisis *today*. When I came to the breakfast table, I decided the only way He could solve this today was to send us some funds through the mail. Yes, that was it; someone would send us some money or a check in a letter. I shared my thoughts about the solution with Debbie, and she humored me with a smile.

Feeling somewhat smug, I went off to my morning classes. When I came home for lunch at noon, I put my books and briefcase down and said melodiously to Debbie, "I'm going to get the mail." She again humored me with a smile as I went out the door and headed for the mailbox. I walked swiftly and popped open the door with great expectation. All the wind went out of my sails as I stared into an empty mailbox. I knew the mailman had come, so I was lost in bewilderment. "Lord, You said You would take care of it today," I said in my spirit. Silence was my answer.

I went back into our mobile home and sat stunned at the table after sharing the bad news with Debbie. We had a quiet lunch under a cloud of discouragement before I left for my afternoon classes. When I returned from my classes, I went and earned fifteen dollars helping Buddy LaPointe with a one-time moving job. On the way home, I shared the whole situation with Buddy. We had grown close by this time and often shared such things with each other. I knew I wasn't fudging with the Lord by telling Buddy as he, Helen, and their two girls were in a similar financial situation.

I had just finished telling our woes as Buddy drove into our driveway to let me off. As we slowed to a stop, Debbie came dancing out onto the small platform at the top of the steps that led into our mobile home, saying, "He did it! He did it!" Buddy was incredulous. "You were just telling me! I can't believe it! You were just telling me!" he bellowed.

Debbie excitedly explained that her Uncle Glen, a very godly man, had called while Buddy and I were doing the moving job and bluntly asked her, "Do you need money?" Debbie did not want to hedge on the Lord, but she could not lie, so she told him that we did. He said, "Good, because I sent you a check in the mail *two days ago.*"

The Lord had indeed answered that day in His own unique and creative way. The funds did come through the mail, but not the way I expected. The amount Glen sent was more than enough to cover all of our bills coming due *and* the dinner at Po' Folks.

This was just the beginning of how the Lord took care of us during our entire stay in Pensacola. One time we came home to find a box of groceries on the porch put together by a couple of our neighbors in the same financial shape as we were. Another time after church, we found one hundred dollars in cash left in our unlocked car. Our car was in a huge parking lot with hundreds of other cars. Even the IRS sent us an unexpected home owner's reimbursement check for over four hundred dollars. There were many birthday, Christmas, and baby gifts of cash and needed items and supplies given and sent to us. Neighbors and Harvey and Neva were constantly giving us a bag of potatoes, a pound of hamburger, a sack of pecans, a turkey for Thanksgiving, or some other needed item. It brings tears to my eyes as I write about this more than twenty-five years later. The Lord and His people are so generous and kind.

On one occasion, we had been praying for a baby carrier for John, and Debbie saw one she liked one Saturday while out shopping. It was priced at twenty-five dollars. We told no one that we were praying for this, and the very next day at church, one of our neighbors came up to Debbie and me and handed us an envelope. They told us it was for buying a baby carrier. We looked inside, and there was a twenty-dollar bill. We decided we could come up with the other five dollars needed to get the carrier Debbie wanted. So Debbie went out the next day to same store to make the purchase. The carrier was on sale for nineteen dollars and ninety-nine cents! Needless to say, we were astonished.

One Friday night, Buddy Lapointe took me out for an all-night fishing excursion off the jetty at Alabama Point, about five miles from where we lived. Buddy was a great fisherman, and that night we caught more fish than we could stuff into the huge Coleman cooler Buddy had brought with us. What a great time we had catching all those fish! It took Buddy hours to clean all of them—he did it alone the next day without even telling me so that I could help—but those fish helped feed us for a while.

The Lord provided in many ways, some big, some small. Sometimes people babysat for us and wouldn't let us pay for it. I found a five-dollar-bill by the side of a very busy road on my way home from classes one day. Dear friends gave us furniture, and the Lord even provided a part-time job for Debbie at a toy store during the Christmas season. The store manager generously allowed Debbie to work during the times I was out of class so I could watch John. He usually just slept while I studied.

In the process of adopting John, we had to have a home study. We were worried the person they sent might not think too highly of the fact that neither of us had a job, I was going to graduate school, *and* we had a baby. But God sent a free-spirited young lady who took no issue with anything. She did not even want to see the list of things I had prepared to show how the Lord was taking good care of us. She also informed us about a system of interstate compacts that existed in the United States to work with interstate adoptions. All the states in the US were separated into groups, and it was much easier to do an interstate adoption with states that were from the same group. This concerned us with Oregon and Florida being so far apart. We thought there was no way they could be in the same group; but they were. The adoption went so incredibly smoothly, we were constantly amazed.

The days and months passed swiftly at Pensacola. The work at the college was really hard, but it went well. The friends we made and the fellowship we enjoyed were very sweet, but sometime in December, toward the end of the first semester, I began to sense the calling of the Lord to go back to Pendleton. At first I thought I was just getting tired of the difficulties and stress of graduate school, but one night it came to a climax. The pressure to go back to Pendleton was so great I couldn't sleep. I talked to Debbie about it several times that night. We had no place to stay, as our house in Pendleton was rented; and there was no job for me, as the people at the Pendleton Baptist Church had hired an administrator to take my place. I was concerned about leaving the college without finishing my degree, but I did sense we had learned what the Lord had sent us to Pensacola to learn. We were actually living out the Beit Shalom challenge in a small but significant way. The pressure this night was so intense, I stayed up until six-thirty in the morning. I intermittently prayed and went into the bedroom to talk to Debbie as she tried to get some sleep.

With no resolution, I finally fell asleep at six-thirty, and the alarm clock woke me up at eight o'clock. Debbie and I wondered what the meaning of the previous night had been. When I came into the mobile home the following evening after class, Debbie was on the phone with a very serious look on her face. I perceived immediately that something was wrong and sat down quietly to listen to her end of the conversation. I gathered that she was talking to someone from Pendleton, and when she got off the phone she explained that Clara Burton had called intending just to ask us how we were doing and have a friendly talk. However, not too far into the conversation, Clara, who is very strong emotionally, had broken down crying. She told Debbie that the man they hired to take my place as administrator of the Christian school had made a huge mess of things. They ended up having to let him go. Clara asked Debbie if we would come back to Pendleton and take over the leadership of the school once more. Debbie shared about the sleepless night I'd just had and said we would talk about the situation.

We were stunned by these revelations, but we now understood what the pressure to go back to Pendleton was all about. We quickly agreed that we needed to go. The next night the pastor from the church in Pendleton called to officially ask us to come back. We confirmed with him that we would. The next day, we began to take care of the details to end our time in Pensacola. We did not know where we were going to live once we got there, but the Lord would soon make everything abundantly clear.

Chapter 10

PENDLETON AND BEYOND

During our time in Pensacola, the Lord made it abundantly clear that He was more than able to take care of us. Yet in our journey of faith, there was so much more to learn. The Lord is always perfect in teaching us what we need at just the right time if our hearts are open to Him, no matter how frail or foolish we are prone to be. As long as we need them, He provides men to be as Elijah was to Elisha, like Larry Gordon and John Samson were in my life. He *never* leaves us or forsakes us no matter how difficult things may seem at any given moment.

It was hard to leave Pensacola; we had made many wonderful friends. It was especially hard to leave Buddy and Helen, but we were so thankful that the Lord had placed us in rentals right across the street from each other for nearly five months. We had grown very close during that relatively short time.

The Lord provided us with the funds to make the long trip back to Oregon by helping us quickly sell our little Mazda station wagon. It was no longer big enough to carry all the possessions we wanted to take back to Pendleton for our growing little family. We bought an older, larger Chrysler station wagon and had enough money left over from the two transactions to get us back to Pendleton. We even had enough funds left after the trip to keep us until we received our first paychecks from the Christian school, but nothing more.

It took us eleven days to drive from Pensacola to Pendleton, a trip that was not without some adventure along the way. We were only eighty-five miles out of Pensacola when our car began to overheat. When I looked under the hood, there was a small leak in the radiator, so we stopped at a service center and bought a little container of Stop Leak. I emptied its contents into the radiator, hoping the solution was as simple as that. Not only did that not keep our engine from overheating, but it made it worse. We found out a little later that our problem was actually caused by a clogged radiator.

As the car continued to overheat, we were told to take it to a shop that was a few miles south of us. The car would get so hot that we had to pull over every mile or so just to let it cool down. As we waited by the side of the road, it seemed like every other car stopped or slowed down to see if we needed help. One kind gentleman gave us a five-gallon bucket of water for our boiling radiator. We learned that Southern hospitality was no myth.

As we limped our car down the road, we also got caught in the middle of a forest fire. It had been an extremely dry autumn in the South, and there were fires in many places. As we waited on the shoulder of the road, smoke started pouring toward us, and several fire engines loaded with firefighters pulled up around us. As men scrambled toward the oncoming fire, one of them told us that we really needed to move our car. I explained our dilemma to him, and he hurried off to fight the fire that was getting very near to the road. We were right in its path. We hobbled our car out of the way just as the massive flames began to shoot across the road.

We finally got our car to a shop in Biloxi, Mississippi. The serviceman thought our problem was caused by our thermostat going out, so he changed it. When that didn't solve the problem, he decided that our radiator was clogged and we needed to get it rodded out. Unfortunately, their shop was not equipped to do that job. It was getting late in the afternoon on New Year's Eve of 1984, and we thought it would be difficult to find anyone still open. All shops would be closed for the holiday in the morning as well. Our fears were quickly relieved as he told us his cousin had a radiator shop just fifteen miles down the road in Pascagoula. He said he would give him a call to send his tow truck up to tow us over to his shop.

In less than half an hour, we were riding in the cab of a tow truck with the serviceman's cousin on our way to Pascagoula, Mississippi, conversing like we were old friends. When we arrived at the shop, the owner gave us a tour as his assistant worked on our car. He showed us his prize antique hot rod in one of the rooms. He was already starting his New Year's celebration as he showed us around and offered me a drink of whiskey right from the bottle! I kindly turned him down. He was not offended. When the work on our car was done, it ran perfectly for the rest of the trip. We were only charged $125 for the work at both shops and the towing. We were overwhelmed by the kindness of everyone, and we thanked them profusely.

When the work on the car was done, we found a motel nearby, as it was now early in the evening. We welcomed in 1985 in Pascagoula, Mississippi, with feelings of peace and joy. We had just experienced our Father's care and loving-kindness once more.

The following day we wanted to make up for our lost time, so we got up fairly early and headed west. When we got to Houston, Texas, we stopped to fill our gas tank. As I stepped out of the car, an icy wind hit me with a chill reminder that we were not in Florida any longer.

As we continued west on Interstate 10, we took a "shortcut" through the hill country of Texas, traveling west on US 290 toward Johnson City, the hometown of former president Lyndon B. Johnson. As we traveled along the highway, Debbie commented that it looked like there was frost forming on the edges of the car windows. I said it simply could not be this far south. When we arrived at a motel in Johnson City, nearly 650 miles from our starting point, I stepped out of the car and slipped on the near half-inch of solid ice that had formed on the roads as we were driving. Who knows how long we had been driving on it, pulling a trailer, with no snow tires on the car!

I carefully made my way to the office to check in. Freezing rain began to fall as we got ourselves settled into the cozy little motel room. When we awoke the next morning, there was a solid sheet of ice two inches thick covering the roads and almost everything else. After procuring breakfast for all of us, I warily made my way to a Sears store that was right across the street from the motel. I felt fortunate to have it so close as I went inside to inquire about tires.

I asked the man behind the counter if they had any snow tires. He said they did not, so I asked him if they had any tire chains. He laughingly said, "No, this is *Texas.*" I was not especially amused as I went back to the motel to tell Debbie that we would be staying until the ice melted from the roads.

The motel room was warm and had two double beds, a bathroom, an easy chair, and a black-and-white television set. A fast-food restaurant right next to the Sears provided us with food, and the television helped pass the time. We were set to weather the storm.

As we waited, I reflected on the journey thus far. I was disappointed that I had not been able to finish the master's degree, but I felt I had learned the lessons of depending on the Lord for everything over an extended period of time while in Pensacola. I knew these lessons would be used again in the near future. We were looking forward to returning to Pendleton among family and friends, but I strongly sensed we wouldn't be there long.

After two days, the weather warmed. The ice turned into soft slush on the road, so we set off again for Oregon. We traveled almost four hundred miles that day and made it to the home of our former pastor, Charlie Wasson, just about fifteen miles north of El Paso, Texas. Finally, on January 11, 1985, we drove into Pendleton, steering through some patches of black ice as we went. I took it easy, and we had no trouble.

My mother had invited us to stay with her on the farm until we could find a place of our own. It was somewhat crowded, but we enjoyed her company, and Mom cherished the time with John, her newest and eighth grandchild. For me, it was nice to be back at the farm among family.

We had arrived in Pendleton on a Friday, and the following Monday we started back working at the Christian school. One of the problems that existed when we returned was a number of students enrolled in the school who had no real interest in Christianity and were in a rebellious state of mind. After only two days back, I warned seven students in specific terms that they had one week to improve their ways or they would not be allowed to continue attending. Only one of them improved, so the other six were dismissed from the school. This sent a serious message to the rest of the students that we were going to be distinctly Christian in nature. From that point on, the the school year went pretty smoothly.

When we returned to the school, I made it clear to those in charge that I would only finish the rest of the current school year for them. I felt certain that the Lord was calling me to help start a church and a Christian school somewhere else. I also told them to search for someone to take my place.

After we had stayed a few weeks with my mother at the farm, a friend of ours from the church, who had moved to another town, talked with us about staying in his spacious, nearly new house in Pendleton. He had not yet been able to sell it. He said that he would charge us no rent if we would just stay in the house, take care of it, and pay the utilities. How could we refuse such a generous offer? Within a few days we moved into this beautiful house just a few blocks from the school. The Lord had again graciously and abundantly provided.

In March, we had a week off from school for spring vacation, and we spent the week with Debbie's mother in Gresham. About halfway through the week, the main shaft in the engine of our station wagon snapped in two. This was no small repair job we could entrust to just anybody. The only nearby mechanic I felt was trustworthy for the job was Bill Oleen (one of the "threefold cord"). Bill had moved his family to Hood River, Oregon, just a year or so previously and was working as a mechanic for a car dealer there. When I called Bill to see if he could help me, he told me that he was amazed at the timing of my call. The Lord had just convinced him to open his own auto repair shop, and I was his first customer!

We towed the car to Bill's new auto shop and visited for a while. Bill mentioned that he was part of a group that was starting a new church and Christian school in the area. He invited us to come to the church service the following Sunday. Bill knew of my calling to start just such a work, but the connection went right over my head.

So I told Bill that we wanted to get back to Pendleton before Sunday to have a day or two to rest before we started classes again on Monday. He gave us a loaner car, and we went back to Gresham.

As the rest of the week went by, for reasons I cannot explain to this day (other than the Lord's persuasion), Debbie and I stayed in Gresham until Sunday. We stopped off at Hood River on the way home to attend the church service with Bill. At the end of the service they had a sharing time, and Bill stood up and introduced Debbie, John, and me. At the end of the introduction, he stated that God was calling Debbie and I to help start a church and Christian school somewhere.

I was surprised at that announcement, but it suddenly dawned on me what Bill was doing. I wondered if this was where the Lord wanted me. My heart almost leaped out of my chest at the possibility. Could this really be the fulfillment of the vision the Lord had been growing in me for over four years? Before I could completely fathom the full impact of this, the service ended and a man named Dick Smith approached me immediately. He explained that he was part of a committee trying to start a Christian school in Hood River. He asked all kinds of questions about my credentials and work experiences relating to Christian education, and then he asked me if I was interested in coming back to Hood River for an interview for the administration of the school they were attempting to start.

After conferring with Debbie, we agreed to come. Two weeks later, we were back in Hood River meeting and talking with all the members of the school committee about the position. At the end of the weekend, Dick asked me if I would consider taking it. We agreed that Debbie and I would pray about it for one week before we would give him an answer.

At the end of exactly one week, Dick called me to see if I would accept the position. Debbie and I had sought the Lord during that week, and we had great peace this was what the Lord wanted us to do. The unusual way it had all come about also convinced us that this was the Lord's will.

To convince us further, we had an unusual experience just a week or two later. We decided we were going to move to Hood River a few days after the school year ended in Pendleton, and we settled on leaving on June 10, 1985. We knew we needed to notify our friend who had so generously let us stay in his house. Before we could call him, he called us and very apologetically informed us that he had sold the house. He said we needed to move out by June 11! I began to laugh and relieved his anxiety by explaining all that had developed. We were all, once again, greatly amazed at the Lord's ability to "cause all things to work together for good to those who love God, to those who are called according to His purposes" (Romans 8:28, NASB).

In many ways, we were living out principles we'd learned from Brother John Samson. Our lives continued to intersect in other ways as well. Before we left for Hood River, I had a strange experience regarding Rosalie's sister, Mabel. Debbie and I had come home after a day of teaching. We were changing from our school clothes into casual wear when I suddenly had a deep impression within my spirit that something very serious had happened to Mabel. I was tying my shoe at the time, and I stood straight up and told Debbie what I'd felt. She looked at me with surprise but said nothing.

The next day Brother John called from England and told me that Mabel had suffered a massive stroke the day before and passed away. After some sorrowful conversation, I asked Brother John exactly when it had happened. It had occurred the exact time I knew something had happened to Mabel the day before. This event, we would learn, was the beginning of a very difficult period in the life of Brother John.

Chapter 11

A SCHOOL AND CHURCH IN HOOD RIVER

When the Lord took Debbie and me on our trip to Great Britain and Israel, He grew our faith in a simple and comfortable way. The trip was not a life-or-death choice; it was a great blessing, a huge bonus, if you will. Then He led us through the faith lessons at Pensacola. We learned that the Lord could sustain us when our well-being depended on Him. We saw Him meet our needs more than sufficiently for nearly four-and-a-half months over three thousand miles from home. This was more of the "wait and see," and it was the deepening of the Beit Shalom challenge in our lives. The Beit Shalom challenge is the challenge of our faith. It is the challenge to depend less and less upon ourselves and our own wits and to depend more and more upon the Father in our spiritual journey of faith with the Lord. Our circumstances are completely engineered by Him and are but the trappings of His loving guidance along His ways. And He was about to take us even deeper into our journey.

When Debbie, John, and I arrived in Hood River, we had most of our belongings in one large trailer and a pickup truck. We had come down the week before and hurriedly found a three-bedroom ranch-style house on Eliot Drive. The people we rented the house from had not cleaned it before they left. When we arrived, we found several people from the church inside cleaning the carpets, the bathroom, the kitchen cupboards, and more. What a wonderful welcome to our new home!

After just a few days at the house, though, we found that the power to the kitchen was insufficient. We could not use two appliances at the same time without causing the breaker to trip. The house had some other problems, also, so we found a large, old house on Belmont Drive called the Oak Lodge, possibly because of the large oak tree in the front yard. It had over half an acre of land and a barn in the back, all for only thirty dollars more per month. With the Lord's help, we were accepted from among several families who also wanted to rent the place. We had spent nearly all of our money moving into the first house, but through the generosity of a few individuals involved with the school, we were able to pay the required first and last month's rent and a two hundred dollar deposit in order to move in. After only three weeks in the Eliot house, we moved into the house on Belmont Drive. This became our home for the next ten-and-a-half years.

From the start, Hood River was an exercise in faith. There were no funds to pay us any salary during the first summer because we had not yet started the school. After prayer and discussion with people from the school and the church, it was decided that our needs would be made known to the church. Since all of the people on the school committee attended the church, we would ask the Lord to work through His people there to supply our needs.

All this went well for the first month or so, but there came a time when the giving toward our needs disappeared almost entirely. We sought the Lord about it, but we did not get any answers. Then I remembered that the Pendleton church had not reimbursed me for expenses for some school training I had taken while I was the administrator there. I became resentful about this, thinking about how badly we needed those funds. I asked the Lord what to do about the situation, and His Spirit whispered within me, "Forgive them the debt." I couldn't believe that I had correctly heard the Lord. So, in my shallowness of the moment, I asked the Lord to show me this really was His will by having a blue Ford pickup truck drive past our house exactly one minute from that moment.

I started a countdown as I sat in our front room, looking out the big picture window that looked straight toward the road that went past our house. With ten seconds to go, I could hear a vehicle approaching the house from the east. As you may have guessed, exactly when the countdown hit zero, a blue Ford pickup truck drove past our house. I was stunned and a little shaken, but I picked up the phone right then and called the Pendleton church. I told them they did not have to pay the money they owed me. They were surprised and pleased as they had been going through a very hard time financially and regretted they had not been able to repay me. I felt very silly and ashamed after hearing that, and we had no more financial troubles the rest of the summer.

We held many school committee meetings that summer discussing how we wanted the school to be run. One of the main issues was whether we would charge a set tuition fee for attendance or not. We did not want finances to be the sole issue in deciding whether a child could attend, yet the school needed to have adequate funding from month to month. So we decided to ask the families of the children we accepted into the school to pray together. We would let the Lord direct them in their giving to the school each month. Then we asked all staff members to be willing to accept whatever percentage of their salary the Lord provided. If 85 percent of the funds came in during a particular month, then each staff person would receive 85 percent of his or her assigned salary. If 120 percent of the needed amount came in the next month, we would make up the 15 percent that had lacked the month before, and we would pay the entire salary for the current month. We would leave the remaining 5 percent for the salaries of the coming month.

Some people thought this plan was pretty shaky, but most really liked it, and some got really excited about it. I believe the Lord honored this, and we used this system for the next sixteen years. It was a great adventure of faith. The Lord saw us through good times and rough times. He supplied all of our needs whether physical, spiritual, or emotional; whatever we needed, He sustained us and blessed us generously.

A month before we opened the school, the Lord led us to a building that adequately served the needs of the church and school for the first fourteen-and-a-half years. Through a series of yearly faith offerings, we were able to pay off the building in just four years. The people of the church came together the first month and put in hundreds of hours fixing, remodeling, and decorating the church and school. The workmanship was outstanding. The transformation of the building was truly amazing because "the people had a mind to work" (Nehemiah 4:6, NASB). It so reminded me of the spirit of Beit Shalom—how the people so willingly worked hard at all of the tasks with such humility and unity.

When we took over the building, another church had been renting it for their church services each week. They wondered if we wanted them to find another place. Even though our churches had some substantial differences in doctrine, we did not think they were worth dying for or even dividing over. We also thought working together would be a good witness for Christ in the community. They agreed. So we held our church services at an early hour, they had theirs later, and we combined for Sunday school between the two. The school used the building during the week. We also agreed that during the Sunday school time, we would be sensitive to our theological differences. We never had a problem in this area. Even though these ideas were not entirely mine, I am sure that Brother John's example of overcoming his father's prejudice against Catholicism and working so well with the monks at the Latrun Monastery helped me to easily accept this arrangement. Danilo van Woerden's success in bringing the churches together in Jerusalem also had some influence on this decision.

Our church also decided not to charge the other church any rent, but we asked them to help out with some of the improvements and repairs along the way. This agreement worked beautifully for over two years. It also allowed the other church, Abundant Life Fellowship, to save enough money to buy their own building. People in the community did take note of this cooperation. Occasionally some told us that they appreciated it, and some came in to ask our pastor how we were able to make it work so well.

Our church adopted the name Shepherd of the Valley Bible Church, and the school became known as Shepherd of the Valley Bible Church Family Education Ministries. The school's name was such a mouthful that we often joked it was a graduation requirement for the eighth graders to be able to say it in full!

Because of all the work done on the building, we had to start the school year a week later than we planned. Just before we began classes in the fall of 1985, we got word that an anonymous donor had given four thousand dollars to the school. We were elated. This was completely unexpected and helped the school get off to a wonderful start. It seemed to signify God's special approval on our endeavor.

We had hired a young lady from California just out of college to teach a combined first and second grade class. When we started, we had just eleven students enrolled. Debbie had five kindergartners for half-days on Mondays, Tuesdays, and Thursdays. Mary, the first and second grade teacher, had three students, and I had three students in a combined fifth and sixth grade class. It was a small beginning, but the attendance grew throughout that first year until we had twenty-two students at midyear. At the end of the school year, one family moved away, and we ended with eighteen students.

One of the fifth graders during the year gave her heart to the Lord and never looked back. Today she is the facilities manager of a church in Colorado Springs with over ten thousand in attendance. It was thrilling to have the school up and running and watching the Lord do so many special things.

We also started the year with a hodgepodge of furniture and desks. One day after classes in the second week of school, Bill Oleen drove by and shouted out his van window that the local telephone company was going to give us their office furniture. The telephone company replaced all their office furniture every five years or so. When they did, they would donate all of their used furniture to a nonprofit organization in the community. The man in charge of this operation was a Christian. When he heard we were starting a new Christian school, he donated all the furniture to our school. They delivered it about a week later.

When I arrived at the building that morning, I saw quite a lot of furniture on the east porch. I thought this was a very generous donation, but I was not seeing all of the furniture! As I got to the porch, I was directed into the lobby, which was crammed full. There was furniture all the way across the back of the sanctuary, and it filled the alcove on the other side as well. There were tables, office chairs, and desks, several different kinds of filing and storage cabinets, and much more. I couldn't believe what I was seeing. Most of the furniture was in great shape. There was plenty to supply both the school and the church. It was truly a wonderful blessing and encouragement.

The first year after moving into the building, the church grew from about eighty-five people attending the services each Sunday to about one hundred and twenty. We wanted the church to be led by a board of elders, so we selected two. Tim was our preaching elder, or pastor, as most churches called this position. Cliff Taylor was the other elder. Shortly thereafter we hired another man to be a co-pastor with Tim. In the spring of that year, I was asked to be an elder. I accepted the call and was confirmed after a process that took about two weeks.

At the beginning of the first school year, 1985–1986, we asked the elders if the school could become a ministry of the church under their authority. They agreed, and I was given the title of minister of education. This was basically the same as being the principal of the school. I both taught classes and administrated. The school committee became the school board and oversaw the general operations of the school.

The Lord saw us through that first year beautifully. The tuition given plus gifts from church members and others covered about 85 percent of our assigned salaries. Whenever there was a shortfall, the Lord provided what we needed through other sources such as personal gifts, refunds, or unexpected windfalls. The timing and amounts of such provisions matched the needs so well that I kept a notebook during that first year to track these events. The Lord matched the timing almost to the day and the amounts almost to the dollar. We lacked nothing.

The first four or five years at the school, I was paid a salary ten months of the year, and the rest of the staff was paid for nine months. We would do odd jobs during the summer months or just take some time off for travel, rest, or vacations as the Lord provided. God always provided jobs when we needed them, the funds for travel when He called us to go, or the funds to just take time off for vacations or rest.

During the summer of 1986, after the first school year, Brother John came over in July to lead a dedication ceremony for little John. The dedication service was magnificent, and the presence of the Spirit of God was strong. The service began with our good friends, Rob and Shirley Bagge, singing a medley of "Jesus Loves Me," "Jesus, Name Above All Names," and "Be Glorified" in beautiful two-part harmony.

After a short prayer, Brother John challenged Debbie and me to be dedicated to God so little John would be dedicated to Him also. Then he led us through a series of vows to bring up little John in the nurture and admonition of the Lord, followed by another prayer and a blessing. Brother John's words and spirit were so powerful, some people were literally sitting on the edges of their seats with a look of utter astonishment on their faces.

Brother John shared with us that Rosalie's health had started to deteriorate since the death of her sister. Her eyesight and her hearing were diminishing, but the doctors could find no physical cause for either. They thought it resulted from grieving for her sister. We felt so bad for Brother John. We often called to see how Rosalie was doing, and we prayed for both of them.

During that summer, another Christian school in Hood River closed, and Shepherd of the Valley inherited most of students. We also added a seventh grade to the fifth and sixth grade classroom. We did away with the kindergarten because we no longer had room for that class with the increased enrollment. Our enrollment in the fall of 1986 bumped up to thirty-three students. We now had three full-time teachers and a handful of volunteer aides. Debbie helped with the volunteer work now that she was no longer in charge of the kindergarten. This allowed for a little more time to focus on our home and being a mom. What a wonderful mother she was, and still is!

We kept in contact with Buddy and Helen Lapointe through the months, and the Lord provided the funds to visit them where they now lived in the Florida Keys during our two-week Christmas vacation. That winter was very snowy and cold, so it was wonderful to have a warm, sunny break to see our dear friends.

A few months later, during our spring break in March of 1987, Brother John came to Hood River again. We visited late into the evening every night. Sometimes we sang hymns, with Brother John playing the piano or me playing the guitar or both. Debbie kept us well supplied with delicious treats. During the daytime, we took day trips to some of the beautiful sights around the Hood River Valley or visited and had lunch or dinner with friends. Each time Brother John came, it was as if he had never been gone; we picked up where we had left off.

While Brother John was at our house that spring, we planned another trip to England for the coming summer. At the end of his visit, Brother John and I flew to Vermont to spend some time with Rob Nichols and his family in Burlington. It was so good to see Rob again and to meet his lovely wife and young son. We spent many hours visiting and reminiscing about Beit Shalom and Larry Gordon. During the daytime, we sometimes hiked around the beautiful northern Vermont countryside, and for one whole day we toured the majestic 2,400-acre estate of Georg and Maria Von Trapp. All too soon, Brother John had to return to England, and I returned to Oregon alone.

The rest of the 1986–1987 school year went very well. After classes closed at the end of May, we took about a dozen of the students from the upper grades on a week-long trip to the Wallowa Mountains in northeastern Oregon. This was the second of sixteen year-end trips we took. We had many great adventures on those trips, and this one was no exception. We hiked in the majestic Wallowa Mountains, played on Wallowa Lake, roller-skated, raced go-carts, and even rode a gondola to the top of 8,150-foot Mount Howard for a spectacular panorama of the surrounding mountains. We fed deer; chased raccoons, squirrels, and chipmunks from our food tables; sang; roasted wieners and marshmallows at our campfire; and much more. We came home exhausted and dirty, but very happy. We have many fond memories from all of the year-end trips. The idea for them started in Pendleton, with Brother John and Rosalie's work with young people as my inspiration. We grew so close to many of the students on these trips; I believe many eternal bonds were formed. It proved a great way to close out each year.

For the next two weeks, Debbie and I prepared to go to England to see Brother John. The Lord had provided for the trip through a very generous gift from Debbie's mother, a tax refund, and a few other smaller anonymous gifts. We were able to rent our house while we were gone to some people who came to Hood River for the now world-famous windsurfing. We left for England just before noon on June 18, the day of our tenth wedding anniversary, and arrived the next morning at Gatwick International Airport in south London. We had a joyous reunion with Brother John at the airport before he drove us to his home in Hove.

We arrived on a Friday and spent the next few days in Hove and Brighton. On Wednesday, Debbie, little John, and I flew from London to Maastricht, Holland, for a twelve-day trip touring parts of western Europe. We took the train into Belgium and back into Holland before we rented a car in Amsterdam and drove through Holland, Belgium, Germany, Denmark, Sweden, and Norway.

We rode in a taxi on our way to the car rental place in Amsterdam. As we neared our destination, we told the driver we really wanted to see the Anne Frank House. Only a few blocks from the rental place, he pointed to his left and said, "There is your house."

When we arrived at our hotel in Hirtshals, Denmark, we had no idea that we had to reserve a spot on the ferry which would take us to Sweden. Reservations had to be done a week in advance. The hotel clerk, upon discovering our dilemma, made several calls and got us a reservation for the next day! It was amazing and fun to watch the Lord provide in so many details of the trip. We felt very adventurous as we toured so many places with only a road map and the Lord's guidance and blessings. He seemed to challenge us to venture a little further and do more on each trip we took.

Now we had been to England for the second of what would eventually be eight trips there. We had ventured beyond England into six other countries on our own. Eventually I would make international trips on my own. The Lord was continuing to teach us that He could provide for the necessities of life and much more. He also showed us we could lean with simple dependence upon Him to guide, protect, and bless. The blessing is not so much in the material part of life as it is in the abiding sense of His daily, moment-by-moment presence. He loves to be intimately involved with each of us, even in the minute details of our lives. We need to learn more and more to depend on Him for everything as we follow His quiet leading.

Chapter 12

A DEATH AND A BIRTH

In the third school year at Shepherd of the Valley, we added the eighth grade to the program. We still had only three full-time teachers to cover all eight grades. That stretched us, but we had some good aides who regularly came in and assisted with teaching some of the subjects. This was a huge help and gave the students more quality in their educational experience. Our faith grew as the Lord continually provided the needed funding for the school ministry.

The enrollment at the school was now in the upper thirties, and through the years it continually increased. The last year, before we merged with another school, enrollment had increased into the low sixties. The finances were more up and down during the third year. At one point the giving got so low we held an all-night prayer vigil, and the Lord provided the funds to make up for our shortfall that very night. Overall, though, things were steady, and the Lord amply saw us through all of it.

Brother John and I routinely called each other at least once every month. Through the months of the 1987–1988 school year, he shared with me how Rosalie's health was continuing to deteriorate. When Debbie, little John, and I had been there she seemed pretty healthy generally, though she had some trouble with her hearing and was nearly blind. But her mind was very sharp indeed. One afternoon during our last trip to England, Rosalie and I had played a friendly game of chess. She seemed to be bumbling as she made what I thought were some fairly poor moves. After a dozen moves or so, she suddenly moved her bishop across almost the entire board from one corner to the other and trapped my king in the corner. I was able to checkmate her only one move before she would have checkmated me. After the game she gaily said, "Oh well, I suppose I could have played better if I could see a little clearer." Feeling fortunate to have won that match, I did not press my luck playing any more chess with her on that trip!

Through the fall and winter, Rosalie's health continued to decline until she had become almost totally bedridden early in the spring of 1988. Finally, on April 16, Brother John called while Debbie was giving me a haircut in the kitchen of the Belmont house. I could tell by Debbie's responses that Rosalie had passed into the presence of the Lord Jesus. I began to weep, and a song came to me at that moment that Brother John had taught us while we were in Pendleton. It was from Psalm 16:11: "In thy presence is fulness of joy; at thy right hand there are pleasures for evermore."

When I talked to John, he described to me in detail how Rosalie had passed. He told me he had checked on her that morning, and she seemed to be doing well. So he went on his daily morning walk, and as he was walking, he had a vision of Rosalie in his mind. He could see her clearly, and she was healthy and radiant with joy. She said to John, "In His presence there's fulness of joy; at His right hand there are pleasures for evermore."

Much startled, I related to Brother John the experience I'd had when I first understood that Rosalie had passed away. I went on to tell him I would get to England as soon as I could. He thanked me over and over before we ended the phone call. I felt so bad for Brother John, knowing how much pain he was in, even though he understood Rosalie was now in the very best of all places.

The Lord provided the funds through some very generous friends, and I was able to get a seat on a jet headed for England in less than a week. When I arrived at the house, Brother John hugged me tightly for a long time. We went up the stairs to Rosalie's bedroom where she was lying in state. I told Brother John she looked very beautiful. I could see her still face with her body wrapped neatly in the bed blankets, but Rosalie wasn't there. It was a very hard moment. We both just stood in sorrowful silence for a few moments. A little while later, John Chambers came to the house, and we all went up to Rosalie's room together. After a brief moment of silence, John Chambers ever so sweetly leaned over Rosalie and softly said near her face, "Don't worry, Rosalie, we'll take good care of Brother John now."

The world was now a poorer place without the great prayer warrior Rosalie Cole Samson, yet it is much richer as her legacy endures. I still wonder how many young ladies through the Girls' Guild were not only taught how to live a better, more skillful life, but were drawn into God's kingdom through this blessed soul's life. I wonder how many of their children and grandchildren know the Lord today or have joined Rosalie in the heavenly realms themselves because of her great faith.

As I write of her death more than twenty-five years later, I cannot stop the flood of tears. There is such extreme solace and gratitude to the Lord in knowing that Brother John and Rosalie have now been reunited for more than twelve years. As Philippians 4:6–7 promises, there *is* a peace that transcends all circumstances that comes only from the Lord.

A Death and a Birth

There were many people at Rosalie's memorial. The service was solemn, but it was bathed in hope. The graveside service was especially beautiful. The pastor gave some comforting words. Rosalie's coffin was gently lowered into the grave covered with many lovely red roses, placed by those who loved her dearly. Rosalie was laid to rest next to the graves of her father, mother, and sister Mabel in a cemetery that was about a mile from Brother John's house in Hove.

Brother John struggled much at times after Rosalie's passing, as one would expect. He had not only lost his soul mate and the love of his life for the past forty-nine-plus years, he had lost his most ardent prayer warrior. After a few months, Debbie and I invited Brother John to come to Hood River to live with us. After some prayer and thought, John graciously declined. We understood that even though Rosalie was gone, New Orleans was still his beloved home.

※ ※ ※

Sometime previous to that school year, Debbie and I grew in our desire to adopt another child. We went to a specialist for several appointments and procedures. It seemed we were not going to have any biological children. After we shared our desire to adopt with the people from the church and school, some of the blessed ladies committed to pray for our desire to be met.

In early January of 1988, Debbie and I heard from a relative that the fourteen-year-old daughter of a friend of hers was pregnant. The girl was considering giving up the baby for adoption. After praying about it, Debbie and I sent word that we were interested in adopting the baby. A few days later, we heard that the birth mother had agreed. We were both ecstatic.

In March, we contacted a pregnancy resource center in Portland. They recommended a lawyer who worked with them in facilitating adoptions. Our lawyer hired another to represent the interests of the birth mother. With the help of the Lord, we paid for both of them over a relatively short period of time.

Three months later, on June 17, 1988, Joel Philip Winters came into the world at 5:29 in the afternoon. He weighed eight pounds, two ounces and was twenty-one inches long. When the birth mother went into labor, Debbie called a good friend of ours and exclaimed, "We're in labor! We're in labor!" Debbie, little John, and I met Joel at the hospital in Portland when he was just forty-two hours old. He was sound asleep, and after several moments of oohs and aahs, he greeted us with a huge yawn. He was simply beautiful.

We were amazed that the Lord had now given us two beautiful children. It brought to mind Psalm 68:5, that God is a Father to the fatherless. He lovingly and graciously adopts us into his family through Jesus Christ (Ephesians 1:5) and supplies family for us in this life as well. I have been without an earthly father since I was twelve years old, so I have a pretty good idea of what it means to be fatherless; but we are all born spiritually fatherless. Yet God willingly brings us into His family if we will accept it. Now the Lord had brought two precious little boys into our family. The responsibility seemed immense, but we knew the Lord had brought them to us. We knew He would help us bring them up in His nurture and admonition, even though the road at times would be very rough.

John was an extremely easy child to raise, and we had become overconfident about our parenting skills. Joel was going to be a challenge. Even though he had many wonderful qualities, he humbled us. When he was only two days old, he turned himself over onto his tummy while in his bassinet. He then lifted his head as if to get a look at the great big world awaiting him. When I saw this, added to the fact that he had cried almost the entire night before, I turned to Debbie and said, "I think we're going to have our hands full with this one."

Some people say that we need to be careful what we say because our words may become prophetic. Joel cried for hours every night for the first two weeks of his life. Someone told us he probably had his days and nights switched around. He was sleeping mostly in the daytime, so we kept him awake as much as we could for a few days. This largely relieved the problem of crying each night. It was good to sleep again.

When Joel was just over two weeks old, the kind people of the church gave us a surprise baby shower after a potluck dinner following the church services that Sunday. They had a beautiful cake made with "Welcome Joel Winters" written on it with frosting, and they "showered" us with many generous gifts.

When Joel was four months old, in October of 1988, Brother John again came to Hood River to see our newest addition. The fourth year of school was already underway, and Brother John spoke at one of our Wednesday chapels. The students really enjoyed hearing and meeting Brother John, especially since most of them had heard stories about him, Larry Gordon, and Beit Shalom so many times already. Many of them stayed long after chapel so they could talk to him. Some just wanted to be near the great man of faith.

The 1988–1989 school year passed by without any major problems, and during spring break in late March, Brother John came once more to Hood River to stay with us. We spent most of the week at the Oregon coast, and Brother John stayed with us into early April. We had a marvelous time of sweet fellowship as we spent time on the beach with Debbie and the boys and wandered through myriads of little shops. Rough waters, however, were coming for Brother John. There were also dark clouds forming over Shepherd of the Valley Bible Church.

Chapter 13

A STORM IN THE VALLEY

In the 1989–1990 school year at Shepherd of the Valley, the Lord provided another full-time teacher, which brought our number of full-time positions to four. We were averaging over 90 percent of our assigned salaries. God always made up more than what we lacked. In fact, during one particular week, the Lord showed me some unusual measures of grace. One Sunday at church I was lamenting the fact that I owned only one suit and it was getting a little rough at the edges. Just then a friend of mine walked by in a nice suit, and in my heart I yearned to have such a suit. Two days later, the same man handed me an envelope and told me to go buy a suit! There were enough funds in that envelope to get two from a store in Portland that was having a sale.

A little later during the same week, we had some mechanical troubles with both of our cars. As I was driving one a few days earlier, I passed a nice car going in the opposite direction. I again lamented not having a car nicer than our two old ones. Two days later, another friend of mine heard about our mechanical problems, took me to a car dealer, and bought us a car. In addition, another friend told me how I could fix the other two. By the end of the week, I had two new suits and three running cars. The Lord is kind in spite of our pity parties sometimes!

Even though the school was doing pretty well, some serious divisions were developing in the church. Some in the congregation wanted to follow the teachings and methods of a famous Christian leader in our country; others did not. Some felt that the man was unbalanced. Both sides became entrenched. Many meetings were held, and three more men were invited by the elders to help sort out the problem. However, the situation did not improve; rather, it became more and more intense. I think the Lord was teaching me patience and endurance, two things often learned only by trials.

Brother John came to stay with us for two weeks when we had our spring break in late March of 1990. By then the situation was so intense that he took us down to a travel agent and booked flights for our entire family to stay at his house in England for eight weeks during the coming summer. While Brother John was with us, he led a beautiful service dedicating Joel to the Lord. The situation at the church was hard.

Harsh words were spoken, feelings were hurt, and friendships were broken. At times I found it very difficult to pray. I just wanted people to come together and find the Lord's direction and follow it. In time I learned that some situations will not resolve, even with God's help, if those involved refuse to humble themselves and submit to the Lord. He only wants what is best for us. At times I wondered if my time in Hood River would come to an end. But God would once again prove Himself bigger than our problems.

In the middle of May, 1990, we went to a children's home in Montana for eleven days on our year-end trip. It was one of our best. We helped with many projects at the 1100-acre ranch in the mornings and enjoyed many fun activities during the afternoons. We saw bison, elk, and other animals on a large bison preserve across the road from the ranch. One afternoon, together with the children at the home, we launched model rockets we had assembled during the school year. We also visited an old mission church and the fort in Missoula. Some of the students even hiked near a place where grizzly bears were known to cross. This brought back memories of Larry's horrible demise and caused me to shudder for a moment. I graciously declined going anywhere near such a place. The whole experience, though, made me desire to start a children's home all the more. Though I didn't know it then, the Lord was planting seeds: a group of us would return almost seventeen years later to investigate that very possibility.

※ ※ ※

When we arrived at Gatwick, Brother John was amazed at the amount of luggage we had brought for our growing family. He mused on whether we could get everyone and everything into his fairly small car. We did, and we talked nonstop while driving from the airport to New Orleans. It was wonderful to be at the house again with Brother John. It wasn't long, though, before we noticed how much he was missing Rosalie.

As the days passed, Debbie and I noticed how Brother John would suddenly excuse himself from a room where he and I were visiting only a moment or two after Debbie joined us. In the past, Brother John had told me more than once how much Debbie reminded him of Rosalie. I explained to Debbie that he was missing Rosalie so much that it was painful for him to be in her presence at times. We still had many times of great fellowship as we'd had in the past, but it became obvious to us that Brother John was struggling.

Brother John had also generously purchased tickets for Tom and Clara Burton to come to England. At the end of the second week of our stay, the Burtons arrived. It was so thrilling to have them in England. It was like some of the great times we'd had in Pendleton, but now we were all here together at New Orleans. With Brother John, Debbie, and Clara joining forces, we had some outstanding meals together. On several evenings, we sang some of our favorite hymns and choruses, punctuated with stories of cherished memories, often well into the night.

We continued the great fellowship over the next two or three days while the Burtons adjusted to the new time zone. Then Brother John encouraged us to plan a trip north into Scotland. The thought of going up to Scotland and staying again at Mrs. Laird's bed-and-breakfast while seeing the sights of Edinburgh with the Burtons and Brother John was exciting indeed. I couldn't wait to see the Highlands again.

As we were planning this wonderful adventure, Brother John surprised us by announcing he would not be accompanying us on the trip. We were stunned. He gave no explanation, and we were baffled by this sudden change of plans. We pleaded with him to come with us, but he wouldn't budge.

Brother John wanted very much for the Burtons to go and see his home country, but for us to go without him was unthinkable. Instead of going to Scotland, we decided to visit Germany and spend some time with friends there. The Burtons had to leave before we did, and the rest of our time with our friends passed too swiftly before we rode the train back to Oostende and crossed the channel to England.

After we disembarked from the hovercraft in Dover, we were standing outside the boarding area talking about getting a train for the long trip to Hove. There was no direct route, so we would have go to Victoria Station in London and get another train to take us back to Hove. The trip normally wasn't too hard, but after traveling by train from Mulheim to Oostende and taking the hovercraft from Oostende to Dover, we were all were pretty tired. We were about to purchase tickets for the train when a taxi driver stepped up and asked us where we were going. I knew there was no way we could afford a taxi all the way to Hove, but the taxi driver asked us how much our train trip would cost. When I told him, he thought for a moment and said he would drive us for the same price. We jumped at his kind offer. This would save us an hour or two of travel time and keep us from having to change trains in London with all our luggage and the boys.

The taxi driver not only gave us a relaxing ride along the beautiful south coast of England, but he showed us many of the points of interest along the way. It was a delightful trip, and the driver told us many interesting stories about the history of places along the coast. We were very glad to give him a generous tip at the end of the trip, and we lavished him with heartfelt thanks.

We were not yet settled in at New Orleans when Brother John announced he was going to spend some time up in Scotland because he needed some time alone. He also said he had made arrangements for us to stay the week with John and Wendy Chambers in Worthing. We were bewildered by all of this, but we agreed to the plan out of respect for Brother John's request for time alone, and we did want to spend some time with the Chambers family.

We had a very special week with the Chambers, but toward the end Debbie and I realized our funds for the trip were getting low. We had planned to stay another five weeks in England. Joel was still having a hard time adjusting to England's time zone, and Debbie was getting homesick. On top of all of this, we received a letter from some close friends in Hood River. They were seriously considering leaving the church because the situation there was not getting resolved. With all this happening, we decided to cut our trip short. After some discussion one night, we went out the next day to a travel agency and shortened our trip by three weeks. This would still give us five full weeks in England, including the next two with Brother John.

Two days later we returned to Brother John's house and gently broke the news of our early departure to him. He wasn't terribly upset, but it did bother him. Another couple from Pendleton earlier that year had also shortened a trip they were taking with him because of a bad experience while in Israel. I tried to assure Brother John it was not personal, but he still felt some rejection.

Our last two weeks with Brother John passed quickly. We had many great times of fellowship, but there were also times when Brother John was agitated. The last night we were there, Debbie and I fixed him our favorite dinner, leg of lamb with potatoes, vegetables, and Scottish trifle. Brother John was so touched by this gesture, he grabbed and hugged me so hard he nearly broke my glasses.

The next day, as Debbie and I were scurrying around the house trying to get everything ready for the long trip ahead, Brother John was so unsettled that he called his doctor to come see him. He told me he felt as if he was going to have a nervous breakdown. This alarmed me greatly, but I felt completely helpless to know what to do. Brother John assured me he would be all right until the doctor got there, so we hesitantly said good-bye and left for the airport.

I called Brother John shortly after we arrived at home. He said the doctor had told him he'd been stressed for so long that he had used up his adrenaline reserves. He only had energy to function normally while his body was producing more adrenaline. The rest of the time he was completely exhausted. He also told me the doctor had prescribed some medicine to help him recover and encouraged him to get as much rest as he could. He assured me that he would be all right, and we verbalized our love in the Lord for each other before we hung up. It was the last coherent phone call I had with Brother John for over a year.

Chapter 14

A Little Angel and a Long Silence

When we returned to Hood River, things at the church were still very tense. One of the elders told me he was surprised that we had come back. He'd thought we were gone for good. That was never our intention. We were refreshed by our time away, and we were ready to come back and help the church through this troubled time.

After we returned to our home on Belmont Drive, we got a surprising phone call from Charlie Wasson, our former pastor from Pendleton. Charlie had been pastoring in Anthony, New Mexico, for about eight years now. Even though Debbie and I were godparents to Charlie's children, we hadn't spoken for quite some time. Debbie still recognized Charlie's voice when she answered the phone.

Charlie explained there was a Hispanic woman in his church who had been abandoned by her husband and left to care for their seven children. In the desperation of her situation, the woman had an affair with another man and was now carrying his child. This man also left her, so she was seriously considering giving up her unborn child for adoption. Charlie wanted to know if we would consider adopting the baby.

To say we were surprised would be a gross understatement. If this adoption worked out, it would be our third private adoption of a newborn. Statistically that rarely happens; but with the Lord, *all* things are possible. Charlie explained more fully the circumstances of the situation. He thought the baby would be born sometime in August or September. Debbie said we would discuss the possibility of adopting the baby and would call them back soon.

After the phone call, with the overwhelming thought of being privileged to have such a wonderful opportunity, it took us less than two minutes to decide we definitely wanted to pursue adopting the baby. The prospect of adding a third precious child to our family was extremely exciting.

After discussing and praying about it, we called Charlie the next morning to tell him we would love to adopt the baby if at all possible. Before ending the call, Debbie told Charlie that if the adoption worked out, she knew the baby would be a girl. Charlie told her that if the baby was a girl, he thought the mother would be less likely to give her up for adoption. This concerned us, but we still wanted to go ahead.

The summer quickly melded into the next school year, Shepherd of the Valley's fifth. Debbie called the Wassons once in the ensuing weeks to see what was happening. They had very little contact with the baby's mother and didn't have anything they could share with us. In early October, our church had a family camp at a lakeside church facility called Camp Morrow. While we were there, some of the ladies of the church asked Debbie if we had heard anything about the baby. She said we had not and thought the mother had probably already had the baby and decided to keep her. It was already past the date Charlie and Sue had thought the baby was going to be born.

On the Monday after family camp, Sue Wasson called without identifying herself. She told Debbie, "You're in labor." Debbie recognized Sue's voice immediately and became very excited. The baby's mother had walked two miles to Sue's house and said she was in labor. Sue immediately drove her to the county hospital in El Paso and called Debbie right after getting the birth mother admitted. After talking to Sue, Debbie called several of our friends to announce she was "in labor."

A little over six hours later, Charlie called and asked Debbie if she was sitting down. Before he could continue, Debbie told him it was a girl. He asked how she knew, and she replied that she just did. She was right. A beautiful baby girl had been born at eight o'clock in the evening of Monday, October 8, 1990. She weighed just five pounds, eleven ounces and was eighteen-and-a-half inches long.

In the next few hours, a flurry of phone calls came from the Wassons , keeping us abreast of the condition of the little angel. In the first call after the announcement of the birth, we were told the baby's kidneys and liver were not functioning well. She was having some trouble with her breathing, so they put her into an intensive care unit. Later, we were told she had swallowed some of the amniotic fluid, which caused her to develop pneumonia. So they put her on a regimen of antibiotics. Finally, she stabilized and began to improve quickly.

It looked like the baby was going to be in the hospital for at least a few days, so Debbie and I scrambled to get a lawyer for the adoption and airline tickets to El Paso. At the same time, Sue Wasson made a search for a lawyer to handle the paperwork for the birth mother. Twelve days later, Debbie and I boarded a jet at the Portland airport for what proved to be an incredible journey.

By the time we departed, the baby had been in the hospital for nine days. She was then released into the care of Charlie and Sue, who were already certified foster parents. Our flight itinerary took us through Denver, where we had to catch another plane to complete our trip. When we got there, we found that our connecting flight to El Paso had been canceled due to a snowstorm. The airport staff helped us get seats on another flight, but it delayed us for seven hours. That time proved to be crucial.

When we arrived at El Paso, we collected our luggage and headed down the concourse to meet Charlie. We stopped so that Debbie could use the restroom. Before she returned I saw Charlie walking toward us. I went to greet him with a hug to celebrate the moment, but Charlie acted as if he was going to walk right by. The serious look on his face told me something was terribly wrong. When Charlie stopped in front of me, he was still facing to my right. He said something about us being delayed too long. I knew we couldn't have done anything about the delay, but rather than wasting time on that point, I asked Charlie what was wrong. He told me the birth mother had changed her mind. While we were delayed in Denver, she became agitated and decided not to give her baby up for adoption.

With a crushed heart, I turned to look for Debbie. She was approaching us from about thirty feet away. I went to her and told her the birth mother had changed her mind. It broke her heart as well. All the way from the airport to the Wassons' house, Debbie and I held each other in the backseat of their minivan and wept. Charlie tried to console us, but none of his words penetrated our numbness and sorrow.

When we got to the house, Sue silently opened the door and motioned toward the baby. We walked toward the most beautiful baby girl we had ever seen, sleeping peacefully on her side. She was in a little bassinet with her tiny hands curled together in front of her face as if she was praying. When Debbie knelt down and leaned over her to get a closer look, she burst into the most mournful wail I had ever heard from her. It was too much for me. I left the house headed for who-knows-where; I just had to get away. Charlie tried to follow me to see where I was going, but I told him not to come. I had to be alone for a while. I was extremely angry, and I blamed God. I went behind a shed twenty or thirty yards from the house and literally shouted at God. How could He allow such a thing to happen? How could He allow my sweet wife to suffer like this? The only answer He gave me was silence. Our Lord never shouts back; and if we keep shouting, we will never hear Him.

After venting long enough to exhaust my anger, I went back to the house to comfort Debbie. I needed at least as much comfort for myself. We cried and tried to pray the rest of the night until we finally fell asleep from emotional exhaustion. I couldn't help wondering where God was.

The next day was Sunday, and we somehow made it through the church service.

We didn't take in much of what went on there. We kept praying through the afternoon, hoping that the birth mother would change her mind. She called and informed Charlie and Sue that she was coming Monday afternoon to pick up the baby.

Charlie tried to convince us to call a lawyer to fight for custody through the courts. I didn't believe we could possibly win, and we were too emotionally drained to consider such a thing. I was so defeated I refused to even hold the baby. I feared it would only make it more painful when we left El Paso without her.

Sometime Sunday evening the Lord began to challenge me to act in faith. The thought occurred to me that if I really believed God was going to give us this precious baby, I needed to pick her up and hold her. Just then Sue said it was time for the baby to be fed, and she asked me if I wanted to feed her. I took the little girl into my arms, sat on the couch in the living room, and fed and held her for the next hour. I swayed heavily between believing the Lord was really going to let us have her and grieving over the thought of losing her.

On Monday afternoon, the birth mother came with her best friend and her seventeen-year-old son to get the baby. Amazingly, both of them tried to persuade her to let us have the baby. We did not plead with her; we simply shared with her some of the few plans we had for the baby's life. This went on for over an hour.

Texas law required the birth mother to physically hand the baby to the adoptive parents. At one point, I looked down on the coffee table in front of us and saw a children's Bible lying on it. It had a picture of Jesus on its cover surrounded by children, and He was holding one child on His lap. When I saw the picture, I said in my mind, *God, if You are real, have her hand the baby to my wife right now.* I was amazed at myself for delivering such a forceful ultimatum to the almighty Creator of the universe. I was even more amazed when I saw the birth mother give the baby a final hug. Then she held the baby out toward Debbie and said in Spanish the equivalent of "You, adoption." Debbie was confused, so Sue quickly explained what the birth mother was communicating. Debbie was both stunned and elated as she took the precious bundle into her arms. I understood immediately and shouted praises as I burst into tears of joy. The room immediately transformed from an atmosphere of quiet sorrow and tension into a bedlam of utmost joy. It completely overshadowed the birth mother's sense of loss.

We thanked the birth mother, her friend, and her son extensively and promised we would give our best love and care to her little girl. She seemed to be consoled a little by these words. Soon they left, and an immense celebration erupted in the Wasson household. We couldn't believe Leahanna Rachelle (pronounced Lee-anna Ruhshell) was actually ours. Suddenly, God was very real, and in His mercy and compassion He had not been offended by the rash words of one of His children. Instead, He had shown His great kindness once more.

We quickly discovered, after contacting our lawyer, that we had one final legal detail to take care of before we could take Leahanna home—an interstate compact. A legal agreement between Oregon and Texas was necessary to legally transport Leahanna to our home. It usually took about two weeks to get a compact completed. This was Monday, and we were scheduled to fly out on Wednesday.

The lawyer told us he would do what he could, but he doubted it could be done in such a short time. We thanked him and called many friends to announce the good news. We asked them to pray about the interstate compact. In the afternoon of the next day, the lawyer called and said the interstate compact had been completed. He was almost more surprised than we were!

The trip home was like a dream. All the people at the airports and on the airplanes were so kind and considerate toward us and our sixteen-day-old angel. She seemed so tiny and fragile, yet she was beautiful. Waiting at the Portland airport to welcome us home were Debbie's mother, sister, and best friend. What a great reunion and first-time meeting! The next several days at home were filled with visits and phone calls from those who wanted to meet Leahanna, congratulate us, and wish us well.

There was one person very close to us, however, who we did not hear from—Brother John. If fact, we had not heard from him for some time. I had tried to call him before we left for Texas, but he didn't answer the phone. We also tried to call him several times after we got home for several months, but to no avail. It all became very strange. Sometimes I would call and no one would pick up the phone. On other occasions, someone did pick up the phone, but no one spoke. At times, I would only hear the chimes from Brother John's wall clock in the background. I imagined all kinds of things that might have happened to Brother John. Did he have a stroke? Did he have a mental breakdown? Was he dying?

After many months of this, I got a frightening call one night. When I answered the phone, all I heard was Brother John saying slowly with much excruciation, "Scott…Scott…come." He repeated it two or three times. I tried to get out of him what was wrong, but he only repeated the words. Then we were disconnected. I tried to call back, but no one answered. This frightened and upset me immensely.

I tried to think what to do. I couldn't afford all the time it would take to get a trip to England organized and underway, so I called the British Red Cross and asked them to please look in on Brother John. Several hours later, the Red Cross called and said they had stopped at his house and he seemed to be all right. They described to me the man they had talked to, and the description fit. Now I was really confused; I didn't know what to make of all this.

I still could not get through to Brother John by phone, so I called and asked John Chambers to look in on him more than once. Whenever he did, Brother John seemed to be all right. More than a year later, in the late fall of 1991, I called Brother John once more, and he answered. I asked him if he was all right and what had been happening for the past several months. He assured me he had been all right and was in good health, but he gave no explanation for the strangeness of the preceding months. We never spoke about it again.

These events really confused me, and I thought about them for years. Eventually the Lord gave me some understanding from a devotional book that Larry Gordon gave me just days before he was killed. In Oswald Chambers' *My Utmost for His Highest*, I read a devotional entitled "The Price of Vision." It began with Isaiah 6:1: "In the year that King Uzziah died, I saw also the Lord." The text continued:

> Our soul's history with God is frequently the history of the "passing of the hero." Over and over again God has to remove our friends in order to bring Himself in their place, and that is where we faint and fail and get discouraged. Take it personally: In the year that the one who stood to me for all that God was died—I gave up everything? I became ill? I got disheartened? or—I saw the Lord?…It must be God first, God second, and God third, until the life is faced steadily with God and no one else is of any account whatsoever. 'In all the world there is none but thee, my God, there is none but thee.'
>
> Keep paying the price. Let God see that you are willing to live up to the vision.

God had removed Larry Gordon from my life. One day He would remove Brother John. Would I cave in to self-pity, or would I still trust God? These events helped me to realize it was a question I would one day face, just as I had with Larry Gordon.

Chapter 15

ANGELS AROUND THE WORLD

Shortly after we returned home with our little angel, the church held a well-attended baby shower for Leahanna at a friend's home. The atmosphere was greatly celebratory because many in the church had prayed for us intensely when the adoption looked like it wasn't going to work out. We were touched deeply by the acts of love poured upon us.

In the first few weeks of Leahanna's life, we expected some weakness due to her small size and rough start in life. After two or three weeks, there were hints that she was not developing well. She was still only drinking two ounces of formula every two hours, and it took her forty-five minutes to do that. Debbie and I took turns feeding her so we could each get a little more sleep.

As the weeks passed, we did not see proper progress in her development. She was not able to turn herself over or lift her head when she should have been able to do such things. When we put her down, she would just lie there instead of moving about like babies her age would normally do. We also noticed that loud noises didn't startle her.

After three months, Debbie took her to the doctor and expressed some of our concerns to him. He checked her thoroughly and tested her reflexes. When he clapped his hands loudly in front of her face with no response, he gave a look of concern. Debbie perceived it and asked what he thought might be wrong. He said he didn't know exactly, but there was something. He wanted us to watch her closely and keep track of any concerns we had.

Leahanna made progress, but it was very slow. Soon after the doctor's appointment, she began to respond appropriately to loud noises, but she was not learning how to crawl. A former student of mine helped Leahanna conquer crawling while she babysat for us. She didn't learn to walk until she was twenty-one months old.

Over the months, Leahanna had numerous ear infections and other maladies, so we saw the doctor fairly often. His concerns grew, and by the time Leahanna was almost two years old, he referred her to a pediatric neurologist at a Portland hospital's child development center. The doctor at the center gave her a thorough examination and ran some blood tests. These showed no abnormalities, so she scheduled Leahanna for a CT scan in two weeks.

The CT scan was difficult for our little girl. Since she was so young, they put her under with anesthetics so she would not move. For the drive home from the hospital, Debbie put her in a car seat. As she awakened from the anesthetic, she was so disoriented she screamed all the way from Portland to Hood River.

About a week later, the neurologists called with results. Leahanna had a rare congenital defect called agenesis of the corpus callosum. In this defect, the corpus callosum, or tissue that connects the hemispheres of the brain, only partially forms or does not form at all. Leahanna's corpus callosum had not formed at all. She also had a type of malformation of the cerebellum, which controls motor functions and some other functions, called Dandy-Walker syndrome.

This sounded bad, but the list of possible effects from these disorders sounded even worse. Two of the worst were the possibilities of Leahanna having either a stroke or seizures. Either of these could have the devastating effect of causing her to lie in a fetal position in bed for the rest of her life. Needless to say, we were alarmed.

Debbie and I shared what the neurologist told us with many of our friends and family members. A multitude of people prayed for Leahanna. Her progress and development were slow, but she did progress. We made contact with a national organization that helped people understand and work with the effects of agenesis of the corpus callosum. Leahanna also qualified for early intervention services, so we got her into regular sessions of physical, occupational, and speech therapy. These helped her immensely. I cannot emphasize enough the importance of early intervention for special-needs children.

The neurologist also told us that if Leahanna made it to the age of five without having any strokes or seizures, she probably would never have them. As I write this, my beautiful daughter is twenty-two years old. She has far surpassed all expectations. Leahanna is a wonderful violin player who can play a song perfectly after hearing it only once or twice. The year before last she made the dean's list in her first quarter at the local community college. She still has her struggles in some areas because of her agenesis, but in other areas she excels because of it. In many ways, as at least one neurologist acknowledged, she is a living miracle.

Leahanna loves the Lord and reads His Word diligently almost every day. At times she has had some serious struggles, but she has turned those into a means of helping others through similar struggles. I see her faith growing stronger *because* of her difficulties. The miracle of Leahanna's success and wonderful disposition encouraged Debbie and I to adopt three more special-needs children over the next nine years. We have seen the Lord do wonderful things in all these children. They are angels. As I did some research for this chapter on the Internet, I came across an organization helping families dealing with agenesis. It is called "Angels Around the World." It is an apt name.

A little over a year ago as of this writing, Leahanna met a young man at a Bible study. His name is Andrew Wilde. He taught himself to play the violin, and he plays beautifully. Last summer they played together in outstanding harmony as the sole musicians at a close friend's wedding. Andrew shared with us that he went through struggles earlier in his life that were very similar to Leahanna's. He says God healed him, and he hasn't suffered since. Because he understands so well what Leahanna is going through, he is very compassionate and caring toward her. There is serious talk about them having a wedding of their own in the future. It is not a matter of *if* there will be a wedding, just when. We are pretty sure he fell from heaven! The principles of Beit Shalom are proving true in our children's lives as well: our Father knows our needs and will provide for them, miraculously at times, as only He is able to do.

Chapter 16

THE ROAD TO ROMANIA

During the 1990–1991 school year, the Lord continued to bring students and provide funds for salaries and supplies. We discontinued the first and second grade classes in cooperation with another school in Hood River using the same curriculum and program. They were holding classes for preschool through the second grade, so we held classes for grades three through eight. This worked pretty well for its duration, but it was a hardship for those families who had to divide children between the two schools. As a result of this arrangement, we had only three paid teaching positions and fewer volunteer aides.

During this time, the majority of the church decided not to follow the teachings and methods of the Christian leader which had caused some serious divisions in the church. As a result, the pastor resigned, and a few families left the church. Some of the fallout caused years of hard feelings, but in time a lot of healing took place. As an elder, the situation was very stressful for me, but the Lord taught me many lessons regarding difficult situations. The most important lesson I learned was to depend on God and follow His ways, not my own wits.

We hired a retired pastor who had a lot of maturity and a gentle spirit to be our interim pastor. Richard Schwab brought a lot of wisdom and experience to our church. He helped us heal from the critical situation we had been through. Under his leadership, we grew both individually and as a church, and the school had a smooth and pleasant school year as a result.

During this school year, the Lord began to challenge me to pray bigger prayers. I had grown up during the Cold War and had a fairly sizable disdain for the Soviet Union and communism in general. The Lord began to show me that most people under communist dictatorships were not in favor of these regimes; they just suffered under them. So He began to impress upon me to pray for the end of communism (which at this point was really a dictatorial socialism) on our entire planet.

In the summer of 1991, the Burtons invited our growing family to spend a week at the Oregon coast with them in a large rental house in Seaside. We gladly joined them, and during the week I walked down to a little store each morning to pick up a newspaper. The second day, the headlines and much of the paper were splashed with the news of the collapse of the Soviet Union. For the next five days I read with amazement every word of the many articles detailing this historic event. The Lord began to grow in me a love for the people of Russia and a strong desire to minister to them. In time, I became almost consumed with the hope and prayer of one day sharing the gospel of Jesus Christ with the people of Russia. The end of the Soviet Union was officially declared on December 25, 1991.

In the fall of the 1991–1992 school year, the school added the first and second grade class back into the ministry. As a result, we hired Natalie Snider as the combined first and second grade teacher. What a blessing she was! We served together for ten years at the school. At times, I referred to Natalie as a "female Larry Gordon." She loved the Lord uncompromisingly (and still does—she and her husband, Greg, are currently serving as missionaries on Isla Mujeres, an island off the coast of southern Mexico near Cancun), and the love of Jesus flowed through her constantly.

Greg and Natalie were professional skiers and came to the Hood River area to work for a friend of theirs who owned a small ski resort on Mount Hood. The year they came was the first of three years of the lowest levels of snow on record in the mountains around Hood River. The resort went bankrupt, so Greg started working for the local school district, and Natalie came to work for the school. Greg ministered with Natalie when he could, and the two of them became a great spiritual boon for the school and the entire Mid-Columbia area. The school ministry doubled its attendance during the years they were involved and grew even more in the spiritual realm. Natalie always challenged me to know and live better the ways of the Lord. They were an outstanding addition to the school ministry.

Since I had reestablished contact with Brother John, I was talking to him by phone at least once a month again. In the spring of 1992, he started talking to me about coming over to England to help him take a load of supplies into Romania to start a coffee shop. He had met a group of people from a church in Vulcani, Romania while traveling with a group from Worthing Tabernacle on a short-term mission. They had gone to help after the overthrow of the communist government in 1989 and the resulting economic chaos. The Vulcani church had a fantastic choir, and he was so impressed that he arranged to take the entire group and some of their family members on a tour of Great Britain and Israel.

I was thrilled at the thought of traveling to Romania with Brother John. Even though we were now talking by phone, I had not seen him in person since I had lost contact with him. I really wanted to see him face-to-face and spend time with him again. There was a unique depth of spirit in the connection I had with Brother John that I'd had with no other person other than Larry Gordon. The Spirit of God was so strong in these men. Anyone seeking God at any level could not help being drawn and challenged into a deeper walk after spending time with them. To me, this was thrilling.

Travel and ministry had always attracted me also, and the Lord had taught me by now that travel was something I could do. Romania had been much in the news since the revolution in 1989. The Berlin Wall and the Iron Curtain fell about the same time. Traveling to post-communist Romania with Brother John to minister to the people was an irresistible adventure, impossible to refuse. So I started to pray for the Lord to provide the finances for the trip. Almost immediately, the Lord provided enough funds to go on the trip and take care of Debbie and the children at home while I was gone. Then the school experienced some financial difficulties, and the money provided for the trip had to be used to pay bills. This confused and upset me, but a few weeks later the school finances improved significantly, and the funds needed for the trip were restored fully.

School ended on Friday, May 29, 1992. On Thursday, June 11, Debbie, John, Joel, and Leahanna accompanied me to Portland to take off for Romania. It was a brief but sorrowful parting. John was now almost eight years old; Joel was eleven days short of turning four; and Leahanna was twenty months old. There were many hugs and kisses before I headed toward the check-in counter. I carried two heavy suitcases, each containing over fifty Romanian Bibles (which the church had purchased to send with me) and a few clothes and other supplies for the trip.

I flew to Dallas first, where I had a short layover before flying the last long leg of the trip to London. After a short night on the plane, I arrived at the London-Gatwick Airport at eleven-thirty in the morning. I was met by Brother John and Cristian Sigheartau, one of the Romanian choir members. Cris had come to England to help Brother John at the house while Brother John helped him get his degree from London Bible College. Cris was very wise and gracious at twenty-one years old, and he seemed to be just what Brother John needed after losing Rosalie.

I enjoyed getting to know Cris while driving to Brother John's home. It was wonderful to be at New Orleans once more, and it was so good to be with Brother John again. He seemed to be doing so well. Thoughts of his struggle after Rosalie's death were distant in the warmness of the sun and the present camaraderie. However, it was not the end of his struggles.

After a short sleep that night, I awoke at 2 a.m. and had a wonderful time with the Lord, praying, reading the Scriptures, and listening to the Lord in the quiet solitude. Right at 4 a.m. the birds began to sing and chatter in the trees and hedges that surrounded the ancient St. Leonard's churchyard adjacent to John's property. At 4:30, I stood on the bed and looked out the skylight just in time to see a red fox ambling through the hedgerow behind the old church in the dim morning light.

After enjoying a couple of hours of this early morning symphony, I got ready for the day and went downstairs to join Cris and Brother John for breakfast. We spent a leisurely morning visiting as we wandered through the shops of Hove and Brighton. That evening we went over our plans and packed for the trip to Romania the next morning. We were going to travel to Antwerp, Belgium, to pick up a large van for touring around Europe with the choir. We would fill the van with as much equipment and supplies as we could for the coffee shop that Brother John was helping start. The plan was to sell soups, sandwiches, coffees, and teas at the shop and give away as much Christian literature as any customer wanted. The employees would always be ready to engage anyone in spiritual discussions without being pushy. In his previous trips into Romania, Brother John had discovered a great hunger for the Lord in many of the people. He thought the coffee shop would be one way to satisfy their hunger. The choir would be another effective avenue for spreading the gospel. We all felt strongly this was the Lord's direction for the trip. We soon discovered He had planned even more for us.

We also planned the route we would drive on the long journey across Europe. When we were satisfied that we had adequately attended to all the details, we headed to bed to get a good night's rest for the challenging days that lay ahead of us. Still not adjusted to England's time zone, I awoke at three in the morning. I read my Bible, and for the second day in a row, the Lord impressed upon me Psalm 2:8: "Ask of me, and I shall give thee the heathen for thine inheritance, and the uttermost parts of the earth for thy possession." I wondered what it meant.

After breakfast, Brother John, Cris, and I loaded our luggage into a taxi and rode to the Hove train station. We were going to take the train to Dover on the south coast via Victoria station in London. From Dover, we were going to ride on a jet foil across the English Channel to the coast of Belgium, where we would take a train again into Antwerp to pick up the van. The van would be our mode of transportation for the rest of the trip. We planned to fly back to England.

When we arrived at the Hove station, we took our luggage and walked down through an underground tunnel to the platform where we were to catch the train to Victoria Station. Just after we put our luggage down, Brother John exclaimed with panic in his voice that he had left a small, red carrying bag in the cab. He quickly explained that the bag contained all the papers for crossing all the borders between Belgium and Romania and funds for our trip, over twenty thousand dollars.

Brother John and Cris ran to see if they could catch the cab driver before he left while I stayed with the luggage. With a feeling of hopelessness, I began to say a panic prayer. Almost before I started to pray, I saw someone across the tracks out of the corner of my eye. He seemed to be waving something red. As I turned, I beheld the taxi driver waving the red bag, trying to get my attention. Almost jumping up and down, I waved back and began to shout toward the tunnel for Cris and Brother John. The taxi driver seemed to understand what was happening and began to look for them. A few seconds later they appeared. They approached the driver jubilantly with great relief and many, many thanks. Brother John rewarded him handsomely, and they returned to the platform only a few minutes before our train arrived. The trip had hardly begun, and the Lord had already rescued us from disaster through an honest cab driver.

The rest of the trip to Dover was uneventful except for seeing the famed Orient Express at Victoria Station. After we arrived in Dover, we boarded what appeared to be a boat. At first I thought it was the jet foil, but it turned out to be our boarding area as we waited for the jet foil to arrive. Cris and I had never been on a jet foil, so Brother John had arranged for us to ride on this one as a special treat. Jet foils are hydrofoils that lift up on struts as they are propelled by jet engines. They travel about four times as fast as a conventional ferry. The trip was a blast.

About an hour later we landed in Oostende, Belgium. We were soon on the train to Antwerp. Just over an hour later, we rolled into the large station in the middle of the city. We made our way outside and found a modest hotel just across the street. After we settled into our room, we had some dinner and took a relaxing evening walk before returning to retire for the night. God was good to us that day; His plans would get even better.

In the morning, we went to a car dealer to pick up the eighteen-passenger van which was to be used to haul the equipment for the coffee shop to Romania. When we arrived at the dealership, we were taken into a large warehouse with many new cars lined up in rows. We were shown the new van, and the man at the dealership gave me the keys to drive it out of the warehouse. The van was parked very close to a row of new cars just behind it, and when I turned the key to start it, I did not realize it was a stick shift. It was in reverse, and when I tried to start the van, it jerked backward and hit two new cars behind it. I suddenly felt very ill.

I jumped out of the van, and dumbstruck, we quickly surveyed the damage to all three vehicles. The back bumper of the van had a small crease in it about a foot long, and the two cars behind had each sustained damage to one of their headlights. The damage was minor, and we had insurance, but it was very upsetting. The man from the car dealership said he would talk to the owner to see what needed to be done. We would return the next morning to fill out insurance forms and do whatever was necessary to take care of everything.

We spent the rest of the morning securing most of the supplies intended for the coffee shop, as well as food for our trip across much of Europe. I was really discouraged about the accident, so late in the morning I asked Brother John and Cris to pray with me. After we prayed, Brother John asked me in a kind but firm way if I was done fretting. I was surprised by his question but quickly understood he was trying to encourage me to forget about it and move on. I did.

Fairly early the next morning, we made our way back to the car dealership to take care of the damage. To our surprise, the man at the dealership said the owner had sent his apologies for not having the van brought out to the front of the building. He asked if we would be willing to take care of the damage to the van if they took care of the damage to the cars. We readily agreed to this arrangement and left the dealership in amazement, heartily praising the Lord. He had delivered us once more in His mercy and compassion.

We spent the rest of the morning and the early afternoon picking up more supplies for the coffee shop and food for the trip. By two-thirty, we were on our way. We drove through Liege, Belgium, and stopped to make sandwiches for a late lunch just off the road shortly after we crossed into Germany. After our lunch break, we drove through Koln, Germany, and stayed at a nice bed-and-breakfast in a small town just outside of Koln.

We continued our journey the next morning right after breakfast. We drove over 750 kilometers (nearly 500 miles) through the rest of Germany and into Austria before we turned off the autobahn toward the small village of Mitter. It was an arduous journey because we could not go faster than fifty-five miles per hour as we broke in the van's new engine, laboriously slow for the autobahn. We also had a long delay at the German-Austrian border because we discovered we had left the folder full of papers needed to cross all the borders back at the bed-and-breakfast. We couldn't retrace the nearly 500 miles we had just traveled, so we had to start all over filling out new papers. We later called the owner of the bed-and-breakfast and asked him to send the papers to Cris's family in Romania, as we did not know where else in our uncertain destinations each day he could send them. Someone in Cris's family would have to drive three or four hours to get the papers to our point of entry at the Romanian border.

As we neared the village of Mitter, we asked a man at the side of the road if there was someplace we could stay the night. He told us there was a hotel right in Mitter. As we slowly drove past the only three roads that turned into the little town, we looked carefully down each one, trying to find the hotel. We did not see anything that looked like a hotel, so as we were leaving the village, we looked for a place to turn around. As we turned onto a road, we noticed a little sign with the word "Zimmer" printed on it. (Zimmer is the German word for bed-and-breakfast.) As we crawled forward to see where the sign was pointing, a car in the other lane slowed for a stop sign. We signaled to the lady in the car and asked if she knew how far down the road it might be. She said it was a nice Zimmer and was only about a quarter-mile away. After our long day, a stay in the country sounded much better than a hotel in town! So we ventured forth and found a well-kept bed-and-breakfast in a beautiful, serene country setting.

After we put our bags in our room, we took a peaceful walk up a road through the lush green countryside. Finding the bed-and-breakfast in this setting was truly a blessing from the Lord. We saw some deer on our walk. Later we saw them again grazing out in the fields as we watched from a window in our room.

In the morning, the lady who owned the Zimmer, along with her husband, made us an enormous, delicious breakfast. She served several courses of food with grace and kindness. When we went to settle our account, she charged us the equivalent of only twenty-five US dollars for everything. Brother John insisted on paying her more, even though she was almost distraught at the thought.

After we loaded our luggage back into the van, we headed east toward Vienna. At first, we drove through some picturesque forested mountains that reminded me of my home state of Oregon. We then descended and drove through the beautiful city. I was sorry we did not have time to stop and see some of the sights. On the other side of Vienna, we drove down into plains of golden, ripening wheat. We prayed we would have no trouble, even without our papers, as we approached the Hungarian border.

The Hungarian guards were curt and serious. After a brief wait, a short, stout man came out of the border station in what appeared to be the uniform of a fairly high-ranking officer. He asked us what we were carrying in the van. We told him we had a stove and some equipment for a coffee shop in Romania. He turned his face to the side without changing his stern expression and looked down the road into Hungary. After a few moments of thought, he simply said, "Good-bye." Surprised by this, we started down the road. Moments later we were laughing with joy and praising the Lord for helping us through the border crossing with such incredible ease.

After a hundred more miles of driving through wheat lands, we approached the outskirts of Hungary's capital city of Budapest. I saw a split in the road ahead and asked Brother John whether I should go left or right. He somewhat frantically said that he could not remember. When he had traveled this route the year before, he was on a bus with the church group. He could not remember which way to go. The split in the road was upon us, so I quickly prayed, "Help me, Lord," and veered to the right.

Budapest was a sprawling city of about two million people, and I felt more than a little intimidated about finding our way through. None of us knew a single Hungarian word. We drove in silence for a short while, looking intently for some hint that we were on the right road. After only about a quarter of a mile, we saw a sign on the right shoulder written in English. It was the first English of any kind we had encountered since entering the country. It said, "Travel information 1/4 mile ahead." We were astonished and elated.

We easily found the travel information center, and we found the employees were *Italians* who spoke English perfectly. The owner of the center was a vivacious Hungarian man who told us to call him "Charlie." Charlie proved to be a most amazing blessing from the Lord.

We explained that we needed a place to stay for the night, but we didn't want to park the van, with all of the equipment in it, out on the street. Charlie said he owned an apartment building less than a block away, and it had a courtyard in the middle with plenty of off-street parking, all behind a locked gate. We also told Charlie we were trying to get to the Romanian border, but we needed to get an oil change for the van. Charlie brought out a map of the entire city from underneath the counter and unfolded it in front of us. He showed us where we were and where we needed to go to reach the border. We were right on the route to the border, and about two miles down this same highway was one of only five service stations in the entire city where we could get our oil changed!

We were amazed and ecstatic at how the Lord had so completely provided everything for us and more. When Charlie showed us the apartment, it was a spacious, completely furnished suite (with dishes and all) on the second floor. It faced the courtyard away from the noise on the street. It also had a phone, and Charlie helped me call my family back home. It was so good to hear the voices of Debbie and the children. It was the evening of our fifteenth anniversary and the day after Joel's fourth birthday.

After all that had happened, we felt so confident in the Lord's care for us that we called Cris's family in Romania and told them *not* to bring the customs papers to the border. We knew the Lord would help us through without them. He is always leading us in ways to trust Him more.

After taking care of all the business in our room, Charlie left, and we went out to find a place to eat dinner. Halfway between the apartment and the visitor's center, we found a beautiful, quiet little restaurant. It had private booths with white tablecloths and chairs with ornately carved wooden backs. I had a very good steak while John had lamb and Cris had pork chops. While we ate, I marveled at how the Lord had brought a man born in Scotland in 1912, a man born in the western United States in 1953, and a man born in Romania in 1971 together for dinner in Budapest, Hungary, in 1992. The entire dinner for all three of us cost only twelve dollars.

In the morning, we woke up refreshed and took our bags to the van after some breakfast. Charlie charged us only twenty-five dollars for the room and sent us on our way to Romania. I think he might have been an angel sent by God.

Shortly after we started out of Budapest, we found the service station Charlie had shown us on the map. They told us they didn't do oil changes after all, but soon after we left, we made a wrong turn. Before we could get back onto the right road, we found another service station that *did* do oil changes. If we had not been in that part of the city looking for the first service station and made the "wrong turn," we never would have found the second service station. Half an hour later, we were leaving Budapest and heading for the Romanian border.

After driving about a hundred miles through the Hungarian countryside, we came to a small town right on the border, about ten miles west of Oradea, Romania. The road took us right toward the border station. As we neared the station, we saw three long lines of vehicles at a standstill just ahead of us. After three blocks, the lines turned a corner to the left, so we couldn't see the border station. There were no signs directing us into any of the lines, so we didn't know where to queue up. The line on the far right had all semitrucks in it, so we assumed that was the wrong line. The other two lines were both made up of cars. I asked Cris and John which line they thought I should follow, but they had no idea. The last time I'd had to choose which way to go, I'd chosen the right. This time I would try the left. I pulled the van into the far left lane. I chose wrong.

After we rounded the corner, we saw that our line came to an end. Every once in a while an official in a military uniform came up to the lead car and had some sort of discussion. He would eventually let that car merge into the line to the right. Our line was moving excruciatingly slowly, and we were still about a quarter of a mile from the border station. Since we had a lot of time on our hands, Brother John and Cris decided to walk to the station to get a head start on filling out any papers we needed to get through this last border. I stayed with the van while they were gone. I was a bit frustrated with the long wait and the lack of proper signage to direct us, but the Lord was about to stretch my faith again.

When Brother John and Cris came back from the station, they shared about the unusual experience they'd just had. While they were filling out a certain paper with two of the soldiers, they came to a blank which asked Brother John to state his occupation. He said he was a pastor. They didn't understand what a pastor was, so Cris explained that Brother John was a priest, a word more familiar to Romanians. A large man in an officer's uniform nearby overheard him. When he realized that Brother John was a "priest," he came up to him, put his arm around his shoulders, and said, "I'm your friend."

Border guards were seldom known to be religious, let alone Christian. In fact, they were usually quite the opposite, often being corrupt and taking bribes to "help" some people get through. Some of the guards at this station even proved that. But when this man, who was in charge of the entire station, heard that Brother John was a "priest," he not only put his arm around him, but he insisted on filling out our papers for us!

Brother John and Cris came back to the car jubilant, but our celebration was soon cut short. We had come to the front of our line, and there was no place to go. The man in the uniform came to our car and started shouting something at me in Romanian. I asked Cris what he had said, and he told me the guard had informed us, in no uncertain terms, that we were in the wrong line. We had pretty well figured that out, but Cris told me the guard also wanted to see my passport. I gave it to him, and he brusquely shoved it into a leather pouch on his belt and walked away angrily.

I was more than a little unsettled and asked Cris what we should do. Cris said he did not know, so we just stayed put. I could not go on without my passport, and the guard had given us no indication of what to do. There we sat, confused, upset, and worried. We prayed and committed it all to the Lord.

After a few minutes, the guard came back to our car and said something in a rather low voice. His demeanor seemed quite different, and I thought he was still speaking in Romanian, so I asked Cris what he had said. "Coca Cola," Cris told me. I looked at him questioningly, "Coca Cola?" Cris said, "Yes, he wants you to give him some Coca Cola." It was beginning to dawn on me what was going on, but I was still apprehensive because we had no Coca Cola with us. Cris communicated with the guard that we had none. The guard said, "Chocolate."

At this, Brother John sprang up from his seat and hopped out of the van saying, "Chocolate; we've got chocolate." A moment later he opened the back of the van and grabbed two one-pound Belgian chocolate bars out of one of our grocery boxes. I had bought them back in Antwerp to share with my family when I got home. I was a little incensed that Brother John had grabbed *my* chocolate for the bribe, but I was not about to fuss about it just then.

Brother John got back into the van and handed me the chocolate bars. I reluctantly gave them to the guard. He quickly stashed them in his pouch, then took out my passport and returned it to me. The sense of loss regarding the chocolate bars was replaced by the joy of getting my passport back. Before I knew it, the guard was blowing his whistle and holding his hand up toward the car in the line to the right of us.

A short while later, it was our turn to pull up to the station to talk with more guards. Immediately, two men who looked like junior officers came out and asked us what we had in the van as they took our papers. Cris started to explain when they both started yelling at him. Cris was still trying kindly to explain to them what we were doing when a large figure overshadowed the junior officers and barked something at them. They quickly disappeared from the scene, and the large fellow bowed toward us with a smile as he motioned for us to pass through the station. He said something kindly to Cris as he gave him some of the papers back. It was the man in charge of the entire station who had helped Brother John and Cris fill out the papers.

The big man motioned us forward. Just ahead, all the cars were pulling off to be searched. I asked Cris if the big man wanted us to go completely through the station without stopping. I did not want to give these last guards any reason to think about using the AK-47s they had strapped to their shoulders! Cris assured me that it was all right to go.

Slowly, I started to move forward, keeping my eyes on the guards. They paid no attention to us, so I sped up as I passed the last of the cars being searched. I watched in the rearview mirror as the car behind us was directed to pull over. They opened his trunk, pulling out and searching bag after bag. In a little more than two hours, we had made it through the Romanian border. Once more, we were elated. Once more, the Lord had gotten us through. It was marvelous seeing the Lord helping us through all these trials. It seemed we were living out our own Beit Shalom story.

Chapter 17

ROMANIA

We thoroughly enjoyed the scenic countryside as we drove through Romania toward Vulcani. The fields and mountains were so green. Some of the fields had rows of neatly stacked hay, while a few others had small, sporadic crews hoeing or plowing with horses. There were ornate, onion-topped churches, and we saw the ruins of an ancient castle on top of a prominent hill. It was a beautiful country, and now in the infancy of newly found freedom.

We arrived at Vulcani about an hour after dark and meandered through the town until we came to the apartment complex where Cris's family lived. His parents and his sister's family resided in separate buildings about a block apart. Even though I had just met them, they welcomed me as warmly as they did Brother John and Cris. There were shouts of joy and many hugs. I had rarely, if ever, met such gracious people.

Cris and Brother John settled into the apartment with Cris's mother. I was given a place to stay with Cris's sister, Angela, her husband, Peter, and their two sweet, quiet daughters. Inside, the apartments were small but cozy and nicely furnished. After arriving at Peter and Angela's apartment, I presented the Bibles to them. They received the Bibles with quiet joy and great appreciation. They carefully packed them away until the coffee shop was finished. We decided we would give them to anyone who showed a definite interest in the Christian life. I was glad I didn't have to pack them around anymore!

We visited for a while and turned in for the night. We were pretty tired from the long day of travel and getting through the border with God's help. I was deeply impressed with how the Lord had taken good care of us. Part of a verse from 1 Peter 1:5 began to make an impression upon my mind: "Kept by the power of God."

Peter and Angela let me sleep on a comfortable daybed in their living room, as their apartment had only two bedrooms. I slept soundly, and Angela fed us a bountiful breakfast after I woke up.

The morning held the promise of a beautiful day. After breakfast, Brother John and I walked down to a marketplace a few blocks from the apartments. I was impressed at the contrast of the robust colors of the fruits and vegetables against the backdrop of dull, shabby buildings, crude tables, and drab clothing. We also found things to be absurdly inexpensive. Though a few women were inspecting the produce with some intensity, most of the people seemed much more interested in engaging in conversation than in buying or selling their wares. These were the ordinary people of Romania in their workaday world. God loved them as intensely as He loves all of us. Now they were experiencing a freedom most of them had never known. It was a joy watching them enjoy each other's company. Would this develop into a more godly culture? Could we help bring them a little closer to God?

After our foray to the market, Brother John and I went back to the apartments for lunch and spent the afternoon visiting the unfinished coffee shop with Cris, Angela, Peter, and a few others. In the evening, we went to the church to see the choir during an evening practice session. There were shouts of joy and many deep hugs at the sight of Brother John. It had been over a year since the choir members had seen him. It was great fun to watch the jubilation.

After several minutes of celebrating their reunion, the choir settled into the rigors of practice. On this night, sixteen members were present, with Angela leading them and Peter accompanying on the organ. I was amazed at the sound they produced. They sounded like a choir of fifty or more, all in perfect pitch and harmony. I now fully realized why Brother John had taken them on tour throughout Israel and Great Britain.

When the choir broke up into parts practice, Brother John and I went outside and climbed to the top of a hill about a block from the church. This vantage point gave us a panoramic view of Vulcani and the surrounding area. Vulcani is set against a backdrop of lush green foothills leading to the Carpathian Mountains. The city was full of dreary apartment complexes mixed with the worn structures of industry. It was a poignant juxtaposition of the ravages of man against the beauty of God's creation.

After visiting with the choir after the practice session, we went to Cris's parents' tiny apartment, consisting of only two small rooms, a tiny kitchen, a bathroom, and a vestibule. We visited for a while before going to bed. This had been home to Cris, his two sisters, and his parents during his younger years. Cris's father, George, was staying with the other sister, Safta, in Bistrita (in north-central Romania) to get some dental work done.

In the morning we attended a service at the church, and what an incredible service it was! It lasted almost three hours, interspersed with prayers, songs, and speakers. People prayed out loud on their knees and sat attentively forward on hard, wooden pews while the speakers shared, and the congregation sang their hearts out during the hymns. *Seven* of us spoke during that service, including Brother John and me. You literally could have heard a pin drop while we were speaking.

I was told that while under communism, the only Christian services of any kind allowed in Romania were funeral services. The people would walk up and down several streets of their town or city during the services, stopping often to allow pastors to preach a sermonette. It was the only opportunity they had to share the Christian faith. Now that they had the freedom to worship in churches, they did not take it for granted.

After church, Brother John, Cris, Delia (Cris's girlfriend and future wife), and I visited an orphanage in the neighboring town of Uricani. The buildings and playground were in poor shape, and the children were dressed in odd combinations of donated clothing. The girls' hair had been shorn because of head lice. There were children of all ages, from infants through late teens. They were all starved for love. Several of them shadowed us from the moment we arrived. I was told they were hoping we would take them home with us. It was truly heartrending.

One little girl, Helen (pronounced Ay-lun), clung to me the whole time we were there. She was precious. She seemed about seven or eight years old. Cris told me she was ten. He said all the children in the orphanages in Romania (and there were many at that time) tended to look younger than they were because of poor nutrition. I was also informed that not all the children were without parents. Many had been orphaned in the revolution, but some were left by their parents, who simply did not have the means to care for them. But God had not forgotten them. Since the revolution, many people from the United States and other countries had adopted Romanian children from this orphanage and many others in the country. Our Lord truly is a Father to the fatherless.

The next morning we visited the mayor of Vulcani. We discussed some possible relations with the West to help develop the city. We also stopped by a hospital and prayed over some very sick children. In the afternoon, Brother John, Cris, and I picked up two members of the choir and their daughters, and together we headed for Bistrita to see Cris's sister and father. We drove through Cluj, Dej, and Beclean before reaching Bistrita late in the day.

We drove to the home of some of Cris's relatives in the country after lunch the next day, laboriously driving twelve kilometers down a bumpy dirt-and-gravel road through beautiful countryside. Near the end of the drive, we sloshed through a small river in our van to get to their house. At this time, country living in Romania was very primitive and rustic. Rural life was set in valleys with huge fields of produce against large, steep, very green hills. Farm workers would get up before light and walk or ride in wagons or on bicycles to the large fields, sometimes a few miles away. They worked until it was dark. They hoed the fields by hand and plowed them with a single-blade plow drawn by a horse. They had no insecticide, so they cleared the plants of insects by hand. Some of the larger collective farms near Bucharest and other large cities in Romania used tractors and farm implements. These farms had no such luxury.

The house was very rustic, with a single electrical wire running to it for lights. His relatives had no running water; they drew it from a well with a bucket. They cooked and heated the house with a woodstove, and cooked on another woodstove outside during the summertime to keep the house cool. They had no cars, only a horse-drawn wagon or two. Cris's brother-in-law demonstrated how to harvest grain with a scythe. It was a simple but hard life.

We spent the afternoon there before we drove back through the river and down the rough road to Bistrita. In the cool of the evening, we had a final night of pleasant fellowship with Cris's family. After many hugs and good-byes the next morning, we started the long trip back to Vulcani. We battled through thick traffic of wagons, trucks, bicycles, and pedestrians on the rugged roads of our route. Almost all of the roads we traveled on in Romania were rough, but the beautiful scenery along the way made the trip enjoyable.

On Saturday, June 27, we prepared the van for a trip to Bucharest that would begin on Sunday morning. We went to the choir practice at the church early in the evening, and I said my good-byes to the choir members. I would not be returning to Vulcani from Bucharest. We spent the remaining time with Cris's family. In the morning, I said my final good-byes to Peter, Angela, their two daughters, and Mrs. Sigheartau before we headed for Bucharest. The trip was long but pleasant, and we had no serious difficulties along the way. I was already missing the people of Vulcani.

When we arrived at Bucharest, Brother John, Cris, and I checked into one room and Delia into another. We were on the fifth floor of a dormitory which belonged to a Baptist seminary. The building had no elevator, so it was quite a trek up the stairs! The seminary was already established well in only two-and-a-half years since the overthrow of communism. We rested in our rooms for a while before we attended an evening service in a church nearby. Brother John and I both spoke, along with two other foreigners and two men from the church. The service was every bit as impressive as the one we attended in Vulcani. The way the men from the church spoke with such passion and the congregation listened so intently challenged me. We've had so much freedom in America for so long, I think we largely take it for granted. I saw nothing of that complacency here. I was moved to see so many people value their faith so deeply.

After the service, we spent the remainder of the day with Liviu Caprar and his wife. They were a delightful couple in their late twenties or early thirties. Liviu was the headmaster of a Christian secondary school that held classes in a building behind one of the larger churches in Bucharest. The school had only been in existence for two years, and they already had 125 students in attendance.

The next morning after breakfast, I went with Liviu to tour his school. I was impressed at the academic level the students had achieved. The building and the rooms were very basic but well kept. The Baptist church in front of the school was a large, magnificent building with a beautiful oak sanctuary.

In one of the rooms of the church, there were fifteen or twenty people seated around two large tables positioned end-to-end. They were stuffing envelopes with reading materials. I asked Liviu what they were doing, and he explained that the people of the church had run an ad on the only television station in Romania. The station was run by the state, and the ad stated the church would send information explaining the basics of the Christian life to any child who inquired. They had been overwhelmed with over two million responses. The people in the room volunteered to mail the information to every single respondent.

After the tour of the school and church, Liviu took me to a large store downtown so I could buy some gifts for my family. He also showed me a few of the significant sights around the city. Then we headed back to the seminary for a final good-bye to Cris, Delia, and Brother John before they returned to Vulcani. I planned to stay the night alone at the seminary and take a taxi the next morning to the airport to begin my long journey home. Brother John had warned me not to get back any later than noon if I wanted to see them before they returned to Vulcani. They did not want to leave too late in the day for the long journey back. The things Liviu showed me took longer than anticipated, and we didn't get back to the seminary until almost one o'clock. Brother John, Cris, and Delia were gone. I would not see any of them again for nearly eight years.

Liviu had misunderstood about the necessity of getting back by noon, and when he found out what had happened, he was very sorry and extremely apologetic. I told him not to fret about it because it was really my fault. Since I had no other plans for the remainder of the day, Liviu and I had an inexpensive but nice lunch at a restaurant nearby. He dropped me off at the seminary afterward. Liviu was so gracious; he impressed me as one whom the Lord would use in a great way in the future. I did hear about Liviu in the not-too-distant future in an unusual way that confirmed my impression.

After Liviu left, I went up to the nearly empty room in the dormitory and lay down on my bed to read. I had been reading *Hudson Taylor's Spiritual Secret* on the trip. As I read now, I became extremely tired. I laid the book on my chest and fell into a deep sleep. I woke to a definite sense of the divine Presence in the room. The room was gray and shadowy when I awoke, but after a few moments the sun broke out from behind some clouds and blazed through the window onto a wall across from my bed. The whole room blazed with a glory that was overwhelming. Just when I thought I could stand no more, a cloud covered the sun again. After a few moments, the sun came out from behind the cloud and the whole glorious experience began again. Then, after a few more moments, a cloud covered the sun once more.

This cycle repeated itself a half-dozen times or more. The last time the room filled with the glory and the light, I felt I could stand no more of the overwhelming Presence. I didn't know what to do, but a thought occurred to me to pick up the book that was lying on my chest and start reading it again. It was a strange thought under the circumstances, but that's what I did. As I began, on that very page I read Psalm 2:8: "Ask of me, and I shall give thee the heathen for thine inheritance, and the uttermost parts of the earth for thy possession." It was the very verse the Lord had impressed upon me at the beginning of the trip. I was stunned and even more overwhelmed; then an exceptional calm came over the whole room. What had I just experienced? Once more I was impressed by the Scripture from 1 Peter 1:5: "Kept by the power of God."

After a long while of pondering all of this, the sunlight began to fade into the grayness of evening. I felt hungry, so I went downstairs to find a restaurant somewhere. Before I left the building, I was met by an American girl named Tina who was staying at the seminary for the summer. She had been volunteering at an orphanage and became fond of a teenage boy she had worked with there. She had decided to adopt him and take him back to the United States. This was quite an undertaking which would take several months to accomplish, so the seminary provided her with a room for a low price while she went through the adoption process.

After we talked for a bit, she invited me to join her and a few of the seminary staff for pizza she was making. She said it would be somewhat of a risk because it was hard to find the right cheeses and ingredients to make a good pizza in Romania.

I laughed and agreed to stay, and we all enjoyed some pretty unusual pizza together.

After our unique dinner, I went up to my room and read for the rest of the evening. I was thrilled with the prospect of being reunited with my family in only three more days. It had been an incredible journey, but I was more than ready to see them.

I slept well and rose early enough to get to the airport a few hours before my flight was scheduled to take off. After breakfast, with the help of the staff, I called for a taxi to pick me up. When I arrived at the airport, I was amazed at how empty it was for such a large city. Then I remembered how destitute most of the Romanian people were.

After I checked in for my flight, I waited for nearly two hours before we were allowed to board the plane. I was amazed again at how old the plane was and how few passengers were on board. Even though we were already past our scheduled take-off time, we sat for another half-hour before we started to taxi down the runway. I said a silent prayer, asking the Lord to help us arrive safely at London.

After three hours of uneventful flight and another hour of trains and a ride in a taxi, I made it safely to Brother John's house in Hove, blessed New Orleans. From there, it was only a couple of days before I returned to the place I longed for—home! I quickly settled in and went shopping in Hove before coming back to the house for a short rest. When I awoke, I called my family back home. It was *so* good to hear their voices. When I finished talking to them, I went to a little restaurant a few blocks from Brother John's house for fish and chips. I returned to New Orleans for a quiet evening and a good night's rest, still "kept by the power of God."

Everything had gone so well. The Lord had done some amazing things. He had taught me an even deeper dependence on Him alone and revealed Himself in an amazing way. I have since shared these stories many times, trying to demonstrate to people that the Lord can be depended on *all the time and in every circumstance.* Three weeks to the day after the trip ended, I read once more in one of my morning devotional readings, "…kept by the power of God."

Chapter 18

A DAUGHTER AND A DOG

I returned from Romania on July 2, 1992. I had been gone for twenty-two days. While I was away, John finished his first year of T-ball, Joel had his fourth birthday, and Leahanna spoke her first word: "Da-da." It was hard to miss these things, but when the Lord calls, we must go.

It was the school's eighth year, and the church called a new pastor to lead Shepherd of the Valley. After his first year, he directed our church to focus on the school as its main ministry. This gave the school a needed boost, greatly stabilizing the finances and helping it develop in many ways. It was still a faith ministry, but now the church helped with the finances if a need arose. This also gave the school and church together a single ministry focus. We never had another shortfall for the remaining nine years of the school, and the Lord greatly blessed the church through the years for its faith and generosity.

During October each year, the staff attended a teacher convention put on by the Association of Christian Schools International (ACSI). There were many training seminars and general sessions with dynamic speakers for hundreds of Christian schools from all over the Pacific Northwest and beyond. Over 1500 teachers, administrators, and support staff were in attendance each year. It lasted for two very full days. We traveled over sixty miles from Hood River to Portland and back each day while attending the convention.

During one of the general sessions this year, a staff member from ACSI talked about a partnership they had formed with a school in Romania. The purpose of the partnership was to help supply the school with educational materials, Bibles, and other supplies. They invited all the schools to participate with the collection.

When the speaker said "Romania," I gave him my undivided attention. When he said the leader of the school was *Liviu Caprar*, I nearly jumped out of my chair. I excitedly told the entire staff this was the young man I had met in Romania. I explained that he had given me a tour of the school the speaker was referring to. Then they flashed a picture of Liviu on the large screen at the front of the enormous meeting room. Almost bursting, I blurted, "That's him! That's him!" The rest of the staff got excited as they began to understand what I was babbling about.

The Lord was doing other things behind the scenes at the same time. While attending the convention, I had no idea a baby girl would be born seventeen days later less than two miles from the convention center who would one day become our daughter.

The school year progressed smoothly, and the Lord provided in abundance for all of our financial needs and supplies. In the spring of 1993, as I came home from school one day, John and Joel were excitedly playing with a large dog in our front yard. It was a beautiful Siberian husky, barely out of the puppy stage, leashed to our porch's pillar.

As I got out of my pickup truck and walked toward the boys, Debbie was coming out of the front door. The boys shouted in unison, "Can we keep him? Can we keep him?" I could see the dog was reciprocating the boys' excitement but was still pretty gentle toward them. My own lifelong love for huskies made me amenable to the idea. I looked up from the dog and the boys at Debbie, but her expression was not quite as enthusiastic.

I turned back toward the bedlam of boys and dog and could see that the dog was wearing a nice collar with some tags on it. As I petted the dog and inspected the tags, I told the boys the dog probably belonged to someone else. That didn't deter them in the least, and the "Can we keep him?" chorus erupted again. So I told them we would talk about it later. Then a new chorus of "Please, please, please?" began to ring out.

I laughed and walked away from the joyful riot. Debbie was not thrilled at the idea of taking on the responsibility of caring for a large dog, but she could not resist the elation of the boys. I found myself hopeful too: could this be the the dog I had dreamed of owning since the fourth grade? Maybe it was silly to even hope. We both knew what our landlady had said when we inquired about having a cat or dog at the house: a one-hundred-dollar nonrefundable deposit for a cat, and absolutely no dog would be allowed.

It had been a few years since we had made that inquiry, so Debbie and I decided to put the whole thing before the Lord. We decided we would pray that if the owner would give us the dog, and the landlady would allow us to keep him at the house, we would know it was indeed the Lord's will. Debbie was satisfied with this arrangement, thinking it was impossible to get by either of these hurdles, let alone both. It *had* to be the Lord's will if we got past both! We shared the conditions with the boys, and they erupted with cheers as if it were a done deal. Even Leahanna was getting caught up in all the excitement and joined the cheer. Oh, the faith the children displayed as we prayed! Then, not quite sure what to do next, I called the county animal control department and explained the situation to them. I also told them that if for any reason the owner did not want the dog, we would like to have it. I was surprised by the enthusiastic response from the lady at the department.

Less than fifteen minutes later, the lady from animal control was at the house. She wrote down my name and phone number and then kindly led the dog into the back of her truck. I felt a tinge of sorrow as I watched from the porch.

As the time passed, it seemed less and less likely that the dog would be ours. Then, after about two hours, the phone rang. It was the lady from animal control. To my utter amazement, she said the owner had indeed said we could have the dog. All we had to do was call him and make arrangements to pick the dog up. Now I was getting excited. She gave me his name and phone number before we ended the call.

As I shared the news with Debbie and the children, Debbie was as dumbstruck as I was, and the children exploded into a new round of excitement. I warned them we still had to clear it with the landlady, but I would have had more success communicating that to a post. The children knew we were going to get that dog. It was impossible not to get caught up in their joy.

A few minutes later, I called the owner and found out that our canine "him" was a "her" named Suki, the Japanese word for love. I thought that was an entirely appropriate name. The owner explained that she was a papered, purebred Siberian husky, and he had over four hundred dollars invested in her with her purchase and all of the shots she had been given. He also explained that he loved to take his dogs with him when he jogged each day, but huskies have a large propensity to run off. This was the second time he had been given a ticket for Suki running away during a jog. He didn't want to risk getting any more tickets, so he wanted to give us the dog. I explained to him the need to first clear it with our landlady and said I would call him back.

Within a few minutes, I was on the phone with the landlady, explaining the whole situation to her. As I talked in my easy chair in the living room, Debbie was eying me with great interest from the adjacent sewing room. The landlady graciously acknowledged we had been good renters and that boys needed a dog during their growing-up years. We could have it. With a huge smile on my face, I looked at Debbie and nodded my head up and down with great exaggeration. I thought Debbie's jaw was going to hit the floor. After I hung up, the celebration was immense. Even Debbie joined in at this point.

We immediately called Suki's owner to make arrangements to pick her up the next day. In the morning, I bought a strong leash, and we drove over to her owner's house. He was very kind and enjoyed watching the boys excitedly leash up and pet Suki. After talking briefly about her care, we took home the newest member of our family. She was a perfect addition, and we enjoyed her immensely for the next eleven years. She was also a prime example of how much the Lord truly does care for the little things. God does promise us that if we will delight ourselves in Him, He will give us the desires of our hearts (Psalm 37:4).

The summer of 1993 flew by quickly. Even though I would not see Brother John for some time to come, we still talked on the phone at least once a month. Cris was still staying with Brother John and helping him while finishing his degree at London Bible College. This arrangement worked well for both of them.

The summer melded into the fall of 1993, and Shepherd of the Valley began its ninth year of the school ministry. In October, the social worker who had helped Debbie and I adopt Joel and Leahanna contacted us about a twelve-month-old baby girl available for adoption. She explained that the baby had been born drug-addicted and might have a genetic disorder, even though she was doing well. The social worker asked if we wanted to go to committee to adopt the baby. This meant our family would be one of three presented to a committee in the Department of Human Services Children's Services Division as candidates.

We were immediately excited about the possibility, and after some discussion, we called the social worker back and told her we would like to go to committee for the baby. We had been praying for another child and felt that this invitation could be God's answer to our prayers.

Less than a week later, the social worker called us back with the results of some genetic testing done on the baby. The testing indicated the baby had a genetic disorder called Fragile X syndrome (also called Martin-Bell syndrome). She encouraged us to do some research on Fragile X and call her back later to let her know if we still wanted to proceed.

We were unsettled by this news, even though we had never heard of Fragile X syndrome. A genetic disorder didn't sound very positive. Debbie researched the syndrome and found there were mild and severe forms of Fragile X, but they all involved some type of intellectual disability. Some individuals (usually boys) with Fragile X were diagnosed as autistic.

This news overwhelmed Debbie. Joel was a very active child, and Leahanna wasn't out of the woods yet with the dire possibilities of her maladies. Adopting another high-needs child seemed like more responsibility than we were able to take on. I was disappointed, but I understood the gravity of the situation. So, with heavy hearts, we called the social worker and postponed the adoption.

About six months later, in the spring of 1994, the social worker called and told us they had discovered the baby did not have Fragile X syndrome. She was only a carrier of it. This meant she would only have some mild effects from the disorder, if any at all. By this time, Leahanna was showing good progress in her development and many signs of only mild effects from her agenesis of the corpus callosum and Dandy-Walker syndrome. We called our caseworker and told her we wanted to proceed with the adoption. We were elated.

To help the committee decide which family would be bested suited for the baby girl, we made a photo album of our family and gave it to our caseworker. Within a few weeks, we went to committee. The caseworker encouraged us by telling us she thought we had a very good chance of being chosen. We were getting really excited.

Late in the afternoon, the caseworker came to our house with our family album. Before we could wonder why she was returning it, she told us we had been chosen to be the parents of the baby girl. She had added a bundle of pictures to the album. The caseworker shared with us that a relative of the baby had also gone to committee but was not chosen. The maternal grandmother was going to appeal the committee's decision, but she was sure the grandmother would not win. Before she left, she told us the baby's caseworker from the Portland area would be calling us soon with all the details about what was going to happen.

We were concerned about the appeal, but we felt a deep peace that everything was going to be all right. We trusted the Lord to take care of it all. So, right after the caseworker left, we began to call our friends and relatives about the new addition to our family. The reality of having a fourth child was very exciting indeed.

While Debbie and I were both at school the next day, the caseworker from Portland called. Debbie took the call in the office. He explained that we could not even begin the adoption process until the appeal was completed. He thought it would take about two weeks. He was very confident that the birth grandmother of the baby would not win the appeal. This comforted us as we waited for everything to work out.

The two weeks flew by, and the caseworker called again. The grandmother had appealed all the way to the governor's office and been denied. He went on to explain there had been serious problems in the past concerning her—so bad the Children's Services Division was prepared to do everything they could to keep her from getting custody of the baby.

Now it was time to start the adoption process. The two caseworkers and Debbie and I began to make arrangements for visits at the foster home and our home. Within a month, Lauren Renee Winters would reside permanently with us.

On our first visit to the foster home, we were pleased Lauren had been living in such an atmosphere of love and kindness. The couple had five biological children. They had raised several foster children and adopted two into their family. They adopted two more in the future. We spent three wonderful hours with Lauren, the foster family, and the Portland caseworker. It seemed like just a few moments.

When we started to leave, I gave Lauren to the foster mom. As I did, Lauren reached toward me and made a sad face as if she did not want to leave my arms. We were all surprised by this happening on the very first visit. We knew this was the Lord's seal; this adoption was indeed His will and had His smile of approval upon it.

The next few weeks were a flurry of visits, ours to Lauren's foster home and hers to us. Before the end of May, Lauren came to stay with us permanently. By now she was a beautiful, precious nineteen-month-old redhead who was in the last stages of overcoming the effects of being born addicted to cocaine and heroin.

Chapter 19

THE CALL OF RUSSIA

Adding a fourth child to the growing Winters flock was not without its problems. Lauren was a sweet baby, and once she came into our home permanently, she began to blossom wonderfully. She still had some residual effects from being born drug addicted. She was hypersensitive, which caused her to cry a little more than the average baby, and her cry was seriously loud. Sometimes she cried so loudly that Debbie just could not hold her on her shoulder. It was just too deafening. She would try to comfort her as best she could at arm's length until Lauren began to calm after the initial earsplitting wail. It was a pitiful sight.

The sometimes deafening and long crying bouts just about drove Debbie over the edge the first few weeks we had Lauren. With the help and encouragement of our family doctor (who was a very godly man), we got through that brief period of adjustment without any casualties. Lauren continues to be our blessed drama queen to this day. One of her many friends calls her "Screamer." Lauren is an accomplished ballerina and artist; she graduated from high school with honors and made the dean's list in her first two terms and the president's list the next three.

The summer of 1994 sped by, as we were quite busy with a growing young family. Joel turned six in June, and John turned ten in late August. Leahanna would be four in October, and Lauren was nineteen months old when we adopted her in May. On June 10, we had been in Hood River for exactly nine years. The Lord had blessed us much during those years.

The 1994–1995 school year was the tenth year of the school ministry. The Lord faithfully supplied all our needs in abundance, and He would continue to do so for years to come. Even though we may falter at times, the Lord never does. Though we do not always understand His ways, He always does the very best for each of us. "Weeping may endure for a night, but joy comes in the morning" (Psalm 30:5, NKJV).

During the early months of the school year, I continued to pray for the people of Russia. My desire to share the gospel of Jesus Christ in Russia grew stronger and stronger. Having grown up during the Cold War in the country that was Russia's archenemy, this all seemed so odd to me. I began to realize the Lord really was calling me to go to Russia, but how could it happen?

My ears were open, and I started to collect information that moved me in the right direction. I heard there was an openness to the gospel in Russia and that some of the leaders in Russia's educational department were asking for Christian educators to come into the Russian schools to teach the students about Christianity. I'd also heard at the last ACSI conference about a group called the CoMission, made up of more than eighty major Christian ministries working together with Russia's minister of education to teach a course called "Christian Ethics and Morality" in schools all over the former Soviet Union. All of this was absolutely amazing to me. One of the seminars at this fall's ACSI conference was to be about the CoMission, and I was determined to attend. I felt very strongly this was how the Lord was going to take me into Russia.

When we got to the ACSI conference, which started in late October of 1994, I attended the seminar on the CoMission with great anticipation. They began talking about sending a group of people to teach the course I'd heard about in the former Soviet Union. Then they revealed that they were going to send the group to Kiev—in Ukraine.

I was confused and a bit startled by this announcement. Had I misunderstood the Lord about going to Russia? Did He want me to go to Ukraine instead? I quickly dismissed the idea. I was sure God wanted me to go into Russia. But if the CoMission was not going into Russia this year, was I to wait to see if they would go the next year? Was I to go to Russia with some other organization?

I knew the Lord did not want me to wait even one more year, but I was at a loss as to how the trip could happen any sooner. I buried myself in the work of teaching at the school, but I definitely did not put the possibility of going to Russia out of my mind.

About two weeks later, Debbie and I attended a couples conference at the Cannon Beach Christian Conference Center on the Oregon coast. Debbie had attended several yearly women's conferences there with our church. She had been after me for years to go there with her to a couples conference. In November of this year, we finally got it done.

We enjoyed the conference very much. The center brought in a singer from the Portland area for the conference. His name was Wade Mitchell, and one evening Wade gave a mini-concert for about an hour. About halfway through, Wade took a break from singing and announced that he worked for a mission agency called East-West Ministries International. The ministry took short-term mission trips into Russia and other countries of the former Soviet Union. Debbie and I looked at each other

The Call of Russia

with surprise and listened intently to everything Wade had to say. Wade said he would be willing to talk after the concert with anyone who might be interested in going on a mission trip they were going to take the next summer—into *Russia*.

I had talked to Debbie many times about the call I sensed from the Lord, so she worked hard to keep up with me as I made a beeline for Wade the second the concert was over. We sat and talked for almost an hour about East-West Ministries and the trip they were going to take the following summer. We ended our conversation after we invited Wade to come to our house in Hood River to confirm the plans to go into Russia during the coming summer. I could not have been more thrilled.

The school year went by quickly. Wade visited us on a Sunday afternoon in the late spring of 1995 to help me prepare for the trip. He also gave a very enjoyable concert for about an hour at our church that evening. Wade and I spoke on the phone many times and mailed several forms back and forth, getting the passport, visa, and other materials ready for the trip.

The school year ended on Friday, June 2, of 1995. The following week the school took a year-end trip to the Oregon coast. It was a great week; we always had a lot of fun and many meaningful experiences on these year-end trips. We took walks and had a wiener roast with s'mores on the beach. We shopped, had good talks about the Lord each night, and came home exhausted. I spent the next three weeks closing up the school for the summer and getting ready for the trip to Russia. Wade told me we would be going to Kaluga, a city of over three hundred thousand people situated on the Oka River, a little less than one hundred miles south of Moscow.

The main goal of the mission trip was to start an evangelical church in Kaluga. East-West had already done a lot of the groundwork. We were going to go door-to-door throughout the city to tell people about the Lord or invite them to a series of evangelistic meetings we would hold each night. We also hoped to get them plugged into the church we were starting. This fit very nicely with what I felt the Lord was calling me to do.

Personally, this would be the first international trip I had taken completely on my own. I was nervous about it, but I felt the Lord challenging me to do it. I also sensed the Lord was deepening my dependence on Him alone. He was starting to fulfill His Word from the Romanian trip in Psalm 2:8: "Ask of me, and I shall give thee the heathen for thine inheritance, and the uttermost parts of the earth for thy possession."

I had spoken on the phone to Brother John about the upcoming trip, and he was thrilled for me. He asked if there was any chance I could come see him in England on the way home. I felt I just couldn't afford the time, as I was already going to be away from the family for nearly three weeks. I regret that decision to this day.

Early in the morning on Thursday, June 29, Debbie and I and our four children headed for the Portland International Airport. I caught my 10 a.m. flight for Chicago, the first leg of the long journey to Moscow, the capital of Russia. After a teary good-bye at the departure area, I headed inside to check my bags and catch the Boeing 757.

After boarding the crowded jet, I discovered it was over half-filled with teenagers who were headed for the Special Olympics in Chicago. They were so excited. They cheered when the stewardess closed the door. They cheered when the plane started racing down the runway. They cheered again when it lifted off. It was impossible not to get caught up in their joy.

After a short layover in Chicago, I boarded a jam-packed Boeing 747 headed for Frankfurt, Germany. It was a grueling nine-and-a-half-hour flight with just a few fitful naps during the short night. We took off from Chicago at 5 p.m. and landed in Frankfurt at 5:30 the next morning. We crossed seven more time zones (nine altogether) and circled the airport two or three times.

There was a four-hour layover in Frankfurt, so I had breakfast and wandered around the airport before heading to my gate in the international wing. I arrived at the gate about a half-hour early, as I was supposed to meet with a family and a man from Texas who were to be part of our mission team to Russia. The family was J.D. and Anne McCaslin and their fifteen-year-old daughter, Carter. The man was Randy Cox, who would be my roommate for the first two weeks of the trip.

When I got to the gate, there was no one there, so I sat in one of the chairs facing the concourse. I often enjoy just sitting quietly and studying people in various settings. After a few minutes, I saw two men race up to the gate across from mine about two minutes after they shut it for the departure. The attendant coldly told them they were too late. Even though they protested vehemently, the woman stood her ground. I thought that was rather harsh. It worried me, as the people I was supposed to meet had not yet arrived. There were only ten minutes remaining before we were to board our plane to Moscow.

The ten minutes went quickly, and no one from our team came to the gate. We were called to get on a bus that would take us to our plane on the runway. I felt very uneasy as I boarded the Airbus A320 alone. Randy was not only to be my roommate; he was also the one who was supposed to help me get through the airport at Moscow and connect me with the other team members.

I had been given a picture of Randy, so I quickly searched the plane to see if he was already aboard. He was not there. I got very worried as the crew readied the plane for takeoff. I wondered how I could make my way through the Moscow airport alone. How would I meet with other team members I had never seen or met? Even though the plane seemed to be ready, we didn't move for a few more minutes. I grew more tense with each passing minute.

As I sat with these troublesome thoughts swirling in my head, I began to pray. Just then a group of passengers burst through the door. Among them were Randy and the McCaslins. I breathed a huge sigh of relief. I did not even tell them the story of the two gentlemen who were denied boarding their plane. Randy and the McCaslins boarded at least ten minutes after we were scheduled to depart. They settled into their reserved seats right across the aisle from my seat. Only the Lord could do something like that on a plane that large (an Airbus A320 can hold up to 150 passengers in a long, narrow fuselage)! After some brief introductions, we were directed to prepare for takeoff. Immediately we were in the air. Randy, the McCaslins, and I talked and got acquainted for about twenty more minutes before we all rested for most of the remaining flight.

We slept for about two-and-a-half hours before we were awakened for dinner. After three hours of flying and crossing two more time zones, we touched down in Moscow at 6 p.m. on Friday, the thirtieth of June. We soon deplaned into the mass confusion and huge lines of the Moscow International Airport.

Going through passport clearance took over an hour, but finding our luggage and going through customs took only a few minutes. Afterward, we waited over an hour trying to find the person who was supposed to pick us up and take us to our hotel. Finally, we gave up and piled the six of us (including the taxi driver) and all of our luggage (which included five large suitcases and seven other duffel bags, smaller suitcases, and backpacks) into a small taxicab and drove to the magnificent Hotel Rossia. Right across the street from the hotel was St. Basil's Cathedral, sitting majestically on the edge of Red Square. It was just within the wall of the Kremlin, the very heart of Moscow.

In the hotel, we met with teammates Julie Henry from Dallas, Texas, the team's "Girl Friday" who had taken care of all the trip details (visas, passports, airfare, accommodations, meals, etc.); Doug McCary, our team leader, a huge man who had left the FBI to serve full-time with East-West Ministries; Keith Miller, a businessman from Dallas who had come on the first trip to Kaluga to set up this trip; Sue Wilcox, Tracy Potratz, Kim Singer, and Mark Hobson from Atlanta; and a student from Volgagrad (in southwestern Russia) named Inna.

After Julie gave us our room assignments, we settled into our rooms. Then we headed for the subway to get some lunch at the world's largest McDonald's. The subways in Moscow were amazing. We took an escalator, lit by large, beautiful, chandelier-like lights, about two hundred feet into the underground caverns. The walls were mostly white with a few designs trimming them and no advertisements or graffiti at all.

The trains came promptly every fifteen minutes; they were neat and clean as well. We rode for several minutes and only changed trains once on our way to our destination. The restaurant was full of people sitting in several different sections. Each section had a unique theme of American characters from different cartoons and animated movies. It had a seating capacity for about eight hundred people.

By the time we arrived at the restaurant, I was beginning to feel the effects of sleep deprivation pretty well. Even though it was fairly full, we got our food quickly and found an open table immediately. As I attempted to put my tray onto the table in my weariness, I did not realize it was still about eight inches above the surface when I released it. It crashed onto the table, and the large cola on the tray fell to the floor and spilled everywhere. Before I could even figure out what to do, a young man appeared with a mop and bucket and cleaned up my mess for me. A few moments later he reappeared bearing a fresh cola for me. I was very grateful and very impressed.

After we got back from our food forage, we went to our rooms, and I took a refreshing and reviving shower. Then Randy and I talked until one o'clock in the morning. It was only noon back in Oregon and two in the afternoon in Texas, Randy's home state, so even though we were exhausted, we spent several hours getting to know each other and explaining how we had ended up on this mission trip before we went to bed. I was thrilled to be here to share the gospel with the people of Russia even though the thought of going door-to-door to tell them about the Lord made me apprehensive. I deeply hoped and prayed that the people would be open to it.

After only four hours of sleep, I awoke at 5 a.m. with the sun already rising. Randy was up, so we talked for another three hours before heading up for breakfast on the twenty-first floor of the hotel. The view of the Kremlin was outstanding. At breakfast, many of us met the president and founder of East-West Ministries International, John Maisel, for the first time. John had come into Russia as early as 1987 and preached an apologetic sermon entitled "Is Jesus God?" to the staff of the Moscow State University. This was the very heart of atheistic communism in the Soviet Union. About 25 percent of the staff came forward to receive Christ as their personal Savior and Lord at the conclusion of the sermon, something unheard of, and very risky, at that time. This sermon was printed into a booklet about eighty-five pages long. We used it, along with two other booklets, to help bring people to Christ while in Kaluga.

After breakfast, we toured Red Square and part of Moscow before returning to the hotel to have sandwiches for lunch. We spent the afternoon walking through the rest of the Kremlin, which surrounds Red Square. The many churches with their golden onion tops were incredibly beautiful, and several other sights were quite remarkable as well. It amazed me to be walking through what was regarded just over three years ago as a bastion of evil. Moscow was now caught up in the turmoil of attempting to convert a formerly socialist dictatorship into a free market republic, and we were here to start a church and tell people about Jesus Christ. Our God is truly amazing.

Shortly after dinner that night, we went to the Old Moscow Circus and witnessed amazing feats of strength, skill, and agility over body and beast. An eleven-year-old girl twirled eighty-five hula hoops at once. Young men and women did incredible acrobatics while dangling from ropes more than thirty feet above the floor, with no net below them. Others did multiple flips on the trapeze, persuaded large bears to dance, and juggled with all kinds of objects while constantly changing their formation. It was hard to believe all I was seeing.

Carter McCaslin was so exhausted she slept through most of the circus. After making our way back to the hotel through the massive Moscow subway system, we visited a short while and turned in for the night. The purpose of those two days in Moscow was to get acclimated to the culture and the time difference. We were eleven hours ahead of Oregon time, and the adjustment was somewhat difficult.

I woke up at four-thirty in the morning after another short night. I had a wonderful quiet time with the Lord, reading the Scriptures and praying while trying to hear His quiet voice. At seven o'clock I readied myself for breakfast. It was Sunday, July 2, and after an enjoyable breakfast of cucumbers, tomatoes, cheese, ham, bread, an omelet of sorts, and chai (the Russian word for "tea"), we headed out to hold a church service in another part of Moscow.

After another pleasant ride on the subway and a short walk, we found where we were going to hold our church service…a parking lot. We had one difficulty to overcome: it was now pouring rain. Some people who owned a building being remodeled right next door saw our plight and let us have our service in their foyer. About two hundred of us worshiped the Lord there. John Maisel gave a challenging sermon on courage, taken from the first chapter of Joshua. Our team was made up of thirteen Americans, four Russian men who were students from a Bible training school that East-West had started in Moscow the previous year, and four interpreters. We met with Wade Mitchell's father, Ron, in Kaluga, along with seven or eight other interpreters. Four people from a church in Kaluga, who wanted to help and learn our methods of church planting and evangelism, also joined us. A few more helpers were added later to bring our team total to forty-two people.

Our luggage was stowed in compartments under the passenger section of the bus, and a large storage space at the back of our bus was filled with dozens of boxes of booklets, tracts, and Russian Bibles. We gave these to anyone in Kaluga who would accept them. We soon found they accepted them readily.

Two booklets were transcripts of two excellent apologetic sermons written and preached by John Maisel: "Is Jesus God?" and "Can I Know for Sure?" Both were about eighty-five pages long. The tracts were Bill Bright's "The Four Spiritual Laws" translated into Russian. We also had several boxes of Russian Bibles.

We traveled for about three hours in a southwesterly direction from Moscow through the Russian countryside of vast forests, mostly birch, pine, and fir. Farms, some sizable, which grew grains, hay, and vegetables, were sprinkled here and there along the way. I was impressed with the immensity of the country. Romania had more hills and mountains that kept the scenery fairly close. This area of Russia had vast forests and plains that stretched for miles.

At last, we arrived in Kaluga and settled into the fairly crude rooms of the Kaluga Hotel. Still not entirely adjusted to the time zone, I took a long nap in the room Randy and I shared. Afterward, we headed downstairs for dinner and a planning meeting, where we met some of our interpreters. The dinner and meeting were held in a large room with an adjoining bar. We had rented the entire area, so the bar was closed while we met. At the beginning of the meeting, John Maisel told us 90 percent of being a Christian was just showing up. At first this statement confused me, but as our time in Russia passed, it made more and more sense. He also advised us that two things were essential while ministering in Russia: flexibility and a good sense of humor. I soon learned how true this statement was!

During the rest of the meeting, we were given our building assignments and instructions on what to say as we visited each apartment. We were to invite the occupants to the evangelistic meetings we were going to hold for the next five nights at the cultural center in Kaluga. We were also to give them some of the booklets if they were open to discussing spiritual matters. If they prayed to receive the Lord, we could give them a Russian Bible if they did not already own one.

After being given several other general instructions and going over the schedule for the day and the week, we ended the meeting by getting acquainted with our translators. Some were language students from a nearby university, and others were believers from a church in Kaluga who wanted to learn how to evangelize as well as translate. We were told that about half our translators from the university did not know the Lord, even though they were willing to work with us. We paid all of our translators at the end of the week. They all were very nice people and did an extremely capable job of translating.

After the meeting adjourned, we spent about a half-hour in the lobby of the floor where our rooms were located. Our music team practiced some of the Russian choruses they would sing during the upcoming meetings. The three Russian female floor attendants smiled broadly as they listened. Then we headed for our rooms to hopefully get a good night's rest.

When Randy and I got to our room, it was quite hot and stuffy, with no air-conditioning or fans. So we opened our windows to let in the cool night air and an army of mosquitoes. There were no screens on the windows. Needless to say, we had a very fitful night's sleep trying to fight off the B-52-sized mosquitoes *(slight* exaggeration intended).

After only two or three hours of sleep and many battles with persistently pesky mosquitoes, Randy and I got up to get ready for the day ahead. At breakfast, we learned that Tracy Potratz and Kim Singer, who were on the music team and were scheduled to give their testimonies at the evening meeting, had not slept at all. John Maisel offered to let them stay at the hotel to rest, but they kindly refused, determined to serve the Lord. We were just beginning to have "flexibility and have a sense of humor."

As the day progressed, we also learned that one of our main speakers for the music team had disappeared in Voronezh (a city in southwestern Russia where part of our team had been ministering the week before they joined us in Kaluga); a planned evangelistic meeting with about two hundred children from a Pioneer Club had been canceled without explanation; only two hundred of the eleven hundred invitations to our meetings had been printed; seven or eight of our translators were not able to be with us until the next day because they had to take their final exams for the year; and our best translator, a young lady named Olga, had had to leave suddenly and go back to Moscow because of a family problem. We had scheduled a large bus to take us and all of our music equipment across town to the cultural center each day. We numbered about twenty and would grow to forty-two by the end of the week. An old, sixteen-passenger bus pulled up to the hotel.

It was time again to be flexible with a good sense of humor. With only three remaining translators, we canceled our plans to visit our assigned buildings for the morning and split into groups of four or five people with each translator to witness on the streets. Wade had told me in some of our conversations before the trip that they often saw three to five hundred people a day commit their lives to the Lord. I was thinking we would be doing well if even a few people came to the Lord on this day (and maybe the entire trip), the way things were starting out. My faith was small, but our God is big.

We had a brief meeting after we arrived at the cultural center, and then we hit the streets to invite people to our meetings and talk to them about receiving Jesus Christ as their Lord and Savior. We ran out of invitations by eleven in the morning, so we started writing the time and place of the meetings on the backs of the tracts. Doug McCary led a ten- or eleven-year-old boy to the Lord by explaining to him how God had set the rainbow in the sky after the great flood. We saw him several more times during the week and always referred to him as "the rainbow boy." Several individuals and small groups of people listened intently as we explained about the meetings and talked about the Lord. God was just beginning to move.

All of us met together for lunch at a restaurant and shared accounts of what the Lord had been doing throughout the morning. Things were getting exciting, but first we had to learn a little more flexibility. After lunch we were instructed to go to the cultural center and wait about an hour for the rest of our invitations to arrive. They arrived at three o'clock, but their lateness did not hinder the Lord. With what was left of the afternoon, we went to our assigned buildings and began to invite people to our meetings and tell them about the Lord. I left with my translator, a young woman named Tanya, to find the building assigned to me. After a short while, we found what we thought was the right place.

We went in through the front door into a dimly lit foyer. A stairway led to the upper floors of the building, and two doors led to separate wings of the first floor. We entered the door to the right, and when it closed behind us, we found ourselves in a narrow, pitch-black hallway. Without even a faint light seeping in, we felt our way along the right wall until we came to a doorway. We knocked on it twice, but no one came. So we made our way to the second door. The result was the same. We fumbled our way to the end of the hallway before we found someone who answered his door.

As soon as the young man appeared in the doorway, I got nervous. What should I say? We had been trained to introduce ourselves and invite people to the meetings. After a quick emergency prayer, I began with Tanya's help to explain who we were and what we were doing. Before I got halfway through my little speech, he said a few words to Tanya and abruptly left the doorway. I thought, *Great, the first person we talk to, and he leaves us standing at the door.* Before I went too far with this line of thinking, I asked Tanya what he had said. She told me he had asked us to wait for a moment because he wanted his wife to hear what we were saying.

Before my surprise could wear off, he was back with his wife. We told them both who we were, and we invited them to the meeting that was going to start in just a few hours. Emboldened by their receptiveness, I went on to tell them about Jesus Christ and how to become one of His followers. To my utter astonishment, they both prayed and committed their lives to the Lord.

Energized by this amazing event, we went through as much of the building as we could before going to the cultural center to help set up for the meeting. Before we left the building, five people committed their lives to following the Lord. I was beyond amazed; I was ecstatic. I had never in my life seen such openness to spiritual matters. Perhaps seventy-five years of socialism had created an immense hunger for the Lord. I would soon find that, for whatever the reason, there was an incredible yearning for Jesus Christ in Kaluga.

After a mad rush to set up for the meeting, about two hundred people showed up. About half of them were children and half were adults. The children were taken to another room to be shown a movie about the Lord and then given a talk. The VCR projector did not work, so the people working with the children learned a little more flexibility! When both of the meetings were over, approximately one hundred people had prayed to commit their lives to the Lord. All my negative and unbelieving thoughts were silenced for the rest of the trip. Praise God for His faithfulness! "If we are faithless, He remains faithful; for He cannot deny Himself" (2 Timothy 2:13, NASB).

We had a late dinner after the meetings were over and shared about our experiences that day and all the Lord had done. J.D. McCaslin stood up and said, "Unbelievable!" and then went on to tell of his experience on the way to his assigned building. Every time J.D. stood up to share, he began with this same expression. After he did this three or four times, everyone at the meal would shout "Unbelievable!" each time J.D. stood up to speak.

On this first exclamation, J.D. told how he was on his way to his assigned building when he noticed three or four people about to pass him on the sidewalk. Before they went by, the Spirit of God prompted J.D. to tell them about salvation through Jesus Christ. After he got about halfway through his presentation, another three or four people stopped to listen. He asked the original group if they would mind if he started from the beginning again. They said they would like him to begin anew because they wanted to hear what he had said again. After getting about halfway through his talk a second time, more people stopped to listen. So J.D. asked once more if those listening would mind if he started over a third time. They again repeated that they would like to hear it again. This cycle happened once more before J.D. was able to get through the entire explanation. After he finished, about fifteen people prayed and committed their lives to the Lord. Unbelievable!

In the morning, I woke up at 5:45. It was the Fourth of July, and it was a glorious morning. I took a walk toward the center of Kaluga before joining the others for breakfast at eight. We were given a few more instructions before we packed into the little blue bus and headed for the cultural center. We stuffed more booklets, tracts, and Russian Bibles into our backpacks before we headed out to the buildings and streets.

Tanya and I went to the building we had visited the day before to see if we could find some of the people who had not been home. There was a large number two on the front corner of the building, so we always creatively referred to it as building number two. Tanya proved to be an excellent interpreter. She loved the Lord and knew her Bible well. In that morning, five people committed their lives to the Lord; in the afternoon, five more did the same.

It was an amazing day. Only one lady turned us away without hearing the gospel. One of her neighbors later told me she was a hard-core member of the communist party. We met another lady on the stairway of the building. She confessed to us that she had a problem with drinking. Before we could share with her how Jesus Christ could set her free from her slavery to alcohol and give her eternal life, the hard-core communist lady came down the stairs and pulled her away by her arm. We prayed immediately that we might have another opportunity to speak with the alcoholic lady about the Lord. About three hours later, she again found us on the stairway. She thanked us with hugs and kisses (kisses on the cheek in the Russian tradition) through tears of gratitude for the hope of Christ.

At another apartment, a woman answered the door after I knocked on it and quickly invited us in. As I entered the room, a man who had not a stitch of clothing on was hurriedly trying to cover himself with some sheets while lying on some sort of sleeping couch. I quickly backed out of the room to give the man some privacy and to keep Tanya from entering the room. Tanya was baffled by my strange actions until I explained to her what was going on. Then she felt great relief! The wife of the naked man insisted we come inside, even though her husband was covered with only a sheet. So we reluctantly came into the room, and to my surprise, within a few minutes they both prayed to commit their lives to the Lord.

While knocking on the door of yet another apartment, Tanya and I were warned by a neighbor that a very bad man lived there. Through Tanya, I told the neighbor that Jesus was in the business of making bad men good. He gave us his hearty approval to see the man. A moment later, the door was opened by a very nice middle-aged Russian woman. Her husband was drunk. His name was Slava, and her name was Dusya. Slava wanted me to go drink some vodka with him. After I told him I didn't drink, he sold me two incredibly beautiful wood-burning pictures he had made with a crude wood-burning tool for five dollars. I tried to tell him I thought they were worth much more than that, but he would not hear it. He went on to explain that he wanted me to live with Dusya and him. I told him I could not do that as I had a family back in the United States. He understood and accepted that. After a short while, Tanya and I left; we weren't getting anywhere under the circumstances. I was determined, though, to come back.

At this point, Tanya and I realized we were too late to help set things up at the cultural center. As we hurried to get there for the beginning of the meeting, we noticed people pouring onto the streets from the buildings and alleyways. They were all going in the same direction we were. Then it dawned on us: they were all going to the meeting. That night over four hundred people came to the cultural center. About two hundred of them stayed afterward and committed their lives to following Jesus.

After dinner that night, Wade Mitchell shared an experience he'd had while telling the way of salvation to an elderly woman in a square in the middle of four buildings earlier in the day. She seemed to be the matriarch of the whole area, and when Wade asked her if she wanted to pray to become a follower of the Lord, she barked a command and everyone in the square bowed their heads to pray. When it was explained to Wade what was going on, he asked the *babushka* (the Russian word for grandmother or old woman) if it would be all right if he explained to all the people what they were praying about. She thought that would be all right, so he explained to everyone in the square the plan of salvation. When he was done, once more everyone bowed their heads to pray to commit their lives to the Lord.

Kim Singer gave the account of her and her translator overhearing a woman who ran into another square full of people shouting, "Find the Americans; they are telling everyone about Jesus!" The stories went on and on; praise God for all His amazing goodness!

After breakfast and devotions the next morning, thirty-one of us headed for the cultural center on the little bus. Tanya and I picked up some materials at the center before we headed to our assigned building for the day. The morning was hot, tiring, and discouraging. Only seven people accepted invitations to the meetings. Four of those seemed receptive to the gospel up to the point of praying to commit their lives to Christ, then each abruptly declined. One young man was argumentative. But the Lord still had much in store for the day.

I was encouraged by the accounts others on the team shared at lunch. Right after lunch, Tanya and I talked to a young woman about Christ only one block from the cultural center. She prayed to commit her life to the Lord right there on the sidewalk. We went back to the first building we had visited on Monday afternoon and found five people at home whom we had not visited previously. Three of them prayed to become Christians, one accepted an invitation, and one was a Christian already. One lady who prayed to become a Christian could not hear enough about the Lord. She sat straight up on the edge of her seat as we explained the way of salvation and cried tears of joy when she prayed.

Late in the afternoon we went back to the building where we had been so discouraged in the morning and talked to the neighbor of the man who had been so argumentative. About halfway through our talk, he came into the building and approached his door, which was only a few feet away. As he paused to find his key, the man we were speaking to asked him what he thought of the things we were talking about. To our surprise, he told him he thought we said some pretty good things, and he encouraged the man to attend our meetings. The last lady we talked to before leaving the building for the evening prayed to commit her life to the Lord. We left joyfully praising God.

About two hundred adults and one hundred children attended the meeting that night at the cultural center. John Maisel gave an excellent sermon. At the end, about one hundred adults came to the front of the auditorium and prayed to give their lives to the Lord. About eighty of the children did the same in their meeting. We sang songs of praise to the Lord all the way back to the hotel. We had a great dinner and went to bed physically exhausted but spiritually exhilarated.

After a good night's sleep and a pleasant breakfast together, we packed into the bus and headed for the cultural center. It was already Thursday, July 6. The team would be leaving on Saturday. After picking up some materials, Tanya and I headed back to the building where we'd been the day before. During the morning, two more people prayed to commit their lives to the Lord. Hallelujah!

At lunch, we heard more great accounts of people praying to become followers of Christ. In the afternoon, Tanya and I went back to building number two and covered the entire part of the building which was assigned to us. No one prayed with us, and we were only able to hand out a few invitations to our two remaining meetings. Just as we were leaving to go to a follow-up meeting with some of the people who had committed to the Christian faith earlier in the week, we met a woman we had not yet visited. We talked to her about Christ, and she prayed to receive Him as her Lord and Savior right at the front door. We praised God again for His gracious timing.

By now Wade's father, Ron Mitchell, had come from doing follow-up work in Voronezh to join us in Kaluga. He led a follow-up meeting attended by twelve adults, fifteen children, and some of the team members. I was amazed at how little the people knew about Christianity. Seventy-five years of atheistic socialism had made its mark, but it had also unwittingly created a great hunger for the Lord.

Once more, about two hundred adults and one hundred children attended the evening meeting. Doug McCary did a masterful job preaching that night. My roommate, Randy Cox, gave a very good testimony, and the music team was superb once more. At the end of the meeting, about eighty adults and several children prayed to commit their lives to the Lord. They stayed long afterward to talk more about Jesus to be sure they understood what they were doing. Even more prayed to receive Christ in the aftermeeting. It was absolutely glorious.

After a bumpy ride back to the hotel, we had dinner and another great sharing time about the day's events. We learned that the director of the cultural center had paid out of her own pocket for a local television station to come to the center and interview some of our team members. Afterward, she intimated to some of our team that her heart was pounding as she listened to the interviews. She promised she and her husband would come to Friday's meeting.

We were also told that some of our team members had gone to a disco establishment in the area, and several of the young people had listened to them as they shared the gospel. We went to bed that night having experienced another amazing day of watching our Lord do miraculous things. All we had needed to do was show up.

That night I slept deeply until seven-thirty in the morning. We had breakfast and devotions an hour later than usual. I used the opportunity to ride a bus across town with one of the interpreters to call Debbie and the children. The call was only three minutes long, and it cost me thirty dollars. While I was paying at the front counter, I could see into the back room. They were still using the type of switchboard operators the United States had used more than thirty years before. No wonder it cost so much!

Our little bus carried us to the cultural center by 11 a.m., so Tanya and I went back to building number two once more. We met a lady who had been at the meeting the previous night. She prayed with us to become a follower of Christ. After lunch, we went back to some of the other buildings we had visited previously, and six more people prayed to ask Jesus to be their Lord and Savior.

One of those who prayed was a lady named Masha. We met her at the top of the stairwell in building number four. Had we left the building a minute earlier, we never would have met her; she did not even live in that building! She told us she lived on the other side of the city. Because we took the time to share the gospel with Masha, we met and talked to another lady, named Tatyana, at the bottom of the stairs. Tatyana also prayed to commit her life to the Lord. What a difference one minute made! The Lord's timing is unparalleled.

The last evening meeting was well attended by almost two hundred adults and nearly three hundred children. When the invitation was given for the adults to commit their lives to Christ, almost all of them prayed to receive Christ. In the children's meeting, all of the children committed their lives to the Lord. One of the adults was Slava, the man who was drunk when I visited him. He promised that he would never drink again. The Lord did much in Kaluga that week, and He would do more in the week to come.

After the meeting ended, we jammed forty people and all our sound equipment into the little blue bus for the last time. It was a joyous ride back to the hotel, followed by a good dinner and another excellent time of sharing what the Lord had accomplished during the day. Randy Cox shared that he had been frisked by the police that day and put into their car. His interpreter had to convince them he was not a criminal before they let him go. Randy had invited them to come to the evening meeting. One of the officers promised he would come.

After dinner, we had a long fellowship time in the fourth-floor lobby. For many of us, it was the last time we spent together. It had been an incredible week. There were no accidents, and not one cross word was spoken by anyone on the entire mission team, only constant encouragement. Hundreds of people committed their lives to Christ, and a brand-new church was birthed. We stayed up enjoying each other until two o'clock in the morning.

I got up after a short night's sleep and had breakfast with John Maisel, Randy Cox, and J.D., Anne, and Carter McCaslin. After breakfast, everyone from the mission team except Ron Mitchell, myself, and two interpreters packed into the tiny bus for the departure to Moscow. I fought back tears as we watched them pull away from the front of the hotel. What a blessed group of people.

Ron and I rested in our room for a while after the mission team left. We spent the rest of the morning walking through a marketplace near the hotel. It had hundreds of little booths with patient peddlers in their workaday world. Throngs of people jostled through the market looking for a good buy. Without buying anything, Ron and I made our way back to the hotel for a lunch of snacks in our room.

We rested in the afternoon on both sides of a visit from three of our interpreters. After a big dinner at the hotel's restaurant, Ron and I read and relaxed in our room before retiring for the night. What a wonderful, relaxing day it was after an extremely busy week.

We woke up Sunday morning after a good night's sleep and met our interpreters, Tanya and Julianna, downstairs after breakfast. We rode on a city bus to the cultural center. The bus was packed with people headed for work on the Lord's Day. Andre, the pastor of the newly formed church, met us at the center. We waited outside for some New Testaments to arrive. When they were delivered, we took them to a restaurant where the very first service of the new church was to be held. Fifty people attended the service, including seven of our team members, three of whom were Russians from Kaluga and Moscow; Andre and a friend; sixteen newly converted adults; and twenty-five children. Andre opened with prayer and led us in singing two worship songs with the help of Julianna. Ron and I each spoke before Andre made some closing remarks and ended our worship time with a song and a prayer. The little church was making a very good start.

During the next five days, Ron Mitchell, Tanya, Julianna, and I made many follow-up calls to the people visited the week before. We also met and talked to some new people about the Lord. We met twice with Andre and two men who wanted to help with the new church. One of the men, Alvin, took us out to share the Lord with about 150 children at a summer camp. After Alvin and I had both spoken, every one of the children prayed to become Christians. Some of them indicated afterward that they had prayed before to become Christians but just wanted to do it again. It was wonderful to see such eagerness to follow the Lord.

Tanya and I also stopped by to see Slava and Dusya four more times. At first, Slava said he had not prayed to receive the Lord at the evening meeting he and Dusya attended. He later prayed again with us to commit his life to the Lord during a lunch we all had together. At two of our meetings, Slava had been drinking, one time even after he prayed with us. Some seem to have great difficulty entering the kingdom of God. During one of the visits, Slava signed another of his remarkable wood-burnt pictures with his name and my name and the day we became friends and gave it to me. All three of his wood-burnt pictures hang on the wall of my study to this day.

We also met with a young woman named Margarita who asked many, many good questions. We made an appointment to see her two days later so we could answer all her questions more thoroughly. After lunch, Tanya and I made four more calls in the afternoon. The last lady we saw had prayed to commit her life to the Lord with Tracy Potratz the week before. We reminded her that her sins were forgiven through Christ's atoning death on the cross. She then asked us if Jesus would forgive anything, and we assured her that He would. With her head bowed in deep humility and shame, she asked if He would forgive her for having an abortion. We shared with her from Psalm 103:12 that, "As far as the east is from the west, so far has He removed our transgressions from us" (NASB). After we shared with her a few more Scriptures, she quietly thanked us as the tears rolled down her cheeks. What a striking reminder that God truly does not remember our sins anymore (Hebrews 8:12)!

Tanya and I met with Margarita to talk and have lunch together two days later. Margarita had had so many questions about Christianity when we'd met with her before, I felt led by the Lord to give her a condensed account of God's relationship and dealings with humanity from creation to the end of time. We shared the account for an hour and a half. When I finished, I told her that I had much more I would like to say, but I thought her head was full for now. She said her head was full, but she wanted to hear more. What great thirst she had for the things of the Lord!

Some of the other interpreters visited us throughout the week, some more than once. We even attended the wedding ceremony of one of the interpreters. On Thursday, about twenty minutes after getting back to my room, three of the interpreters, Inna, Lena, and Sergei, came to take Ron and me around the town to show us some of the sights of Kaluga. We said we were too tired to go out, so they stayed and visited for two hours.

During our visit, they confessed that when they had agreed to interpret for us, they'd made a pact not to give in to our Christian beliefs. Inna had made a commitment to the Lord earlier in her life but had drifted away from following Him. During the week they interpreted for us, Inna recommitted her life to the Lord, and Lena prayed to become a Christian for the first time. Sergei said he intended to commit his life to following Jesus, but he wanted a little more time to think about it. We talked about the things of the Lord for almost the entire two hours.

About thirty minutes after they left, another interpreter, Ilena, came to our room and told us the people at the front desk wanted to see us to straighten out a few details. She stayed and talked about the Lord with us for about an hour. She had been confused regarding some things about Christianity. The talk proved to be a very profitable time for her. I pray all of these are still faithfully following the Lord.

During the weekend, I started preparing to go *home*. I hadn't seen my family for nearly three weeks. On Sunday morning, I woke up at 5:45 and did my final packing after a quiet time with the Lord and another breakfast of snacks. After a sorrowful good-bye to Ron, Tanya and I got on a city bus that took us to the Kaluga intercity bus station. We left at eight o'clock and arrived at Moscow around eleven after an uneventful but scenic bus ride.

Tanya helped me check in after we found our way to the hotel. We left my bags at the hotel before taking the metro to two outdoor markets in search of gifts for my family. After two hours of shopping and riding the metro, we returned to the hotel empty-handed, only to find a shop two blocks from the hotel that had just the right gifts for my wife and children.

I paid Tanya for her masterful interpreting for me while we were on the street just outside the hotel. After a sad farewell and agreeing to keep in contact, I went up to my room.

I had a hard time getting to sleep that night, thinking about going home to my family.

The alarm jolted me to consciousness at four in the morning after only three hours of sleep. After breakfast, I gathered my luggage and went down to the front of the hotel. I was supposed to meet a man named Valentine who was scheduled to take me to the airport. When I got downstairs, no one was in front of the hotel except a man across the front drive working on his car. I waited for several minutes, vainly hoping for Valentine to show up. My anxiety level was rising with each minute. At twenty after five, I had barely enough time to get to the airport to catch my plane. Praying like crazy, I called to the man across the parking lot, "Taxi?" He lifted himself from under the hood and said, *"Da,"* yes. I asked him if he could get me to the airport in time to catch a 7:20 flight. Fortunately he could speak English, and he told me we would have to go really fast to make it.

We quickly agreed to a price which was only a little more than what Valentine would have charged me. Then we threw my bags into the trunk and raced for the airport. He drove through the streets of Moscow at seventy miles an hour, slowing only where he thought the police might be on patrol. It helped immensely that the streets were nearly empty this early in the morning. We made it to the airport with just enough time to check in and go through customs before boarding the plane.

I rushed in and checked in at the ticket counter, then sailed through customs and checked my bags with about twenty minutes to spare. The only thing left before boarding was to go through the visa and passport check.

When it was my turn, I stepped up to the booth where a lady in a military uniform was checking passports and visas. She briefly looked at my passport, but she took an inordinate amount of time looking at my visa. After what seemed like forever, she pushed my passport and visa toward me without the exit stamp, said, "Visa expired," and waved me back toward the ticket counters. I understood instantly with great horror that she was not going to let me board the plane. I said with some urgency, "What do I do?" She waved me off again. I said again with great urgency, "What do I do?"

The woman could see I was not going to budge until she got someone to help me, so she called out to a short, stout lady wearing what looked like a high-ranking military officer's uniform. After she briefly spoke with her, I was directed with a hand motion to follow the stout lady. I thought about some of the horror stories I had heard in the past about people under the deposed communist regime being taken into back rooms and beaten with hard rubber clubs while under interrogation. I had pretty much dismissed that thought from my mind when she took me into a back room. The room had a large table in the center with about a dozen people in uniform sitting around it intensely shuffling through stacks of papers. I was relieved to see no rubber clubs. The stout lady handed my papers to one of the people close to the door. She looked at them for about one minute, curtly handed them back to the stout lady, and said a few words to her. The stout lady turned to me and said, "Visa expired."

After that revelation, I asked the stout lady what to do. She also waved me off. Almost in a panic, I loudly asked her again, "What do I do?" She called to a man, who came over immediately to see what the trouble was. He explained to me that I would have to speak to the American consulate to get my visa extended, and then I would have to go to a ticket agent and get my ticket changed. He also informed me the American consul would not be in until nine o'clock. I told him my plane was leaving in less than twenty minutes. He replied flatly, "That is not my problem." I was more than a bit stunned.

The man took me down to a lower level of the airport, filled with trolleys heaped with luggage. He looked at my ticket and in less than two minutes located the trolley with my suitcases on it. After he pulled them off and handed them to me, he led me back upstairs, took me over to a ticket agent, and left. This lady was as stout as the last one and didn't look any friendlier. She spoke English fluently, so I was able to describe my dilemma to her without any difficulties. She looked at my ticket and started searching her computer screen for another booking. She said it would cost me $150 to change my ticket and another $150 to get my visa extended.

I told her I only had sixty dollars left in my pocket, but she made no response as she continued searching for a new booking. The next thing out of her mouth nearly sent me over the edge. She said I couldn't get a flight out of the country until September. It was July 17. I was too upset to speak or even pray.

Noticing my shell shock, she asked to see my ticket once more. Then the miracles started. After thumbing through the pages of my ticket packet for a few moments, she said I had been double-booked for my exit. I could get on the next flight. I almost cried as I remembered Julie Henry telling me I could go out either Monday, July 17, or Tuesday, July 18. I had felt that our work in Kaluga was finished, so I had decided to leave on Monday to get home one day earlier.

I felt like dancing, but before I could, the ticket agent took some visa extension papers and started asking me questions. As she filled in the blanks on this formidable-looking form, she came to a question that asked me to state why I had come to Russia. I balked. I wondered if she was sympathetic to the old communist regime and would be offended at the distinctly Christian activities I had done while in Russia.

I did not want to lie, so I quietly told her I had come to help start a church. Before I could say another word, she grabbed the papers and my ticket and said, "I will take care of this for you." It was now a few minutes past nine, so she went up to the consulate's office and left me standing at the counter. After about twenty minutes, she returned with an extended visa for me. I asked her how much I owed her for the new booking and the visa extension. She said I owed her nothing and went on to explain that there would be no charge for someone who had done something so kind for her country!

I was absolutely jubilant. Then she said I could either fly out at 4:30 that afternoon, stay the night in Frankfurt, Germany, and catch a connecting flight in the morning; or I could stay the night in Moscow and catch an early morning flight out of the country. I was in no mood to spend one more day in Russia, so I told her I wanted to take the flight to Frankfurt. I thanked her exceedingly as she typed up a new ticket for me. She assured me it was she who was more thankful.

I walked slowly around the airport for the next several hours to pass the time. I read the signs on the wall (which were in both Russian and English) so many times that I actually began to understand some of the Russian. About an hour before my boarding time, I went to the gate. I didn't want to take any chance on missing this plane! While I waited, I heard some people near me speaking in English. After listening to them for a little while, I could tell they were Christians. I asked them who they were and why they had come to Russia. They told me they had come with Campus Crusade for Christ and had worked with some of the East-West team members in Volgograd in June. We talked until it was time to board the plane. They were like angels sent from God Himself—not the first, nor the last, angels I have encountered in my journey!

When the plane touched down in Frankfurt four hours later, I was very thankful to be back on western soil. I found a Sheraton Hotel adjoined to the airport, so I checked into a room for a relaxing evening. I tried to call Debbie several times to let her know I would not be coming into Portland on my original flight, but I never did reach her; I had forgotten she and the children would be staying the night with her mother in Gresham. They would go to the airport from her house in the morning. I didn't realize how much trauma this was going to cause. I assumed the people at the airport would be able to tell her what had happened. I could not have been more wrong.

I awoke at 5:45 after a restful night, rejoicing that I would be home with my family this day (even though "this day" was going to be thirty-three hours long after crossing nine time zones). After showering, packing my bag, and trying to call Debbie once more, I checked out of the hotel and went to the airport. I got my boarding pass and had breakfast before a two-hour wait for my departure time.

The time passed fairly swiftly, even though I was anxious to get home. Soon enough, I was boarding a 747-200 for an eleven-hour flight from Frankfurt to San Francisco. It was an excruciatingly long flight, but some of the beautiful sights (even from 38,000 feet) helped to pass the time. We flew north over Iceland and Greenland. The polar cap was a dazzlingly white tundra with beautiful aqua-blue lakes. Then we headed south over Baffin Island, northern Canada, and parts of Alberta and British Columbia before reaching the west coast of the United States.

After we touched down and taxied up to the terminal in San Francisco, I deplaned and went through the passport check and customs before rechecking my bags for the last short leg of the long journey home. The three-hour layover dragged by, but the shuttle flight to Portland took only seventy-five minutes. It was like a long, cool drink after an extended journey through a dry desert to see my family in the arrival lounge after I stepped off the plane. John and Joel burst into a sprint when they saw me, while Leahanna stayed with Debbie as she pushed the stroller with Lauren aboard toward me. What a joyful reunion! I soon knew just how relieved they were to see me.

When Debbie had not heard from me the day before, she had come to the airport with the children to meet me. I did not get off of the plane, so she went to the ticket counter at the gate and inquired about my whereabouts. The lady at the counter told her my name was not on the passenger list. She searched the passenger lists of several other flights to see if I might be on one of them. My name appeared nowhere.

Debbie called our pastor's wife to tell her what had happened before leaving the airport panicked, in tears, with a carload of upset children. She drove all the way back to Hood River to find Wade Mitchell's phone number so she could call him for help (this was before everyone had cell phones and voice mail). When Wade heard what had happened, he too became very worried, knowing how dangerous Moscow could be and that I had been with his father. Wade stayed up making phone calls for most of the night. Finally, at four in the morning, he called Debbie and told her he had located me and I would be in on a flight that day.

I was horrified when I found out what had happened. I felt terrible I had forgotten Debbie was going to stay with her mother the night before she met me at the airport. All was quickly forgiven, and we rejoiced all the more at being reunited.

It was an incredible journey from the beginning to the end, a life-changing event. My faith had grown tremendously after seeing God perform so many miracles, especially the miracles of so many people coming to faith in Christ so readily. It seemed, at that moment, that nothing was impossible with God. But would it continue? Would I still believe God would continue such astounding feats as I entered back into the workaday world of "normal" life? In time, I realized miracles were not as important as the change the Lord had wrought in me. I could never be the same; I had experienced too much.

As I shared with others the extraordinary and miraculous accounts of the trip, many times I wondered if I would ever experience anything like that again. I often concluded I probably would not, but I once more underestimated our amazing heavenly Father. Within two years, the miracle of Russia would happen once more.

Chapter 20

CUBA!

After my return from Russia, the rest of summer 1995 passed by quickly, as summers always do. In September, we began the eleventh year of Shepherd of the Valley Christian School. The Lord continued to provide abundantly for the school ministry. We were able to hire a fourth teacher for the school year, so each teacher taught just two grades.

In mid-October, the pastor of our church resigned suddenly as a result of some serious personal problems. The church leadership asked me to preach until we could arrange for an interim pastor to come. I preached for the next twenty-two Sundays. The Lord gave me the strength for the extra load, but on the first weekend I didn't have to preach, I slept twenty-two of the next twenty-four hours! By March of 1996, we hired Stan Love to be our interim pastor. Our church fell in love with Stan, so in June we made him our permanent pastor. He stayed for thirteen of the church's most fruitful years before he retired.

In December of 1995, with the Lord's provision through a generous relative, we were able to purchase a house in Odell, about seven miles south of Hood River. With the help of many generous friends in the church, we moved into the house in early January of 1996 after some extensive remodeling. It proved to be a wonderful home for the next nearly thirteen years.

In January of 1996, after being in the house for only two weeks, three feet of snow covered the Hood River Valley. We had to close the school for two days while we dug ourselves out. In February, less than a month after the huge snowfall, it began to rain. It rained record rainfalls for the next two weeks, and Oregon was hit with its worst flooding since the record flood of 1964. In some places in the valley, whole hillsides with growing orchards on them gave way. Many roads were closed due to slides, including three of the four roads to get from our house to town. The whole state suffered the highest financial losses in its entire history due to the flooding.

The school incurred some substantial damage from water seepage, and we had to close down for an entire week to make repairs. Fortunately, our new home was on a hill and had no damage other than a little seeping of water into the garage. We were very thankful for God's protection during a time of immense destruction throughout the state.

As the spring progressed, everything eventually dried out, and the school year came to a close with another wonderful year-end trip to the Oregon coast. We worked hard, played hard, and worshiped joyfully. We always came home exhausted. Sometimes I was sick for the entire month of June! Even though there were some hardships, I loved working with the young people. The Lord had fulfilled my vision of helping to start a Christian school and church. I could not have been happier. It was better than I could have dreamed.

The summer of 1996 was full of projects around the house. We replaced the entire roofing on the house, dug and covered over one hundred feet of drainage ditch, poured concrete for two storage areas and a basketball court, and more. By the end of the summer, we had done so many projects on the house it was a relief to go back to school just to get some rest. The Lord, though, had graciously provided for all of it.

The fall of 1996 began the twelfth year for the school. It was fairly uneventful until early November, when my sister Judy suffered a serious stroke at the age of forty-five. She had been a type 1 diabetic since she was thirteen years old. Thirty-two years of enduring the disease had ravaged the tissues of her body. When I heard about her stroke, I left immediately for Pendleton to see her. She could not speak. She had a wide-eyed look of fear as she lay mildly sedated in her hospital bed. She had come to the hospital two days earlier with her blood sugar count extremely high (over five hundred!). The doctor who saw her didn't seem to understand what was happening as he tried to search for the cause of her high count. Then she had the stroke.

During the next few days, she stabilized and improved—so much so that I went home as she seemed to be recovering. Two of her three adult daughters were also there with her. We called often over the next several days. Even though she was improving, she did not regain her ability to speak. Many of us in the church prayed for her continually.

Two weeks later, my son John and I were hunting in the mountains about twenty-five miles southeast of Heppner, in northeast Oregon. It started snowing that day, and when we went to bed in our tent, there was almost a foot of snow on the ground. About two in the morning we were awakened by a state police officer searching for me. He had taken no small risk to find our camp, so I knew something was seriously wrong. He informed me that Judy had taken a very bad turn for the worse and probably would not last much longer.

We decided it was too dangerous to try to get out in the middle of the night, so we waited for daylight. After packing my stuff into my pickup, I left John at the camp with some close friends and headed for Pendleton. It took me hours to get out of the mountains. Even after I reached the lower elevations, the road was very curvy, and there were spots of ice in many places. By the time I got to the hospital, it was early afternoon.

I rushed up to her room and could not find anyone. Finally, two nurses came out of a back room, and I inquired about my sister. They didn't seem to know what to say, so I said, "She's gone." They just sympathetically nodded their heads. I left the hospital in the grip of intense emotional pain and sorrow and went to my niece's apartment in search of my brother. He answered the door shortly after I knocked. I rushed in without a word, and we embraced deeply. We wept hard and long before we finally began to console each other.

The next few days were a blur of wading through deep sorrow and comforting each other. Finally, I had to go home to Hood River to bring my family back for the funeral. It was a comfort to be with them even though we were all sad. Joel was especially sad because Aunt Judy was very special to him. Whenever we went to Pendleton during the last few years, Judy had loved to spoil the boys with gifts, treats, and good times. When I got home, Joel brought out an air rifle Judy had bought for him. He cried as he clutched it tightly to his chest.

Shortly after we arrived in Pendleton, our friends brought John to the Burtons' house, where we were staying. They had a terrible time getting out of the mountains in the ice and snow. A travel trailer jackknifed, but no one was injured. They were able to right the trailer themselves with a winch.

On the morning of the funeral, I was trying to read my Bible, but I was struggling with doubts. Judy had gone through some serious rebellion in her younger years and was pretty abusive with drugs and alcohol for over twenty years. I had tried to help her become a Christian several times, but she was convinced she already was one. Sometimes she called me in the middle of the night drunk or high on something and tried to talk to me about the Lord or some problem she was experiencing at the time.

I had felt like I was never getting anywhere until a time six or seven years ago when she called me in the middle of the day. The moment I heard her voice, I could tell something was different. She was in the middle of her second divorce from her first husband. She had hired a lawyer who was a Christian. When he talked to her about the Lord, she *got it,* and she gave her life to Jesus.

For the next three years, she grew as a child of the Lord. I often referred to that time as the only years of her adult life when she was truly happy. But then she started slipping back into some of her old, angry ways. Who knows for sure, but I believe that thirty-two years of type 1 diabetes had taken too great a toll on her. I really believe the Lord knew it was time for her to come home to heaven.

But those last years left me with some serious doubts regarding Judy's Christianity. I knew sooner or later Judy's daughters would ask, "Where is our mother?" At that moment, I wasn't really sure.

I went to the Lord and pleaded with Him, "I have to know." Every day I read a chapter from the Bible, and that day's reading was Acts, chapter 2. When I pleaded with the Lord, the still, small voice inside me softly whispered, "Read." I looked down at my Bible and began to read. When I came to verse 27, the words screamed at me, "Pay attention! This is your answer!" They read, "Thou wilt not abandon my soul to Hades, nor allow thy Holy One to undergo decay." I nearly laughed with joy. Even though I knew this text was referring to Christ Himself, on this day I read *this* chapter and *this* verse. I had my peace.

Two of Judy's daughters did ask me that day where their mother was, and I was able to share with them the experience I'd had that very morning. They too were given some peace in a very dark hour of their lives. I was once more so thankful to the Lord for His incredible goodness and mercy. Even when we doubt, He does not withhold His tender mercies from us. His loving-kindness is without end and knows no bounds.

※ ※ ※

The holiday season passed swiftly each year, and this year was no different. It was a sorrowful season with the passing of Judy, but time still sped on. Early in 1997, Wade Mitchell contacted me and informed me that East-West Ministries was sending a short-term mission team into a country where they had never been before—Cuba. The idea of going to Cuba intrigued me. I had been in Romania and Russia just a few years after communism fell in each of those countries, but Cuba was still a communist country.

Wade told me that since the Soviet Union fell, Russia had ceased giving Cuba nine billion dollars per year in military aid. Cuba was in a financial world of hurt and had to make nice with the world to attract the dollars of tourists, especially those from the United States. As a result, the government of Cuba had amended its constitution, easing up the restrictions placed on the churches of the island nation. Travel into Cuba was also much easier under the new regulations.

I told Wade I was interested in going. I still felt a strong call from the Lord to share the gospel of Jesus Christ with people who were under repressive regimes. Wade gave me the name of the person in charge of all the details. In the early spring of 1997, I contacted Judi Wheeler, who worked at the Dallas headquarters for East-West Ministries, and she sent me a packet of information about the trip. I went through all of the information thoroughly and felt very strongly that the Lord was calling me to go to Cuba.

One of the ways the Lord confirmed when it was His will for me to go on a mission trip, or any trip for Him, was through finances. If the Lord provided the funds to go on a trip and took care of the financial responsibilities at home while I was gone, it was a strong indication to me that He was behind it. I also made sure the elder board at the church, the school board, and especially my wife were all right with me going on any given trip. They all gave me their approval for the trip to Cuba, so I started praying for the Lord's provision.

As I prayed, I felt compelled to do something I had never done before: ask the elders of the church if I could approach the church body to help send me to Cuba through a special offering. It seemed like a violation of the principles I had learned from the Beit Shalom challenge, so I tried to put it out of my mind. The compulsion only grew stronger, so I decided to put the question to the elder board. I asked the Lord to show me if this was indeed His will by getting the approval of the elders to proceed.

The elders unanimously approved of having the special offering during a church service in early June. The Lord provided me with part of the funds for the trip before the day of the special offering. When the day for the offering arrived, I still needed another $1,800 to fully finance the trip and take care of the bills at home. The offering that day totaled just over $900.

Pastor Stan was a little disappointed the offering had not raised enough to cover the remainder of the costs. I wasn't too discouraged by the shortfall because Debbie and I planned to have a yard sale the next Friday and Saturday to raise more funds to go on the trip. On the last day of the yard sale, Debbie and I found we had raised three hundred of the remaining nine hundred dollars needed. Early in the afternoon a couple from the church came to the yard sale. The husband took me aside and asked me how much more was needed for the trip. I told him we still lacked six hundred dollars. He took out his checkbook and wrote me a check for the full amount. Needless to say, I was overjoyed.

Now everything was set. Two weeks later on Wednesday, June 25, my family and I once more had a sorrowful farewell as they saw me off at the Portland airport. Four hours later, I was met by Judi Wheeler's kind and gracious father, Bill Hall, at the Dallas International Airport.

After a very short night's sleep, Bill drove me to Judi's house where we picked up Judi and another member of the mission team, Lauri Nevius. After everyone and their luggage were in the car, we headed for the airport. When we arrived, we met five more members of the team: Todd Lingren, Will Tomlinson, Tom Prohaska, Nancy Reeves, and Shelley Weber. All were from the Dallas area.

Todd was only twenty-one years old and was the assistant director of the mission trip. I thought he was a little young for that kind of responsibility, but he quickly proved himself to be more than able for the task. Tom worked for East-West Ministries and became a full-time missionary to his family's native Czech Republic shortly after our time in Cuba. Will, Nancy, Shelly, and Lauri were all coming just for this trip, as I was.

Even with the easing of travel restrictions, we still could not fly directly to Cuba because of the embargo the United States had set against it in 1959. So we took a four-hour flight to Cancun, Mexico, to stay the night before flying into Cuba the next day. The flight went by quickly as I slept for almost two hours while we were in the air.

In Cancun, we went through a huge customs line before we headed for our hotel. Once we checked in and put our luggage in our rooms, we got into our swimsuits and headed for the beautiful turquoise waters that lapped onto the sandy shores. The cool seawater was refreshing in the fairly humid heat. The beach was lined with large hotels right on the edge of the sand. Black rock outcroppings sprinkled here and there were beaten by frothy waves. The breakers formed only twenty or thirty feet from the shore. Beyond them, turquoise waters spread into the purple sea in the distance. It was the kind of scene made for tropical postcards. I had always thought the color in those cards was enhanced, but now I knew differently! This was an earthly paradise, soiled only by the depravity of humankind in the artificial glitter of what is often ironically referred to as civilization. The best humanity can offer titillates the flesh but leaves the soul empty. The inspiration of Cancun's natural beauty drew me to the Architect and Builder of the universe and deeply impressed me with His creative abilities.

After a restful night, Will Tomlinson and I got up and had breakfast together in the hotel. Then we hit the beach for another couple of hours of swimming in the cool waters that splashed onto the warm, brown sand. We reluctantly left the waters with plenty of time to shower, pack, and head back to the airport to catch our afternoon flight to Havana. I had a hard time fathoming I would be on Cuban soil in a few short hours.

We met the rest of the team going to Cuba at the airport: Kurt Nelson, Dick Ferrell, Maria Densmore, and Susan Sherburn. The flight took less than an hour. We had barely reached our peak altitude when the plane descended toward Havana.

Kurt was the director of our mission trip, and Dick Ferrel was a businessman who financially supported East-West Ministries. He had come on this trip to see if he was investing wisely. Maria Densmore had spent the first nine years of her life growing up in Cuba. It took her family three years to escape Castro's regime and be reunited in the United States. She had come to Cuba the year before with the group that set up everything for this trip. They found her childhood home, and when she went inside, she broke down and wept. She had quite a burden for the people of Cuba. Susan Sherburn was a grandmotherly type who had felt the call of the Lord to come on the trip.

By the time we got through the airport and customs, it started to get dark. We gathered our group outside on a large concrete patio. We were with several other people who had just arrived in Cuba while we waited for our bus to take us to our hotel. A short Cuban man in a colorful tropical shirt skulked around the crowd and asked questions while we waited. We had been warned the Cuban secret police would do such things, trying to elicit information from travelers for security purposes. This man came to me and commented there was an unusually large number of Americans there that night. I agreed with him while trying to act like I knew nothing about it. Seeing that I was not going to talk much, he moved on shortly before our bus arrived.

On the way to our hotel, we drove by the Plaza de la Revolucion. All we could see in the darkness was a tower and a large statue of Jose Marti in front of it, both lit by floodlights. All of us stayed at the beautiful Hotel Englaterra except Judi Wheeler. She joined another group from East-West Ministries that had already arrived and was spending their time encouraging Christian brothers and sisters in another Cuban city.

After a delectable breakfast in the morning, we loaded our baggage onto our bus and left Havana for a seven-hour ride to Ciego de Avila in the central part of the island. We passed dozens of American cars from the 1950s mixed with smaller Czech-built Skodas and other cars from the defunct Soviet Union. There were dump trucks with hitchhikers or old cars loaded into their dump beds. There were bicyclists and even horse carts. At one stage, we moved into the left lane as some men were drying rice in the right lane. We jokingly decided we wouldn't purchase any Cuban rice on the trip!

The deep green tropical scenery mixed palm trees and lush vegetation with paint-peeled cinder-block shanties under rusty, corrugated tin roofs sprinkled along the road. These were against a backdrop of low, rugged, jungle-covered mountains below an azure sky. There were the occasional abandoned sugar refineries and small villages along the way, and only one sizable city, Santa Clara. Once every five or ten miles a disabled car would be seen on the slanted shoulder of the highway while men struggled in futile labor under a raised hood. Once you leave the environs of Havana, Cuba is a beautiful country full of lovely people who own almost nothing.

We made a short forage for fuel in the poor neighborhoods of Santa Clara and left a restroom attendant with a gospel tract and a brief explanation of salvation through Jesus Christ. Two hours later, we stopped for a break at a roadside rest area with little thatched-grass-roofed huts which sold soda pop and other refreshments. Two men hoping for tips played a guitar and maracas beautifully and sang of their beloved Cuba. We gladly remunerated them for the lovely music before we resumed our long, fascinating journey.

When we finally reached the Hotel Ciego de Avila, the late afternoon was giving way to early evening. We settled into our rooms briefly before heading out to meet the pastor of the church we would work with for the next week. Eduardo was one of the most gracious and humble men I have ever met, quiet in his demeanor and ever the servant at heart. He was not only the pastor of the church, but he had helped almost two dozen fledgling churches in the area as well as working at his full-time job of teaching during the week. His wife, Cila, was also a hardworking servant with a very sweet personality. We also met several of our interpreters and helpers at Eduardo's house: Juan and his brother Ivan, Donato, Orelvis, Ramon (who had hitchhiked for over three hundred miles to come help us), Amado, Ramirez, and Oliveros. Oliveros wanted to start and pastor a church in a nearby town called Venezuela after he finished seminary. He was only twenty years old. After introductions and a short time of visiting, we sat down to an savory meal of fish, potatoes, rice, cucumbers, and freshly marinated beans.

After dinner, we all packed into the bus and headed to the church for a Saturday night worship service. What wonderful, lively singing! What kind, loving people! They gave us such a warm, gracious welcome. I was overwhelmed when I first sat down among Christian brothers in Cuba. The service went on for nearly two hours, but it seemed like just a few minutes. After the service and the long, amazing day we had just experienced, we went back to the hotel for a restful night.

After a *cold* shower and a hearty breakfast, we took the bus to join Eduardo for the Sunday morning worship service at the church. The service was lively. People sang loudly while clapping and listened intently to the sermon. Afterward we went to Eduardo's house for a great lunch of chicken, browned rice, green beans, cucumbers, potatoes, and yucca (a potato-like food). After lunch we rode back to the hotel for a relaxed afternoon and a pizza dinner before heading back to the church for the evening service.

During the evening worship time, Tom, Nancy, and I went out to a small church in Venezuela. Nancy and I shared briefly before the pastor and Tom spoke. After Tom finished speaking, a Haitian lady came forward and said she was going to get rid of all of the idols in her home. There were more than a few Haitians living in Cuba. Some of them had brought the practice of voodoo and some forms of idol worship with them. After the service, we headed back to the hotel for the night.

In the morning we had scrambled eggs and toast for breakfast at the hotel before we rode the bus to the church for a brief meeting. We had come to Cuba to strengthen Eduardo's church and to encourage as many of the fledgling churches in the area and their pastors as we could. We wanted to get into as many Cuban homes as we could to share the good news of Jesus Christ and then direct them to Eduardo's church or one of the smaller churches. After the meeting, the bus let us off in small groups around the city to share Christ with the people of Ciego de Avila. Susan Sherburn and I went with three interpreters into one of the neighborhoods.

We knocked on the door of the first house we came to, and a very pale and frail-looking woman, probably in her early thirties, answered the door. She explained that she lived alone with her ten-year-old son. She also told us she'd had surgery just the day before. We offered to leave and come back later when she felt better, but she said she wanted to hear what we had come to tell her. She said she was a Christian, but when we told her and her son what the Bible said about being a Christian, they wanted to pray right then to receive the Lord as their Savior. Just as we bowed to pray, there was a knock at the door. It was her neighbor and her son who had come to check on her and see who was at her house. I thought that this was a diversion by

Satan to keep the lady and her son from praying to receive the Lord. Again, my faith was challenged that day as not two, but four people received the Lord just a few minutes later!

After the bus collected all of our small groups, we found that a total of twenty-eight people had committed their lives to Christ that morning. Others had promised to come to our meetings at the church in the evenings. There would be many more in the days to come.

After another great lunch of fruit compote, rice, bean soup, poached eggs, green beans, and cucumbers at Eduardo's house, we went back to the hotel to get some rest and escape the intense afternoon heat of the Cuban summer. After dinner at the hotel, we took the bus to the evening meeting at the church. There, we learned of some of the needs of the Cuban Christians. Bibles and study materials were needed for seminary students. Bicycles and flashlights were needed by others to get to their church services and back. Many more needs were brought to our attention, and we were able to meet some of those before we left Cuba. There was a big praise for East-West Ministries helping the church fix its leaky roof. They had been praying for it to get fixed for forty-one years.

After making plans for the rest of the week, we dismissed the meeting and rode back to the hotel. It had been a great day. Twenty-eight new souls had entered the kingdom! Our God is always so very good.

After breakfast the next morning, we went to Eduardo's house, picked up our interpreters, and dispersed to various parts of the city. Susan Sherburn and I went with Juan as our interpreter. At first we had difficulty talking to people about the Lord, so I prayed God would guide us to the right people. When I looked up, I saw a young woman standing in a doorway. We asked if we could talk to her; she said she would give us ten minutes. A friend of hers was inside the house, and not only did she and her friend commit their lives to the Lord, but she excitedly took us to six family members in a house across the street. All six of them prayed to receive Christ as their Lord and Savior as well. Six more people became Christians later that morning at various places. Praise the Lord!

Just before noon, our interpreter talked to a man sitting at a booth along the street. We couldn't understand what they were saying and didn't think too much about it until a car sped from the direction of the local police station and stopped at the booth. Two uniformed men spoke to the man at the booth. This didn't look good, so we started walking away at a quick pace. The uniformed men got back into the car, did a U-turn in the middle of the street, and started speeding toward us. I started praying, and just before the car got to us, it turned a corner and raced off back toward the police station.

Relieved but hot, we sat down on the steps of a house to rest. A moment later, a young couple we had led to the Lord the day before came out and invited us to go inside to escape the heat. We gladly went into the shady interior. They gave us some cold water to drink while we waited for the bus to pick us up. The Lord not only kept us safe, but He kept us refreshed. He is always more than faithful! In the evening our group split up and went to different locations for home meetings. I spoke at one of the meetings. As we talked at the hotel that night, we wondered if it would be safe to go out visiting homes in the morning after the close call Susan and I had had. We decided to pray about it, sleep on it, and make a decision in the morning.

In the morning, during my quiet time with the Lord, my chapter for the day was Acts, chapter 18. When I came to verses 9 and 10, I was startled to read, "Do not be afraid any longer, but go on speaking and do not be silent; for I am with you, and no man will attack you in order to harm you, for I have many people in this city" (NASB). Then the still, small voice said, "There's your answer."

I finished my quiet time and took my Bible to breakfast with me. When Kurt brought up the question of whether we should go out to visit or not, I read the verses that had been impressed upon me during my devotional time. When I finished, Kurt said, "I think we've got our marching orders."

Susan Sherburn and I went with Juan again after praying for protection and much fruit from our morning's labors. We saw an eighty-year-old grandmother and a family of five plus a neighbor girl commit their lives to the Lord in about three hours of visiting. The Lord had proven Himself faithful once more.

After another great lunch at Eduardo's house, we went back to the hotel for a restful afternoon. Maria had been talking to our headwaiter, a man named Nestor, about the Lord. Nestor was a sweet man who folded our napkins into roses, fans, and other beautiful shapes all week long. That afternoon Nestor committed his life to the Lord. After dinner, Maria talked to the three guitar players who serenaded us all week, but they told her they couldn't pray right then because they were working.

After dinner, we went to the meeting at the church, and Nestor came with us. I saw some of the people who had received Christ that week there also. When the meeting was coming to a close, the pastor asked anyone who wanted to receive Christ or anyone who had received Christ that day to come to the front of the church. Nestor almost climbed over the pew in front of him to get to the front of the church!

Seven people in all came forward. Two or three of them committed their lives to the Lord for the first time. It was only Wednesday, and already over one hundred people from Ciego de Avila had committed their lives to the Lord. I was seeing the Lord move in mighty ways just as He had done in Russia. What I had thought was a once-in-a-lifetime experience was happening once more.

On Thursday morning, Amado took Neurma (the song leader at the church), Juan, Susan, and me to some apartment buildings. At one apartment, four people committed their lives to the Lord. At the next apartment, a woman named Margarita received the Lord. She had been invited by the Christian couple who lived there to come and listen to us. She immediately took us to some of her friends to hear what we had to say. They didn't become Christians right then, but it was fun to see her excitement about the Lord so soon after becoming a Christian.

After another great lunch at Eduardo's house, we split up for different activities during the afternoon. Tom, Donato, and I attended a small meeting at the apartments we had been to that morning. Three more people became believers. A total of forty-one souls had come into God's kingdom that day. That gave us a total of 142 new Christians for the week. Hallelujah!

After the meeting, about thirty of us went to a meeting in the small front room of a house. We sang, gave accounts of how God was working, and listened to the Word being preached. We had a wonderful time of fellowship.

During dinner at the hotel, our group was given a fruit basket and a free dessert by the staff. They said they had never met a group like us. We were very touched by these gestures. After dinner, the three men who serenaded us prayed with Maria to receive Jesus Christ as their Lord and Savior. We praised the Lord much again.

At the worship time that night, the people of the church held a farewell service for us. Many from the church spoke and thanked us, and we all spoke and thanked them. When I spoke, I told them I wished I had a suitcase big enough to fit all of them into it to take them back home with me. One little girl was overheard telling her mother she thought she could fit into my suitcase. It was a joyous yet sad time, but we all spoke of looking forward to being together forever in heaven. I longed very much for the Lord Jesus to return at that very moment.

During the week, we had expressed at times our concern for all these new believers. Would they be all right after we left? It was comforting to have a good church well established in Ciego de Avila that could help them, but would they become involved with the church? Would the fear of reprisal from the government keep them back? We would learn once more that the Lord is bigger than all of our concerns.

In the morning, July 4, the assurance came. As I was continuing to read the book of Acts for my devotions, I read chapter 20. As Paul began verse 17, he gave his farewell to the Christians at Ephesus. When I came to verse 32, I read, "And now I commend you to God and to the word of His grace, which is able to build you up and give you the inheritance among all those who are sanctified" (NASB). With this, the Spirit of God assured me the new Christians in Cuba were going to be all right.

After my devotional time, I went to breakfast and shared with the team what the Lord had shown me through His Word. It was very comforting to all. After breakfast, the mission team, our interpreters, some of their family members, and a few people from the church crowded into our bus for a day of rest and fun at a resort a few miles from Ciego de Avila. As we were boarding, Todd gave a gospel tract to a boy watching us get onto the bus. We could see him outside the bus, smiling and struggling to understand what he was reading just as we were ready to leave. Maria could not stand leaving anything so important alone, so she called for the bus driver to wait a few moments. She went out the door, and we all watched and prayed as she ever so lovingly explained what the booklet was saying. Then she closed her eyes and prayed with the boy. A moment later we were on our way to Cayo Coco (Coconut Key), rejoicing that another precious soul entered into God's kingdom.

It was an outstanding day with almost no clouds in the sky. After a few miles, we drove onto a highway built on a jetty that took us to the key. We had to stop at a checkpoint before we were allowed onto the resort island. It took us over an hour to get past the checkpoint because we had some Cubans with us. We were once more amazed at the disparity the Cubans faced in their own homeland. One of our interpreters lamented a few days earlier, "Everything is illegal in Cuba." I prayed and continue to pray for the Lord to comfort the people of Cuba.

We spent a glorious day on dazzlingly white sandy beaches, swimming in crystal-clear water among tropical fish and conch shells. It seemed like the paradise of God. We rented two Jet Skis and took the Cubans on ride after ride. It would probably be the only time in their lives many of them would be able to do this. Oh, that such days would be without end!

Alas, the sun began to sink toward the west. As we loaded onto the bus, the sky started to cloud up rather quickly. Before we were halfway across the jetty, a fierce, hurricane-like storm burst upon us. It rained so hard we could hardly see to drive, and it blew nearly straight sideways. Huge waves crashing against the rocks off the shoulder of the road sprayed us relentlessly with seawater.

Shortly after we reached the mainland, the storm ended. Within a few minutes the sun streamed through the enlarging breaks in the clouds. The only reminders of the fierce storm were the several large puddles of rainwater scattered about.

When we reached the church, we said our final teary farewells to most of the church members and all of the interpreters. Sometimes it is so hard to say good-bye; maybe that is part of the reason eternity beckons us so strongly as time rolls on.

As the bus pulled away from the church, we looked back as long as we could see our friends. Then it was on to Camaguey, further toward the southeastern part of the island. We met the part of our group that had been encouraging the Christians in Baracoa, almost the most eastern part of Cuba. We all joined together in a large church service. All of us were honored with a certificate and a small gift for our service to the Cuban people.

Afterward, we said our final sorrowful farewell to Susan Sherburn and Maria Densmore. Judi Wheeler, Lauri Nevius, and Shelly Weber joined us on the bus for a late ride back to the hotel in Ciego de Avila. The girls told us they'd had a very difficult time in Baracoa because their bus driver was an informant. They also shared with us that 149 souls from Baracoa had entered the kingdom. The remainder of their team members were going out again in the morning.

When we arrived at the hotel, we stumbled to our rooms and fell into bed. What a long but wonderful day it had been! It was a short but restful night. We said our final good-byes to Nestor and the rest of the staff at the Hotel Ciego de Avila in the morning and stopped off at Eduardo's house briefly for one last farewell to him, Cila, Ramon, Amado, and a young woman named Keilah. Keilah openly cried as we left, and she wasn't the only one to shed tears.

Once more, we looked back as long as we could see our brothers and sisters in Christ. Finally, we turned to face the long journey back to Havana.

It had been an amazing and wonderful trip, but we were more than ready to return to our loved ones. Even though I couldn't wait to see Debbie and the children, I fell asleep very quickly.

The alarm jarred us to consciousness at 4:30 in the morning. Our bus driver, Damian, hugged each one of us before he drove off with tears in his eyes. We boarded our plane and soon were flying to Cancun and then back to the US. When we landed at Dallas International Airport, I only had time for a very quick good-bye as I rushed to catch my connecting flight to Portland. They were boarding the plane as I hurried to the gate. It took off shortly after I was seated. Four hours later, I was met at the gate in Portland by Debbie, John, and Joel. The boys could hardly contain themselves as I hugged Debbie. Neither could I.

We collected my bags and drove to Grandma's house, where I was met by two squealing girls. It was a glorious ending to a glorious trip. The Lord had shown Himself once more to be strong indeed. He had stretched my faith well beyond my comfort zone. He had shown me once more how real He is in our lives every day, and how He wants to be deeply involved with us personally. He is an incredible God, and He *is* "able to do exceeding abundantly beyond all that we ask or think, according to the power that works within us" (Ephesians 3:20, NASB).

A few weeks after returning from Cuba, I was informed by one of the mission team members that Juan, who had served as an interpreter for Susan Sherburn and me, was an informant. Now I understood why we were nearly arrested. The Lord protected us, but this meant I could not return to Cuba anytime soon. My return might lead to the entire team getting expelled from Cuba (or worse), and it could cause problems for the Christians who lived there.

Even though I am writing this more than fifteen years after that mission trip took place, the Lord may still have plans for me to return to Cuba. A little over a year ago, I talked with Wade Mitchell at a missions conference in Portland. Later Wade and I got together and talked about the possibility of taking a mission team from the Northwest into Cuba. Our God is simply awesome.

Chapter 21

BACK TO BRITAIN

The three years after the Cuba trip passed fairly peacefully. The children grew; Debbie and I aged a bit more; three more school years began and finished. The school had grown to the point that we sold the building and property in the spring of 2000 and started negotiations to buy land for a site to build a new school and church building.

One significant event during these years was the birth of a baby girl on April 24, 1999, at Emanuel Hospital in Portland. She was born addicted to methamphetamine and cocaine and had a stroke before she was born because of the drugs her birth mother used. She was a miracle, and she would soon be known as Kimberly Joy Kailynn Winters.

Life always gives us our share of tumult. With Jesus' help, we not only get through it, we can even triumph at times. In the end, we find that "Though our outward man is perishing, yet the inward man is being renewed day by day" (2 Corinthians 4:16, NKJV). The Lord has been in the business of giving "beauty for ashes, the oil of joy for mourning, the garment of praise for the spirit of heaviness" for a long, long time (Isaiah 61:3). Some of the fires that create the ashes we start ourselves; some we don't. It doesn't really matter; for those in Christ, His grace *is* sufficient; His power *is* made perfect in weakness (see 2 Corinthians 12:9).

In the early spring of 2000, the Lord put it on my heart to see Brother John again. Even though I had called him at least once every month, I had not seen him in nearly eight years. We had asked him to come stay with us on different occasions, but it never worked out. Now I realized that on his next birthday, which was coming very soon, he would be eighty-eight years old. He sounded as healthy and vigorous as ever on the phone, but he had told me at times that long-distance travel was getting too hard for him.

My son John was now in his freshman year of high school. He had many more memories of Brother John than Joel did, and the girls had never met him. So I thought it would be good for him and me to spend two weeks with Brother John sometime during the summer. Cristian Sigheartau was still living near Brother John, and I hadn't seen either of them since our trip to Romania in 1992. Cris had married his girlfriend Delia, and they now had two daughters, Melissa and Stephanie.

There was only one wrinkle in our plans. John and I had already been making plans to accompany an elderly gentleman on a short-term mission trip to Nogales, Mexico, in early July. After some plotting and praying, we figured we could go to Britain in June and still go on the trip to Mexico in early July. There would be time for one week at home between the trips.

The Lord opened all the doors for both trips to take place, and he also provided the finances. On Wednesday, June 21, 2000, my son John and I flew out of Portland on the first leg of our journey to see Brother John. It had been too long since we had seen each other face-to-face, heart to heart.

After a short layover in Newark, New Jersey, we boarded a Boeing 777 that flew us into Gatwick during a very short night. After we went through customs, we headed out of the international arrival area to meet Brother John and Cris. I was a little shocked when I saw Brother John. He looked frail and had a difficult time walking with a cane. He had told me on occasion that one of his knees was giving him some trouble. It bothered me to see him so; he had always been such a pillar of strength to me.

We hugged long and deeply before slowly making our way to the car. We talked nonstop as Cris drove us to Brother John's home in Hove. Our conversation on the way assured me that even though Brother John's body was failing, he was still strong in spirit. It was so good to be with him and Cris again. It was so good to be back at New Orleans.

After putting our luggage into the Prophet's Chamber, we came down to the kitchen and helped Cris fix some sandwiches for lunch. We continued our rich fellowship as we dined and basked in the warm afternoon sun in the solarium. As we talked, I could see that the garden surrounding Brother John's backyard was not quite up to the standard it had been in previous years, but it still looked nice. We talked until John and I began to tire, as we had pretty much missed an entire night's sleep.

We slept soundly in the Prophet's Chamber for four hours until six o'clock in the evening. Shortly after we awoke, we had dinner with Brother John alone. After dinner, Cris brought Delia and the girls to the house, and we visited well into the night. The fellowship and Cris's girls were very sweet. Melissa was a precocious four-year-old, and Stephanie was an eighteen-month-old toddler bubbling with joy as she babbled her first words in spurts of English and Romanian.

Cris and Delia left around nine, and the two Johns and I visited until around eleven. We went to sleep by midnight, and I woke up once again at four in the morning. I could hear the familiar sound of dozens of birds chirping away merrily in the trees and hedges around St. Leonard's Church next door. I enjoyed the symphony of God's creation for about half an hour as my son slept peacefully across the room. I had a long and peaceful quiet time with the Lord as the light filtered in through the skylight. It gradually filled the room, growing from the grayness of dawn to the fullness of morning's light.

Over the next few days, John and I rested and had great fellowship with Brother John and Cris and his family as we adjusted to England's time zone. On Friday, my son and I flew up to Edinburgh for the weekend. He had never been to Scotland, and I hadn't been there since 1983. I wanted to show him some of the sights around Edinburgh while we were so near. We had a great time together as we toured Edinburgh Castle, hiked up Arthur's Seat, went to the church services at Charlotte Baptist Chapel, and more. It was an enjoyable little excursion, even though I missed spending time with Brother John and the Sigheartaus.

Back at New Orleans, we spent the next few days just relaxing and enjoying each other immensely. Cris and my son John got along famously, as they both enjoyed soccer very much and even played a mini-match in Brother John's backyard.

We had many hours of conversation, and it amazed me how deep was the level of fellowship Brother John and I were able to have all through the years. Even now, though I had not seen him for nearly eight years, it was as if we had not missed a day. He had such keen insight into spiritual matters, I was always challenged to think things through in light of the Scriptures. His gracious ways were so Christlike that I couldn't help but to be drawn to the Lord. Even when we disagreed, we always ended in unity. He never compromised, but our relationship was much more important to him than winning an argument. I had seen him treat others in much the same way. These were the ways of the Lord, and they were the ways of Brother John also. As Tommy Burton often said, "He was a very unique individual."

Alas, our time with Brother John and the Sigheartaus passed all too quickly, and it was time to return home. We left Brother John at New Orleans while Cris drove us to the airport. I wondered if I would see Brother John alive again. I never imagined that I would see him again a little over six months later, the last time I would see him this side of heaven.

Chapter 22

THE FINAL CHAPTER
(BUT NOT THE END)

After a short week at home with Debbie and the other children, John and I spent two very fruitful and busy weeks in Nogales, helping a talented and godly pastor with his work in a fledgling church there. We returned from Nogales on Monday the twenty-fourth of July, which left just enough time to prepare for the sixteenth year of Shepherd of the Valley Christian School. The summer faded quickly, and the school year began on September 5, 2000. It had all the promise of being a very good one, even though it would be the last year the school would be known as Shepherd of the Valley Christian School. We had been negotiating with another Christian school in Hood River about the possibility of merging. Big changes loomed ahead.

The Lord had been extremely faithful during the first fifteen years of the school's existence, and He would be faithful again, many times. The Lord is always faithful, whether we are able to discern it or not. It is we who are not faithful. We can lose our faith in God in good times or bad; but if we remain faithful and seek Him with our whole heart and soul, we will find Him (see Deuteronomy 4:29). If we continue to grow in our faith, we will find Him to be kind, loving, compassionate, and merciful beyond all limits. He *is* that good.

The first month of the school year progressed smoothly, and Debbie and I began to discuss whether to adopt more children or not. It had been over six years since we adopted Lauren. We wanted to adopt at least one more child, but nothing seemed to be happening. We sent out our home study fifty-three times and went to committee once. Even then, we were not chosen to be the adoptive parents.

We had kept up our foster parent certification with the state in hopes of adopting (until an adoption is final, which usually takes about a year, adoptive parents are foster parents by legal definition). It had been so long since we last adopted, we decided not to renew our certification. We thought maybe the Lord wanted us to stop at four.

A new caseworker had begun working with us right after Lauren's adoption, and she had worked very hard trying to help us adopt. About two weeks before our certification expired, she called and said we had been chosen to go to committee for three different children. We were both stunned and extremely delighted.

We asked our caseworker what to do, since we didn't think it would be best for the children if we adopted two or three at once. She told us to let things take their course. We could go to committee for one child at a time, and if we were chosen to be the adoptive parents at any time, we could remove ourselves for consideration for any that might still be remaining.

We studied all the information our caseworker sent us on the three children and prayed about it with several of our friends. We decided to go to committee on all three children and let the Lord show us which one He would choose for us, if any, through the process. We felt strongly, though, that one of the children, a seventeen-month-old girl named Kimmie, was the one the Lord had already chosen for us.

When we went to committee for the first child, a little girl from Newport, we were not chosen to be the adoptive parents. Our caseworker was quite upset about it. She told us that some unfair assumptions had been made by some on the committee because we were Christians and had homeschooled our children at times. She wanted us to file a grievance with the state against the committee, but we trusted this was the Lord's will. The caseworker assured us she was going to do all she could to make sure such a thing would not happen again. We tried to assure her we were all right with the decision.

When the next child went to the second committee, we were not chosen to adopt that child either. Only Kimmie was left. We still felt we were going to be chosen to be her adoptive parents, even though she had more physical issues than the others.

Just before the committee met to make the decision for Kimmie in early November, Debbie checked into Legacy Emanuel Hospital in Portland for a neck surgery we had scheduled months before. She'd had neck pain all of her adult life, and a few months before, it had become unbearable. The doctors discovered she had grown bone spurs on the inside of some of her neck vertebrae. They were going to drill out the spurs, patch the holes, and attach a four-inch titanium rod to plates they would attach to the back of some of the vertebrae in her neck—all of this through a one-inch incision made at the base of the front of her neck.

Our caseworker told us she would call us at eleven o'clock on the morning of Debbie's scheduled surgery to tell us if we had been chosen to be Kimmie's adoptive parents or not. Debbie's surgery went extremely well, and they rolled her from the recovery room into her own room at about nine o'clock. Debbie's mom, her sister Jan, and I were sitting and visiting quietly in the room as Debbie came in and out of consciousness. We had not told her family anything about this latest adoption attempt; they thought we already had too many children. When eleven o'clock approached, I quietly slipped out of the room and went to our car in the parking lot to wait for the much-anticipated call.

Every minute seemed like an hour as I waited. Then, about ten minutes after eleven, my cell phone rang. Our caseworker wasted no time in congratulating us for being chosen to be the adoptive parents of a precious little girl. I thanked her profusely and let out a whoop loud enough to scare the whole city of Portland just after we ended the call.

I hurriedly left the parking area, went straight to the gift shop, and bought Debbie a card to congratulate her on becoming a mommy, along with a ceramic figurine of a child angel. When I came into the room, Debbie was awake, so I handed her the card. As she read it she began to cry quite loudly. Debbie's mom and sister rose out of their seats with their mouths open and expressions on their faces that said, "What in the world did you do to her, you brute?"

I quickly explained to them that we had just been told we were going to be adopting a little girl. Their anxiety quickly turned into surprised shock. They hammered me with a dozen rapid-fire questions, and I tried to answer them as well as I could under the circumstances. While all of this was happening, Debbie was weeping quietly with tears of joy. Kimberly Joy Kailynn Winters had officially entered our lives.

As soon as Debbie was able, we began the visitation process to get to know our new little daughter. We were told by the foster mother that Kimmie was very slow to warm up to strangers. On our first visit to her foster home, Kimmie let me pick her up and hold her, and she sat contentedly on both our laps during the entire visit. The foster mother commented that the first time she talked to Debbie on the phone, she had known we were the ones God had chosen to be Kimmie's parents.

Over the next eight weeks, we visited Kimmie several times and even brought her to our home in Hood River for an overnight stay. Everything went very well, and we were scheduled to pick her up at her foster home to come to our house permanently the day after Christmas. However, there was a huge snowstorm that day, and we had to postpone getting Kimmie for a week. The following Saturday was New Year's Eve, and there was still a lot of snow on the ground, but the roads were all right. So we met Kimmie's foster parents at a restaurant in Cascade Locks, about halfway between our two houses. She was ours forever. We were so thankful to the Lord for His kindness.

Kimmie was born drug addicted with fetal alcohol effects, compounded by the stroke she'd had before she was born. By the time we got her, she was nineteen months old and was making remarkable progress. We were very grateful for the outstanding work the foster parents had done with Kimmie (thank you, Dave and Kristen!), but she hadn't begun to speak yet because of the damage from the stroke. Over the next month, we taught Kimmie some sign language so she could communicate with us. She picked this up quickly and was very happy to be able to "talk."

Even though Kimmie has always seemed quite bright to us, she struggled much when she entered school three years later. She finished kindergarten at the age of seven and still was not reading by the time she was nine years old, even though we put her into special learning programs each year. We prayed for her, but there were times when I wondered if she would ever be able to read.

※ ※ ※

During the spring and summer of 2001, we met dozens of times with the leadership of another Christian school in Hood River to discuss the merging of our two schools. One of the board members had approached me about it after school about a year before. She said she loved the spiritual atmosphere of our school and wanted it for their school. At first, we said no because the plan they offered us was not satisfactory to us. Later, they came back with a very generous plan, so we reignited the discussions. Both of the schools had grown to the point of needing larger facilities. Through hundreds of hours of meetings, we developed a plan to merge the two schools.

Shepherd of the Valley Bible Church and Christian School had already sold our building and property in anticipation of buying some land and building a new facility. The church was meeting in a school auditorium, and the school rented part of another church facility during the week to hold classes. With the funds from the sale, we had bought five acres of some of the nicest land in Hood River. After the purchase, we didn't have enough funds left to build a school and church facility, but the Lord had been so faithful to us through the years, we knew He would provide.

In the merger plan, the other school said that if we donated our land as a site for a new school, they would buy another four-plus acres adjoining it. They would also build a facility large enough to house our merged schools and a dedicated space for our church. Six years later, a lot of very excited people entered a brand-new, more than 45,000-square-foot facility housing both Horizon Christian School and Shepherd of the Valley Bible Church. It is still arguably one of the nicest buildings in Hood River. The merged school immediately had just under 200 students. By the time of this writing, the school has nearly 220 students enrolled in preschool through high school classes.

The Final Chapter (But Not the End)

Shepherd of the Valley Family Education Ministries came to an end at the closing of the 2000–2001 school year. For sixteen years we had served the families of the Mid-Columbia area of Oregon and Washington. Students from over a dozen communities had attended the school without any tuition charge. They gave what the Lord led them to give, and we lacked nothing. To this day, those years are still held in my heart as the best sixteen years of my life. The Lord taught so many the life of faith that began with the Beit Shalom challenge. I still feel some sadness at the thought of our little school with its great family atmosphere being gone, but it seems the Lord did want us to move on. In the end, the decision to merge was largely taken out of my hands, but I really believe it was always in God's hands. It did bring great change to the course of my life and the lives of my family. In the end, as always, the Lord brought great blessings from it.

The first year of the merged school, the administrator from the other school and I were co-administrators of the ministry. We both taught for a half-day and administrated for the other half. We had a part-time superintendent who came in once a week to supervise and advise us. This arrangement sometimes was humorously referred to as the "three-headed monster." The second year of the ministry, a new administrator came in to replace all three of us. The other administrator and I shifted to full-time teaching, and they did away with the part-time superintendent altogether.

I took advantage of not having any administrative duties to continue pursuing the master's degree I had started in Pensacola eighteen years earlier. I got permission to pay for a substitute teacher to take my place every Monday so I could attend classes, and I enrolled in a program at Western Seminary in Portland called "Monday School." I attended classes each Monday in Portland from ten o'clock in the morning until ten at night. Then I taught Tuesday through Friday at the school in Hood River.

Initially, I thought Monday School was a part-time program. It was not. So I was going to seminary full-time and teaching nearly full-time. I created an enormously busy year for myself. By early springtime of 2003, I realized I could not keep up this pace for three more years, the time it would take me to complete the program. I had felt for a while that my time in the school ministry was coming an end. The call to start a children's home had been getting stronger in recent months. Then a man who had helped start the Shepherd of the Valley Christian School contacted me to talk about starting a children's home with him. I told him I wanted to focus on finishing my seminary degree, but I wanted to talk to him again as I neared its completion.

By the summer of 2003, I knew I could not continue to teach and go to seminary at the same time. It was too much. I did not want to cut back on my class load at the seminary. I wanted to finish within the next three years, so I decided to resign my position from school. It was a huge decision, but I felt the school was on stable grounds financially, and I really felt compelled by the Lord to look into the new venture of a children's home. It was a difficult move to make, but I felt strongly it was God's will.

The Lord had already provided me with enough funds to make it through about one more year of seminary without working at all. I felt confident He would help me to finish. He had undertaken so amply for the school ministry and the trips I had taken in the past, I knew I could trust Him to help me finish seminary and take good care of our growing family too.

Two days after I resigned from the school, our pastor, Stan Love, called me. Stan also served as the chairman of the school board, so he'd heard about me resigning and wanted to talk to me about it. He was not happy that I had resigned and neither was I, but about halfway through the conversation he suddenly said, "Hey, you can be the associate pastor for our church." I could hardly believe what I was hearing. I very quickly went from a feeling of fairly deep gloom to utter elation.

We discussed excitedly how I could work part-time for the church to help me through seminary while Stan coached me on the responsibilities of the pastorate. Both aspects deeply thrilled and touched me. To top it all, we were having an all-church business meeting two days later, and Stan said he would prepare the groundwork and bring it up for a decision at that meeting. Just four days after resigning from the school, I became the associate pastor of Shepherd of the Valley Bible Church. They would keep me on staff until I finished seminary, then I was free to pursue the children's home. It was better than anything I could have dreamed up myself.

On top of all of this, in the fall of 2003 Debbie and I discovered a beautiful baby girl available for adoption through a magazine put out by the Boys and Girls Aid Society. Kimmie was so much younger than Lauren, we thought it would be good for her to have a sister closer to her age. Sierrra Marie, eleven months old at the time, was listed with several *possible* maladies in the magazine, and only one other family had inquired about her. After being chosen to go to committee along with the other family, Debbie had the wisdom to contact Sierra's foster mother to find out how well she was really doing. We learned she was a healthy, thriving baby with only a mild form of cerebral palsy. Her foster mother said Sierra was like a flower just beginning to blossom.

Three weeks after we went to committee and only six weeks after we had discovered Sierra, Debbie and I were chosen to be her parents. In the first week of January of 2004, Sierra Marie became Sarah Marie Winters, a permanent blessing to our family.

So with six wonderful children the venture began. I worked extremely hard for the next two years and was able to graduate from seminary with high honors in the spring of 2005. Pastor Stan was careful not to load me up too much from the church side, which was very helpful. The day I graduated from seminary, I had paid all of my school costs on time and was able to keep up on all the financial responsibilities at home too. I am forever indebted and thankful to the Lord, Pastor Stan, and the people of Shepherd of the Valley Bible Church.

The man who had contacted me about starting a children's home began a series of informal meetings with me in the spring of 2005. Our family took a much-needed three-week vacation right after graduation through the Lord's provision. After we returned, we held formal meetings the summer of 2005 to officially start the new ministry by the coming fall. In honor of the men who had so impacted me and set my feet on a journey of faith, the new ministry would be known as Gordon-Samson Children's Ministries.

I started tutoring about a dozen students in the fall of 2005 as we applied for nonprofit status with the IRS. Two of our students were my daughters Leahanna and Lauren, who were twelve and fourteen. We thought having a school up and running would help us get our nonprofit status faster. In time, this proved to be true. We also thought it wise to start the school right away as we jumped through all of the legal hoops to get a home started. That way, we would not have to start two major aspects of the ministry at the same time.

We charged a minimal tuition rate to each of the families, but it was always done on a sliding scale. Each family was charged only what they prayerfully thought they could give. The larger bulk of the cost to run the ministry came from donations from other people. We could not continue the ministry without the donations beyond the tuition giving, so it was a faith ministry.

By the time we started classes in the fall, we had a five-person board in place to oversee the ministry, and in less than six months, we were awarded our nonprofit status. We worked hard at forming our constitution and bylaws in the process. Then we worked hard again at trying to establish the children's home through Oregon's licensing procedures. In the spring of 2006, all of the board members took a trip to the children's home in Montana that Shepherd of the Valley Christian School had visited on one of our year-end trips. We toured their facilities and had a long question-and-answer session with their leadership before we came home.

By the end of the 2006–2007 school year, we had run the school ministry for two years, but we were still having difficulties getting the children's home started. Because of the slowness in getting it up and running, our biggest donor got discouraged and withdrew his support. This put the ministry in great financial jeopardy. We tried hard to make up for the loss during the summer of 2007, but it simply did not happen. We discontinued all aspects of Gordon-Samson Children's Ministries by the end of August that year.

This really confused me. I had thought this was surely the Lord's ultimate fulfillment of His call for me to run a children's home, but it was not to be. During the two years of its existence, we had seen the Lord do some marvelous work in the lives of the students involved, especially in my two daughters. It just didn't seem like it was already time to end the ministry, but the Lord did have something better in mind. When we doubt Him, He always does come through, even if it may not be the way we think it should happen!

For the next few months, I did odd jobs to support my family. I even applied for a position as a Christian school administrator in a town almost two hundred miles from Hood River. I was one of the last two candidates considered for the job. When I was not chosen for the position, my family and many in the church expressed great relief. I was happy to stay in the area that had been my home for the last twenty-three years, but what was I going to do?

As we considered this, a man who had joined our church in recent months resigned his teaching position in a Christian school in The Dalles, a town just twenty miles from Hood River. Debbie encouraged me the last two months of the summer to call the school to see if his former position was still open. I didn't think it would be so late in the summer, but Debbie was persistent. So I finally called the school on Labor Day of 2007. Thinking it really would be a miracle if someone actually answered on a holiday, I was intending on just leaving a message to humor my wife. I was very surprised when a person actually answered the phone. I was even more surprised when the person who answered was the school's administrator, Jeannie Justice! I nervously introduced myself and told her I was inquiring to see if there was a teaching position still open. I told her I had been a teaching administrator of three Christian schools over the past twenty-six years. She excitedly interrupted me and exclaimed that she had been praying for several months for a man to become the administrator of the school. She went on to explain that she felt she had gotten less than a stellar reception at times, being a woman administrator. She also felt that her time as an administrator was coming

The Final Chapter (But Not the End)

to an end as she neared the age of retirement.

After talking for several minutes, we ended the phone call with an arrangement for me to meet with the chairman of the school board to talk about the possibility of working at the school. When I shared with Debbie the course the conversation had taken, we were both quite amazed. I wondered if the Lord really wanted me to become the administrator of a Christian school once more.

I met with the school board chairman, Dave Kinser, the next week, and he told me there was not a position immediately open at the school. They were interested, though, in involving me, so they put me to work substituting whenever there was a need. Over the next three months, I substituted three or four times in the high school learning center and spoke in their chapel service once.

Then on Tuesday, December 10, Jeannie and Dave invited me over to talk some more. I thought they just wanted to discuss further the possibility of me working there sometime in the future. When I arrived, I learned that Jeannie's longtime best friend, Joyce Lee, had come down with cancer. Joyce was the primary teacher at the school. She was already so sick she needed to stop teaching right away. Jeannie wanted to take care of Joyce, so she wanted to relinquish her administrative responsibilities immediately yet continue as the elementary teacher. They hired me on the spot to come in the next day as the administrator and primary teacher. Fascinatingly, the first year I taught at the Pendleton Christian School, I had taught in the primary learning center using the same curriculum and program they were using here!

When I got home and told Debbie the news, she was almost as incredulous as I was. Nevertheless, on Wednesday, December 11, 2007, I began work at Sonrise Academy in The Dalles, Oregon, as the administrator and primary teacher. I felt very blessed to be there, though now I had a whole new student body and their families, staff, and community to get to know. It has proven to be a great blessing.

Joyce's cancer was hard on her, and there was a period of time when it was questionable whether she would survive or not. We prayed for her every day. By the end of the school year in June of 2008, she felt so good she asked if it was possible for her to return to her old position. Just two months before that request, the high school teacher asked me if I thought I could handle the high school learning center the next year. He had been working on a business on the side and felt the Lord was leading him to try it full-time after the school year ended.

After a busy summer shifting into the high school classroom and continuing to learn all I could about the school, I began the 2008–2009 school year as the administrator and high school teacher. Joyce was able to resume her responsibilities in the primary learning center, and Jeannie continued teaching in the elementary learning center. That summer I asked the school board if they would promote Jeannie to the position of assistant administrator as well as elementary teacher. They graciously and heartily approved.

We have all continued in the school to the day of this writing. We added a preschool class and teacher and a nearly full-time general assistant. Three years ago, we hired a new high school teacher, so I took over teaching in the middle school learning center as a position opened up there. About a year ago, I asked Dave Kinser if he was interested in adding a children's home to the ministry, and he told me to go for it. We brought it before the school board a few weeks later. They were so excited about the idea they immediately approved it unanimously.

We have since been searching for some property for a school and a children's home. We don't have any funds right now, but we do have a big God. If it is His will for us to have a facility for both ministries, He will provide a way to make it happen. It did occur to me just a few weeks ago, as I observed the gang of young people—Leahanna and her boyfriend Andrew, Lauren, Joel, and Kimmie—having a ton of fun together at our house, that the Lord had already given me a children's home.

※ ※ ※

In December of 2008, Joyce had been back on the job for over three months. She had recovered well from the cancer up to that point, and a place for a student came open in her learning center. I noticed how remarkable she was as a teacher, and I was reminded of how good the reading program was. So I asked Joyce if she would pray about adding Kimmie to her class to see if she could teach her how to read. By now, Kimmie was almost ten years old.

Joyce prayed about it over the weekend and told me on Monday that the Lord had given her His peace about taking on Kimmie with her high educational needs. Kimmie enrolled in early December of 2008 and finished almost the entire first grade curriculum by the end of the school year in early June of 2009. Joyce with her forty-plus years of expert experience had Kimmie reading in less than two months.

Even though she is still behind her chronological grade level, Kimmie has made the honor roll nearly every quarter since she finished the first grade curriculum. Much credit is due to the amazing God-given skills, hard work, and loving compassion of her two teachers during this time (thank you so much, Joyce Lee and Jeannie Justice!), but the ultimate credit goes to the Lord. We are so thankful to the Lord Jesus for bringing us to Sonrise Academy. As I write this, Kimberly Joy Kailynn Winters is over fourteen years old. She is a thriving, sweet young lady who is very full of the life God granted her.

※ ※ ※

Two weeks after Kimmie came to stay with us permanently in early January of 2001, I received a disturbing phone call from Brother John's nephew Jim Samson. He called to tell me Brother John had just been diagnosed with an advanced case of intestinal cancer. It had metastasized into several of the surrounding tissues. They were going to do surgery immediately to relieve the pain, but the cancer had advanced too far to save him. The doctors expected him to live only two weeks to two months longer.

Needless to say, I was shocked and saddened by this news. I made plans immediately to see Brother John as soon as I could. My son John really wanted to accompany me on this trip to see Brother John one more time this side of heaven, so we made arrangements for both of us to go to England. I called Tommy Burton in Pendleton and told him the sad news. He quickly made arrangements to go to England as well. One week later, John and I landed at Gatwick International Airport in London.

I knew this would be my last trip to England while Brother John was with us on earth. Our journey together had lasted for more than twenty years. We had endured the death of Larry Gordon, and God brought the beauty of a deep, lifelong friendship from those ashes. Brother John taught me the lessons of dependence on God alone from the Beit Shalom accounts during our time in Pendleton. We traveled together to Britain, Israel, and Romania, putting those lessons to the test, and the Lord proved Himself more than faithful every step of the way. I stepped out in faith on my own in Russia, Cuba, and in the school in Hood River, but Brother John was always with me in spirit, in thought, in the journey of life. More importantly, I had learned the Lord really is always with us, whether we believe it or not. As the apostle Paul said in Acts 17:28, "For in Him we live and move and have our being" (NKJV).

Now Brother John and I faced one more step together: death, his death. It was an enormous challenge to me, but I soon experienced another life lesson from Brother John: how to face one's own death with grace, dignity, humility, courage, and honor.

The Quiet Leading

It is a lesson that can only be learned with the help and love of the Lord, which are always there to help us endure all things.

We quickly caught a train from the airport to Hove. As we rode, I had a time of fellowship with the Lord. I read the evening reading from January 8 in a devotional booklet entitled *Daily Light on the Daily Path,* compiled by Samuel Bagster, that Brother John had given me years before. As I read, a text stood out to me from Jude 24 and 25: "Now unto him that is able to keep you from falling, and to present you faultless before the presence of his glory with exceeding joy, to the only wise God our Savior, be glory and majesty, dominion and power, both now and ever. Amen." I knew the Lord had impressed this upon me with regard to Brother John and his condition.

Shortly after we arrived at New Orleans in Hove, Jim Samson drove John and me to the hospital where Brother John was recovering from his surgery. When I entered the room, Brother John was resting peacefully, but even the quiet commotion of us entering the room awakened him. He opened his eyes and calmly smiled at us. The love and strength of that smile chased all the fears and distress from my heart immediately. I knew everything would ultimately be all right.

I went over to Brother John and hugged him with all my heart. When we separated, he held my hands firmly and smiled broadly at me as he had done so many times before. Even in the face of death, he was as strong as ever in spirit. The first thing he told me as we began to visit was how the Lord had impressed upon him Jude 24 and 25, and then he quoted it from memory. I almost interrupted him to tell him the verse before he said it. I shared with him my experience on the train down from Gatwick.

We continued visiting for nearly two hours. As we talked, he told that a lady from the hospital staff had come to talk to him about his physical condition and the inevitability of dying soon. Brother John had answered that he had preached so much about dying that it was time for him to experience it too. His spunk was nothing short of amazing.

Brother John needed to rest, as the surgery had been performed just the day before, so we took our leave and made our way back to New Orleans. John and I settled into the Prophet's Chamber before we came downstairs and had dinner and tea with Jim. He told us the surgery had gone very well, and the doctors thought Brother John would not be in too much pain for at least the next few weeks. They thought they could manage what pain there was through some mild medication. We were thankful to the Lord for that.

The Final Chapter (But Not the End)

Cris Sigheartau came over and visited after dinner. Even though the overall mood was sad, Cris always had an upbeat spirit about him. It was nice to have him with us, even though the situation was hard. Our mutual faith in the Lord and our convictions of eternal life through Christ Jesus gave us the strength we needed.

We continued in fellowship for a few hours before Cris left for his home, and the rest of us went to bed. I was still not over jet lag, so I didn't fall asleep until after I heard Brother John's grandmother clock at the bottom of the stairs chime twelve times.

After less than four hours of sleep, I was awakened by the chorus of birds chirping in the hedges around St. Leonard's. They sang and twittered as if nothing in the world was wrong. It was as if they were saying, "The world will go on; everything will be all right. You'll feel better in time." Maybe this is part of God's melody in the world for those who suffer. Maybe He's saying, "Trust Me; one day everything *will* be all right. You'll see." Then He holds us ever so tightly, close to His heart of hearts. Right now my world was dark and gray, but the sun would come up.

After about thirty minutes, the birds stopped singing as they always did. It was as if their Maestro had tapped the music stand with His baton. The symphony of the day was about to begin. The morning light waxed brighter and brighter as it poured through the skylight. Soon John began to stir from across the room; day was arriving. The peace and calm of the morning would give way to the bustle of the day.

Eventually we both got up and had breakfast in the solarium with Jim. What a beautiful way to start the day—under the warming sun, surrounded by the tender loveliness of the garden. We ate and chatted until John and I had to leave for the railway station in Hove. It was only about a mile from New Orleans, and Tommy Burton would be arriving soon.

When we arrived at the station, Tommy's train had just left for the next stop down the railway. We scanned the sparse crowd inside and spotted Tommy doing the same thing with a suitcase in each hand. There is a particular joy at seeing a familiar face in a faraway place. We called out to Tommy, and he immediately turned and saw us. We hurried over to him to help him with his bags.

After we entered the house, we left the bags by the front door and introduced Tommy to Jim. Then we all sat for some tea and "biscuits" (the British term for cookies) in the tea room. We enjoyed each other's company for over an hour before Tommy, tired from his long journey, went upstairs for a rest. Jim, John, and I cleaned up and put away the tea dishes. Then we prepared the house and Brother John's bedroom for his return from the hospital in the afternoon.

The three of us went to the hospital just after lunch, while Tommy rested, to bring Brother John home. We helped him with great care into and out of the car, and the ride from the hospital went well. Once inside the house, we were able to give him a ride up to his bedroom with the aid of a lift chair that Brother John had installed on the stairway years ago for Rosalie. Now it was there for him.

Once we got Brother John settled into his room, he rested well for the remainder of the afternoon. He came downstairs in the late afternoon for some tea and a little bit of dinner. It was so nice to have him back at New Orleans, even though it was hard to see him so ill. His spirit was good, even though he was feeling very weak and weary. In spite of everything, he was getting stronger each day as he recovered from the surgery. I cherished the time with him very much.

Each night Brother John went to bed at about eight o'clock. I helped him get ready, and then I joined the others downstairs. We visited for another two or three hours while checking frequently on Brother John. When we went to bed, I left the door at the bottom of the stairs leading up to the Prophet's Chamber open. That way Brother John could call to me if he needed anything, and I could easily hear him. I slept very lightly with the effects of jet lag, and I kept an attentive ear for the slightest stir from the bedroom.

Jim had been taking care of Brother John nonstop for about two weeks by the time we arrived at the house. We encouraged him to take a break and go back to his home in Scotland to rest and spend time with his family. So the morning after we arrived, Jim flew to Edinburgh. This left Tommy, John, and me to care for Brother John. Cris came over often to help and spend time with us all. Brother John's doctor came by once every two or three days, so we fared pretty well.

We spent our days taking care of Brother John, cooking meals, and entertaining guests who came by to see him. Others who were a distance away called or sent letters. Brother John had quipped a few times that he thought he had more friends on "the other side" than here on earth. He was getting so many visitors, calls, and letters that he finally had to admit that he might have been wrong. All the love and compassion people were showering on him lifted his spirits even more.

John Chambers came to visit more than once while we were there. Another man, named George Ganders, came by one day and stayed for two or three hours. At one point, he and I were alone, and he shared with me through tears how much he loved Brother John. This was not an uncommon sentiment. Through the years, I heard with my own ears at least seven men say that Brother John was like a spiritual father to each of them. He was all of this and much more to me. Early in the course of our twenty-plus years of deep friendship, we became soul mates as Jonathan and David had done so long ago (see 1 Samuel 18:1). Now death would only separate us physically for a while.

In the middle of one night while I slept lightly, Brother John called my name. When I got to his room, he was breathing heavily; he thought his heart was giving out. I silently prayed for him, and he calmed down to the point of being able to fall back to sleep. I didn't sleep the rest of the night.

I called for the doctor the next day, and he came about two hours later. He checked Brother John thoroughly and couldn't find anything that would have caused the attack the night before. He thought it might have been caused by anxiety or the medication, but he wasn't sure. After the doctor left, Brother John told me he had thought the Lord was going to take him home. He was even somewhat disappointed that He hadn't. His impending passing was not an easy thought for me to contemplate, but I could see that the Lord was preparing Brother John for this eventuality. Only a miracle from God could change this course, and it seemed that was not what He had chosen for Brother John.

Some may think I had lost my faith, but it is not a matter of having enough faith to conjure a miracle from God. Sometimes, for His own good, holy, and loving reasons, God chooses not to heal those He loves, even the choicest of saints. We have a large history of such cases. God also chose not to intervene in the death of His own Son. He had a greater purpose. Likewise, sometimes He has a greater purpose in allowing His saints to suffer and die. We do not always understand those purposes, but if we truly know God, we know that we can trust Him no matter what our circumstances may be.

I was coming to accept Brother John's passing in the very near future. A part of me hated the thought of it, but I knew deep inside I could trust the Lord, even in this. Death is not the worst possible circumstance for those who are the children of God. It is the end of our mortality, but it is the beginning of our eternal state in the heavenly realm, a state of almost incomprehensible blessing (1 Corinthians 2:9–10). As the time of our visitation passed, I came more and more to terms with the eventual passing of Brother John. I experience sadness to this day thinking about it, and I still miss him very much, but I also have joy in knowing that he is in a much, much better place. Not only that, but he is with his beloved Rosalie—and best of all, he is with the Lord Jesus Christ, the Lord of all glory. Brother John is *living* in the very presence of God. That is the very essence of paradise.

Toward the end of our stay, we visited in the living room on a sunny afternoon as we had done many times. On this day, I noticed something very unusual right outside the front window. There was a single rosebush in the center of a small grassy area in the tiny front yard. The rosebush was completely bare except for one large, beautiful white rose in full bloom. There were not even any leaves or buds on the branches of the bush. It was completely bare except for this one fully blossomed white rose.

I had seen it before, but it had never dawned on me how unusual it was to see a rose in the middle of January. It had been twenty-five degrees when we rode on the train down from Gatwick less than two weeks before. I pointed out the rose to the others in the room, and we were all quite amazed at this anomaly of God's creation. I went outside and inspected the bush closely. The plant was completely dormant, not a sign of growth anywhere on it, except for this one, single, lovely white rose.

I was so taken by the rose that I took two pictures of it. I saw it as a sign from the Lord—life, beautiful life, out of that which was dying. Later I looked up the meaning of a white rose. Among its several meanings were "eternal love," "innocence;" and "heavenly." I thought of the eternal love our heavenly Father always has for us, even in the most difficult of times. We also have the innocence of Christ through His shed blood on the cross (see Isaiah 53:5 and Colossians 2:13–14). I was very touched by this sign from the Lord. He is always with us.

When I returned for Brother John's funeral in May of 2001, I inspected the same rosebush. It was full of buds ready to blossom, but every one of them was red. There was not a single white blossom on the entire bush. Red and white roses mean "together, unity." I took this as the Lord's message that even though death had separated Brother John and me, we were still together. At this writing, it has been more than twelve years since Brother John entered into the presence of Jesus. He is still as much a part of me as ever.

Soon, all too soon, our last day at New Orleans was upon us. I savored each and every moment of our fleeting time together on this side of eternity. It had been wonderful, and I knew, without a shadow of doubt, that once I left New Orleans I would not see Brother John alive again until we met in heaven on a distant day in the future. It was a very difficult thought to embrace, but the Lord gives us unusual strength to endure when we need it, if we will allow Him to do so. He is eternally faithful.

Finally, I helped Brother John get ready for bed. I asked him if he would tell

Jesus that I loved Him when he came face-to-face with Him. He smiled and said he would see what he could do. After I left him, he rested peacefully as the rest of us visited for a few more hours downstairs. We said our farewells to Cris when he left at nine o'clock. Tommy, John, and I went to bed about eleven, as John and I had to catch the train from Hove to Gatwick around mid-morning.

My son John fell asleep almost immediately after we retired to the Prophet's Chamber. I lay awake for more than an hour after he fell asleep. The house was peacefully silent. I contemplated many things during this time. It would be the last time I would have the privilege of sleeping in the Prophet's Chamber. I had a general feeling of sorrow as I reflected that night, but I did not cry. There would be many tears shed on the morrow as final departure separated us in body.

Finally, in the deep calm of gentle sorrow, I heard the voice in my spirit I had heard so many years before. The Voice of persistent inspiration and quiet leading whispered once more, "Wait and see."

Postscript
WHERE THE WINTERS FAMILY IS NOW

May 2013…

With four of our six children still living at home with Debbie and me, our home is a center of activity nearly seven days and nights a week. There is hardly a moment when there are not one, two, or more of their friends here with us. We tell our friends we have our own built-in youth group as we often have seven, eight, or more people dining at our table daily. We love almost every minute of it!

John, our oldest, is twenty-eight years old and living in Scottsdale, Arizona. He finished two or three years of college before he joined the National Guard in 2009. He did a ten-month tour of duty in Iraq in 2010–2011 and came back in pretty good shape. He now works in the auto department at a superstore in the Phoenix area and does his weekend warrior exercises once a month in the desert. He is serving his country honorably. He treated Debbie and me to a trip to Alaska two years ago and took me to the Major League All Star game in Phoenix shortly before that. John was married in 2005. Unfortunately, his wife divorced him while he was deployed. He loves the warm winters and hot summers of Arizona and enjoys many of the sports activities in and around Phoenix.

Joel will be twenty-five on June 17 of this year. He returned home from treatment a little over two years ago after some serious difficulties with some personal issues during his late teens and early twenties. Just before returning, he asked the Lord to heal him from his struggles. He has never looked back. He has lived in his own apartment here in The Dalles, Oregon, for over a year and works hard at his current job. He's a pretty happy young man who enjoys spending time with Leahanna's boyfriend, Andrew. He and I have spent a lot of quality time together since he returned home.

Leahanna is a lovely twenty-two-year-old woman. She is living at home while going through a job training program. Just recently, Sonrise Academy began to consider hiring her as a part-time teaching aide. She and Andrew Wilde are madly in love as they court and occasionally play beautiful violin music together at weddings and churches in the area. She attends two local Bible studies and helps with a youth ministry at a church here in town.

Lauren, still our drama queen, is twenty years old and is also living at home while finishing her second year at the local community college. She gave up her ballet to focus on her studies and has made the dean's or president's list every term so far. She is a great self-starter and has worked at part-time jobs and student government while attending college. She recently took a trip with the student council from her school to Philadelphia to see some historic sites and attend seminar classes on student leadership.

Kimberly (Kimmie) is a vivacious fourteen-year-old who loves to try her mother's patience. She works hard on her schoolwork at Sonrise Academy and has made the honor roll almost every quarter since enrolling in December of 2012. She recently returned from the Accelerated Christian Education Regional Convention and brought home a fourth-place ribbon in scrapbooking, a third-place ribbon in flower arranging, and she is the 2013 Regional Junior Convention champion in still-life color photography.

Sarah, our sixth child, is a precocious, witty, hilarious ten-year-old. She is doing extremely well at school and has just begun to follow her sister playing the violin. She recently went through her first adjudication, receiving high praise for her performance. She accompanied Kimmie to the Junior Convention this year and won ribbons in all six of the events she entered. She was especially proud of placing third in Bible memory, having memorized over five hundred consecutive words from the Gospel of John.

Debbie and I are doing our best to keep up with this active bunch. Debbie works very hard creating a warm, lovely home with her many incredible domestic skills as she drives kids all over town and beyond. I am in my sixth year teaching middle and high school students full-time while administrating part-time at Sonrise Academy. It is challenging at times for both of us, but we are enjoying it all immensely as we near our thirty-sixth anniversary. Through all the trials and triumphs, the Lord has been very, very good to us.

A portrait Larry Gordon gave to a few of his closet friends before he left Pendleton.

John and Rosalie Samson in their home (New Orleans), 1983

John and Rosalie Samson's home, "New Orleans." Photo taken during one of our trips to England.

A photo of Beit Shalom taken on our trip to Israel with Brother John (Samson) in 1983.

Brother John Samson and Cristian Sigheartau waiting for the jet foil from England to Belgium on our way to Romania, 1992.

The Winters children in the fall of 1992. Back row (left to right): John and Joel; Front row (left to right): Kimberly, Leahanna, and Lauren

The single white rose that grew on the dormant rose bush in front of Brother John's house in January, 2001.

The entire Winters clan in January, 2012. Back row (left to right): John, Joel, and me; Middle row (left to right): Kimberly and Debbie; Front row (left to right): Sarah, Leahanna, and Lauren.

Acknowledgments

Writing this book has been an eight-year journey. It has been in my heart and soul much longer. There have been hundreds of hours of research and writing invested, with help from many people. I want to acknowledge with gratefulness those who have contributed to this work.

First, I thank my beloved wife, Debbie, for all the hours she spent helping me remember the details of this book and assisting with the wording of so many sentences and paragraphs (including this page). I also thank my dear children John, Joel, Leahanna, Lauren, Kimbery, and Sarah for their help and patience.

I especially thank Lorraine Nelson for the many, many hours she contributed to the first edit of the entire book. Thank you, Andrew Wilde, for helping me find my way around the computer so many times. I am also very thankful to the many others who helped with so many of the details and accounts recorded in this book. I am also indebted to the gracious people of Deep River Books for helping me learn so much about writing, and for all their encouragement along the way.

I am most grateful, though, to the Lord, Jesus Christ, who made all of this possible.

Most of the accounts recorded in this book are the result of arduous hours of research, done to the best of our abilities to give you the exact truth. Sometimes we are at the mercy of the accuracy of our sources. Many of the quotes and details are from videotapes, personal notes, and other sources. However, some are from our collective memories as best we can remember them with the Lord's help. If there are inaccuracies, we are not aware of them, and they are a result of our human frailty. Thank you for your grace and patience in this.

Contact the author at: thequietleading@gmail.com